Psychotherapy with Survivors of Sexual Violence

The role of psychotherapists in creating change for survivors of sexual violence can extend far beyond the rooms in which appointments are provided. *Psychotherapy with Survivors of Sexual Violence* aims to provide psychotherapists with practical guidance that will enable them to work with the prolific societal issue of sexual violence, both in the privacy of clinical practice and the wider world as activists.

Erene Hadjiioannou outlines the components of relational psychotherapy necessary to counter the trauma that brings survivors to services, with a particular focus on empowerment and the freedoms that constitute it. The book defines the neurophysiological systems involved in surviving traumatic experiences and common psychological presentations, including post-traumatic stress disorder.

Hadjiioannou explains the long-standing challenges of delivering psychotherapy to survivors who have reported to the police from various perspectives: understanding the criminal justice system, note-keeping, and survivors' experiences of reporting. Barriers to accessing support, including myths, are examined and the book includes interview quotes from a range of survivors as well as fictional case studies throughout.

Psychotherapy with Survivors of Sexual Violence will be a key text for psychotherapists of all backgrounds working with survivors, and for mental health professionals in training.

Erene Hadjiioannou is an integrative psychotherapist based in the UK. She has specialist experience in supporting adults of any gender to manage the impact of trauma resulting from sexual violence.

Psychotherapy with Survivors of Sexual Violence

Inside and Outside the Room

Erene Hadjiioannou

LONDON AND NEW YORK

First published 2022
by Routledge
2 Park Square, Milton Park, Abingdon, Oxon OX14 4RN

and by Routledge
605 Third Avenue, New York, NY 10158

Routledge is an imprint of the Taylor & Francis Group, an informa business

© 2022 Erene Hadjiioannou

The right of Erene Hadjiioannou to be identified as author of this work has been asserted by her in accordance with sections 77 and 78 of the Copyright, Designs and Patents Act 1988.

All rights reserved. No part of this book may be reprinted or reproduced or utilised in any form or by any electronic, mechanical, or other means, now known or hereafter invented, including photocopying and recording, or in any information storage or retrieval system, without permission in writing from the publishers.

Trademark notice: Product or corporate names may be trademarks or registered trademarks, and are used only for identification and explanation without intent to infringe.

British Library Cataloguing-in-Publication Data
A catalogue record for this book is available from the British Library

Library of Congress Cataloging-in-Publication Data
Names: Hadjiioannou, Erene, author.
Title: Psychotherapy with survivors of sexual violence : inside and outside the room / Erene Hadjiioannou.
Description: Abingdon, Oxon ; New York, NY : Routledge, 2022. | Includes bibliographical references and index. |
Identifiers: LCCN 2021011232 (print) | LCCN 2021011233 (ebook) | ISBN 9781032065885 (hardback) | ISBN 9780367429515 (paperback) | ISBN 9781032065885 (ebook)
Subjects: LCSH: Sexual abuse victims--Rehabilitation--Great Britain--Case studies. | Psychotherapy--Great Britain--Case studies.
Classification: LCC RC560.S44 H33 2022 (print) | LCC RC560.S44 (ebook) | DDC 616.85/83690651--dc23
LC record available at https://lccn.loc.gov/2021011232
LC ebook record available at https://lccn.loc.gov/2021011233

ISBN: 978-1-032-06588-5 (hbk)
ISBN: 978-0-367-42951-5 (pbk)
ISBN: 978-1-003-20294-3 (ebk)

DOI: 10.4324/9781003202943

Typeset in Times New Roman
by Taylor & Francis Books

Contents

Preface		vi
Acknowledgements		viii
1	Sexual violence in context	1
2	The personal impact of sexual violence	26
3	Psychotherapy as activism	42
4	The challenge of myths	64
5	Working relationally with sexual violence in psychotherapy	89
6	Promoting empowerment in psychotherapy	108
7	Delivering pre-trial therapy in the United Kingdom	126
8	Vicarious trauma: Impact and management	155
	Index	170

Preface

Case studies and quotes have been included throughout this book to illustrate aspects of what can take place in psychotherapy with survivors of sexual violence.

These include the words and accounts of real survivors who have been brave, kind, and generous enough to share their personal experiences in order to highlight the core themes of this book. Real names have been changed or retained as per the individual wishes of each person.

To the survivors that did so: I am very grateful to have met you and spoken with you. Thank you so much for your contributions and for inviting me in to let me know more about you.

These survivors want to tell you what is essential when seeing a psychotherapist to recover from sexual violence:

> My therapist gave me her self, which was much more important than what she said. Her eye contact and body language told me that I was accepted and that she was interested. This meant we could connect. Without that interest, I would've been judged. From there I felt everything else could work.
>
> *Rob*

> Psychotherapists and clients should be able to be themselves. They should be able to behave in the ways they feel comfortable and that feel natural without pressure to conform to ideas about how you express yourself in that role.
>
> *Sam*

> What happened to me doesn't define me, even though it can be at the forefront of my therapy and what I bring to therapy sessions.
>
> *Crystal*

> Feeling safe, being heard, and validated. Having a space where someone was sat with me, letting me work it out.
>
> *Amanda*

Someone who validates your feelings and normalises your emotional and physical responses to the traumatic events; someone who is truly trauma-informed. They help you to make sense of your reactions and emotions at the time of the event, as well as helping you to understand why you continue to be impacted by it in the present. Providing psycho-education and giving you autonomy empowers you along the way so you can navigate through your feelings and emotions in relation to yourself, the perpetrator, relationships, faith, and culture.

Tayba

I want to say how important the relationship is, rather than a set approach or theoretical way of doing things. What that relationship can give you and focusing on building that more than anything else is the most important thing.

M

My therapist's willingness to question certain therapeutic boundaries if he could see that these boundaries were becoming barriers to my recovery.

Anna

Acknowledgements

There are many people who deserve a formal thank you for their support and contributions to this book:

Joe, I'm grateful that your unconditional support includes understanding how much my work is a part of being who I am and taking action on the things I believe in.

Jacinta Kent for your solidarity, warmth, and generosity. The therapeutic profession is enriched by having you, your energy, and your point of view. Thank you for helping me meet with survivors to give space to their voices here.

Lucy Coen as someone who has been an integral part of my learning on the criminal justice system in relation to survivors for several years. Thank you for your input on the chapter about pre-trial therapy. I see your unwavering determination in the fight for justice and admire you for it.

Cat Crossley of Clavis and Claustra for all illustrations related to this book, including a 'Shout Out for Survivors' flyer used to invite survivors to share their experiences. You were the right person for the task because of your strong belief in equality for all.

James Taylor for standing alongside me in many ways, for many years. Thank you for having encouraged and validated the ways I have chosen to use my own voice.

To my friends and their patience for reading or listening to excerpts of the book along the way. Thank you for your help in this process as psychotherapists, counsellors, activists, and survivors.

Whilst writing this book the Crown Prosecution Service (CPS) guidelines on delivering 'pre-trial therapy' were revised, with a public consultation taking place for feedback on the proposed revisions in late 2020. In 2019 my work included co-development of a project to address the consequential issues of these guidelines across the legal and therapeutic professions. These issues continue to affect survivors' rights to pursue justice as offered by law and their simultaneous right to access talking therapy as a confidential form of support.

Facilitation of this project began with Anj Handa of Inspiring Women Changemakers who connected me with two amazing people: Tayba Azim and Dorothy Hodgkinson. Together the three of us formed an independent steering group that liaised primarily with legal professionals to try to create positive change within an area that is significantly problematic for survivors and those aiming to assist them.

A report based on our work was submitted in response to the CPS' public consultation, as well as directly to senior figures in the CPS, in October 2020. This report included feedback about the many difficulties in applying the original guidelines from therapists in statutory services, therapists in the third sector, and ISVAs.

Our report included future projections on the difficulties of accessing therapeutic services pre-trial within overloaded legal and mental health systems, including the barriers created by them. We noted the increased need for legal and therapeutic interventions given the steep rise of domestic violence during the social contact restrictions enforced in response to the global Covid-19 pandemic.

As a steering group we are indebted to Stephen Littlewood of KBW Chambers for his enthusiasm and expertise. We appreciate you being aligned with our concerns and finding a way forward with us. I also thank each of you here for our collective effort to improve survivors' rights to legal justice and improve the standard of professional talking therapy for clients who are pre-trial.

We were not the only ones to publicly push back against the problems caused by the CPS guidelines on pre-trial therapy which affect survivors' freedom of speech, privacy, and accessibility of talking therapy services. This collective pushback to injustice and discrimination is part of the ongoing fight for the rights of survivors in a victim-blaming society.

Above all, this book could not exist without the survivors I have met thus far in my career. I am awed by your continued survival in a world that is often re-traumatising, including the systems within it that challenge your right to live freely and safely.

The mental health system should be shaped by you at all levels, including welcoming practitioners with lived experience. There are many of us who want to fully respond to your truths and will support you inside as well as outside of rooms where psychotherapy appointments are offered.

I hope writing this book is an adequate stepping up to respond to what you have shared with me over the past decade. Thank you so much.

Chapter 1

Sexual violence in context

Contextualising our shared dialogue

The intention of this book is to better enable psychotherapists to respond to the needs of survivors of sexual violence via traditional appointments, varying types of psychotherapeutic work in community spaces, and supportive action in the wider world whether one refers to this as activism or by any other term. Furthermore, this book aims to demonstrate how to: alleviate the traumatic impact of sexual violence, increase accessibility of psychotherapy to all survivors, become allies to the process of recovery in public spaces, and collaboratively create social change around an issue that is profoundly disempowering.

There is much to consider in contextualising the dialogue around sexual violence wherever such dialogues occur. The purpose of this is primarily to ensure that all parties understand the nuances of a very complex societal occurrence and its impact on the clients we meet in psychotherapy services. It is also true that sexual violence occurs globally on a prolific scale, meaning that a shared understanding is something to constantly be asserted and re-asserted in service of supporting survivors impacted by it.

The value of lived experience in clients and psychotherapists is vital in evolving our profession, as this is first-hand information gathered from having lived through sexual violence rather than it being known purely theoretically. Such truths can include experiences of disclosure of sexual violence to others in various spaces and trying to access personal or professional support, as both can have positive or adverse effects on the individual. This includes psychotherapy as a space within the wider world.

We can start by contextualising our dialogue as professionals and work towards expanding it outwards to join the global conversations about sexual violence. This back-and-forth process means that our professional language, and therefore how we understand this phenomenon, will change over time. The influence of the internet as a space in the wider world that we each occupy can mean such changes occur much faster than prior to its existence. It also means that the voices of individual survivors can be heard more easily as part of a wider movement of empowerment and change.

Within psychotherapy any words a client uses to refer to their experiences should be respected via the mirrored use of them by their psychotherapist wherever possible. A chosen use of language is a part of finding one's way in their process of recovery. Psychotherapists can then begin to meet individual survivors and honour their subjective lived experiences, in ways rarely found elsewhere within a society that wishes to ignore or further persecute them especially when they speak.

Being survivor-led means integrating survivors' truths into professional practice, and the language used in this book is influenced by this principle. The psychotherapeutic working relationship thus includes being allied with such clients, which involves having professional dialogues directly influenced by subjective accounts. Within psychotherapy this is powerful to the process of change in the client's life and this power can reverberate further into the field too.

This perspective on language also acknowledges that every survivor will use specific words, including naming different types of sexual violence, differently. Sadly, the configurations in which this issue occurs are numerous and varied. Discrepancies in language between survivors can denote a use of words to avoid re-experiencing what happened whilst still needing to refer to it and knowing that words are shaped by cultural understandings of sexual violence. Additionally, there are often disparities between how words are used in the subjective process of psychotherapy versus the more objective arena of the legal system or any other formal process of disclosure.

There are several words and phrases to qualify in order to begin a dialogue of this kind, with all its nuances. In this book 'sexual violence' is an umbrella term that points to the wide range of non-consensual sexual contact a person can experience in their lifetime. The word 'violence' is included to denote that such contact is always violating, although it may not be stereotypically or overtly violent. Furthermore, such violence refers to the kind of forced re-organisation of the self, the intrusion into one's psychological (mind) and physical (body) facets of this self, and the subsequent interruptions to the many domains of one's life.

The impact of sexual violence is often referred to as 'traumatic,' including in everyday conversations. Although a direct nod to diagnostic criteria that can theoretically help psychotherapists understand a client's difficulties, it is true that the personal result of sexual violence does not always come under this category upon professional nor personal evaluation. However, within this book this term is used in order to provide a recognisable broad understanding of the degree of psychological, physical, practical, and relational injuries caused by sexual violence.

Interweaving theory, practical action, case studies of fictional clients, and lived experiences of real survivors within this book reflects the process of relational psychotherapy. Relatedness is not a linear act between selves and is definitely not the case when trust is disrespected through sexual violence.

When any of us relate our selves become visible and become open to receiving other selves in a tangible way. Such visibility can be felt as threatening to the survivor, including to the extent of putting their life at risk, which is why many psychotherapists only meet certain facets of their client's selves.

As relational psychotherapists we aim to meet the person amongst their presenting concerns. We simultaneously aim to enable clients to safely meet all the facets of their self they are disconnected from because of the impact of sexual violence. These meetings are places where the balance between theory and experiential work, characterised by the relationship, occurs within a co-created psychotherapeutic conversation.

At each contact point in the process of relational work psychotherapists and clients make psychological contact with each other. This includes influencing each other's subjective experience at conscious and unconscious levels. Such influencing occurs even when clients are so highly traumatised that they cannot safely engage with the working relationship on a consistent basis, as is the case for many survivors.

Furthermore, influence between selves is not only necessary for effective psychotherapy to take place. It also assists in evolving the profession along with society as we all better understand the impact of sexual violence wherever and however it manifests. A psychotherapist making space for the truths of survivors is inherently vital for therapeutic work and is a mark of commitment to being an ally to this often societally persecuted population.

In the spirit of being allied the words 'client' and 'survivor' are used interchangeably. Both reflect the ever-changing nature of language in public and psychotherapeutic spaces. 'Survivor' in particular is a reflection of widely-accepted vernacular within movements led by those with lived experience and support services at the time of writing.

The use of 'survivor' is also relevant to the overall ethos of the explorations outlined across all chapters as a way to signal empowerment to those who have endured traumatic events, as well as finding ways to live long after these take place. This is in comparison to 'victim,' another commonly-used term, although some clients may resonate more closely with this word at times.

In a book where the legal process is discussed as an overlap to the psychotherapeutic process, using 'survivor' provides a linguistic distinction from the former in practice and experientially. Many clients are re-traumatised by the criminal justice system whereas psychotherapy actively seeks to minimise and alleviate trauma-based responses to internal and external stimuli.

Nonetheless, psychotherapists are encouraged to respect the fact that language has an impact and a meaning specific to the individual client. Therefore, the word 'victim' is not outlawed within psychotherapeutic dialogue especially if this is the term used by a client to refer to themselves.

Also used within this book is the word 'we,' which at times points to the fact that everyone has some contact with the challenges to everyday living raised by varying types of sexual violence. This includes psychotherapists who have lived experience, whether they are transparent about this in their working life or not.

Within psychotherapeutic work this could translate to 'When we are going through something traumatic like sexual violence, it is normal for us to respond in the following ways ...' Being explicit that humans have neurophysiological mechanisms to automatically react to traumatic experiences normalises how we all try to survive them, rather than pathologising individual responses.

Beyond this, 'we' also solidifies the intention of undertaking work to collectively address sexual violence. Psychotherapists do so via appointments as well as having an active presence and participation in other spaces we each occupy personally and professionally. Examples can include informal support outside of traditional services or political activity.

Furthermore, each of the words qualified are deliberately applicable to any person of any gender, including those who identify outside of the categories of cisgender male or female. In this way we respect the truth that there are many types of people who have sexual violence in their history. Psychotherapists can take this as a helpful starting point to theoretically widen their lens on this topic, as well as practically invite a more diverse client base into their services from a place of integrity.

The use of commonly understood psychological terms such as 'presenting concerns' and 'presenting material' need to be explained at this stage. Such terms within this book refer to the client's process of making their subjective experience and multi-faceted self known to their psychotherapist via implicit or explicit means. Clients can communicate these in conscious and unconscious ways.

This process includes the things the client wants to change via psychotherapy, their personal history, and how they relate to their own self or other selves. 'Presenting' in psychotherapy does not necessitate the client simply giving something to their psychotherapist which then only becomes the responsibility of the latter to hold. However, this can be a part of the work at times when disconnection (as the opposite of relatedness) takes place in some way.

The use of the word 'clinical' within this book is used to illustrate the issue of sexual violence as it appears in formalised mental health spaces. However, the use of this terminology does not assume that its appearance, along with the survivors that experience it, only takes place in these kinds of spaces. It is used to encourage the process of applying theory to practice in the reader.

Undertaking psychotherapy with survivors includes being entrusted with the truth of sexual violence. Part of the role of psychotherapists therefore is to step up to what is being shared via an active relational process knowing that the impact of such truths affects the client's experience of their self, relationships with other selves, and contact with the wider world. An overview of challenges that clients often face is examined along the way so that psychotherapists can accommodate a working understanding of these, as they often present as challenges to advancing the shared work.

From wider world issue to individual struggle

Sexual violence is any act from one or multiple people to single or multiple others consisting of intended and/or actual sexual contact without seeking, considering, nor respecting consent. With this broad definition we can consider all the different types of sexual violence people can be subjected to, the diversity of individual survivors, the varying circumstances in which sexual violence occurs, and the many different kinds of people that can be perpetrators. On the ground, psychotherapists can expect to meet survivors who are as varied as the concerns they raise within appointments.

Sexual violence does not occur in a vacuum. It can often be mistakenly viewed as an isolated, random incident in an individual person's life that is easily recovered from. The reality is that its impact becomes concurrent with and interwoven into the life of the survivor. For those who experience sexual violence in the context of pre-existing relationships, or during the process of human trafficking, this may ring especially true. The impact of this global issue on an individual, their relationships, and everyday life is tangible for extensive periods of time.

The global occurrence of sexual violence is so high that its commonality risks it being deemed as normal, but sexual violence is unequivocally not normal. It is not a developmental stage, incident, or life experience that validates a human being. It does not propel people forward in life from a solid internal or external base, particularly as the impact of sexual violence is not easily integrated anywhere at any level. What sexual violence does instead is repeatedly interrupt and disrupt one's sense of self, as well as one's relationships, and life.

A survivor's truth no longer correlates with the various spaces in their life, which leads to adaptative and avoidant behaviours in order to retain some sense of safety. Again, this does not make the survivor abnormal. There is simply no other option within bodies, minds, relationships, and a wider world that are largely unchanging. Adaptive behaviours include navigating the level of actual or perceived threat of repeated unwanted contact from others and can be felt long after the last time threat was sensed.

Whether a survivor's truth is believed, or not, strongly determines the practical process of accessibility to recovery after any disclosure is made. At a personal level, not being believed can be as traumatic or more traumatic than the sexual violence itself. For clients who have an ongoing close proximity to perpetrators, including living with them, this can mean remaining trapped in many ways for long periods of time. The wider world and relationships continue to be organised around the oppressive dynamics that ensure sexual violence goes on unaddressed.

Primal survival mechanisms are excessively activated that make individual bodies and minds feel out of control to the point of disempowerment. A consistently comfortable baseline cannot be found in any spaces within or beyond a client's self and thus regular life becomes inaccessible as well as unbearable. Individual clients present with this to varying degrees from those who cannot participate in life at all, to those who are high functioning.

However it manifests, psychotherapists are invited into a survivor's struggle and process of recovery, at the time they meet. Psychotherapists are offered an insight into a client's life at that point as well as making contact with their past. This of course includes the incidences of sexual violence they have gone through. Once they meet, it is standard to focus on specific elements of the client's presenting concerns in line with what they would like to be different.

Ethically, this is acting in accordance with a client's needs or wishes. The work may be limited to only their initial requests, even as breadth or depth of conversations increase over time. This may be due to the practicalities of what is on offer from the psychotherapist, which in many services may be time-limited and/or non-specialist talking therapy. Psychotherapists may also meet a survivor unexpectedly, for example when a disclosure is made after a referral or assessment is completed.

With any client in any setting there are agreements to be made on how to proceed with the work on offer to maximise the efficacy of psychotherapy as a joint endeavour. There is always a careful balance to be found between focusing on what is emerging for the client, including in an urgent way whilst bearing in mind their overall presentation, history, and relational or attachment style. Interventions can then be tailored according to each client and takes into account their specific needs rather than providing a standardised service.

Barriers within the mental health system

For survivors of sexual violence what is essential to include in shared consciousness with their psychotherapist is their own experiences of disclosure and what accessing suitable talking therapy has been like. Such experiences necessitate psychological or physical contact with others and any contact is less safe following sexual violence, even if the survivor intentionally seeks it out.

It is impossible to work in a relational manner if psychotherapists only focus on symptom alleviation, as this overlooks the humanity of the client. To do so results in the person remaining lost amongst their trauma. A sole focus on symptom alleviation also does not fully prepare the survivor to re-enter the wider world as a multi-faceted self, along with their personal identity. In addition, a person's humanity is violated at the time sexual violence takes place, which emphasises the need for psychotherapists to respond humanely thereafter as a restorative approach to facilitate meeting the person amongst the trauma.

Psychotherapy cannot be considered as a truly separate space from the rest of the world, as its privacy and confidentiality might appear to offer. The mental health system is a human-made system, which unfortunately means that the disempowering dynamics people can perpetuate against each other play out in this arena. Specifically, psychotherapy is not exempt from potentially disempowering those who wish to access it because of the many barriers that clients come up against in receiving help to recover from sexual violence.

Asking about a client's experiences of disclosure and accessing support provides valuable information about the relational dynamics that compound or alleviate the impact of sexual violence upon them. Being told why disclosing or receiving support were not options is similarly revealing. The process of describing the incidents and asking for help, when this has been possible, is at one level a survivor's way of attempting relatedness with another self following these traumatic experiences.

The nature and outcomes of these dynamic interactions are helpful in better responding to an individual client's needs, including repairing person-to-person injuries of the past via the present work. If responded to adequately in psychotherapy, the survivor has a better relational template for engaging comfortably with other selves and spaces in their lives outside of psychotherapy. The reparative component is the experience of trustworthy, non-threatening relational contact that is within their control wherever possible.

Sexual violence often occurs between persons who are known to each other, as well as between strangers. The former is more common and the degree to which people know each other before sexual violence happens varies considerably. In any case it occurs person-to-person and thus should be considered in a relational context so that psychotherapists can understand the complex dynamics that come to life for us to respond to in appointments. Similarly, our theoretical understanding and what we learn from survivors can be extended to decipher the complexity of sexual violence as a prolific phenomenon in the wider world.

The minutiae of these complex dynamics represent the back and forth of human interactions which sadly can include sexual violence from one person to another. What is crucial in beginning our considerations of sexual violence is the context in which it occurs between persons, this being larger human-made systems. To re-frame within this systems context: humanity includes injustices at times, with sexual violence being one example.

Humans shape the world they live in, including explicitly and implicitly exerting influence over the systems that govern communities, whether this be on-the-ground social etiquette or procedures within formal institutions. Hierarchies are simultaneously created that unequally distribute power and define values in limited ways. Unfortunately, the world then becomes shaped by injustices stemming from disempowerment and misplaced value. Embedded injustices of systems are borne from oppressive principles such as patriarchy, racism, heteronormativity, and capitalism, to name a few.

The further individuals fall outside the categories of: non-disabled, white, middle/upper class, cisgender, gender conforming, speaking the primary language of their country of residence, and heterosexual, the less often they are afforded their equal right to spaces in the world to exist safely and freely. Similar considerations can be made with regards to other categories such as religion, faith, spirituality, age, and non-monogamy.

Individuals who are different to those that have powerfully constructed human-made systems are likely to have accumulated experiences of injustice within them throughout their lives. When it comes to accessing and engaging with psychotherapy as a human-made system the same principle applies. For many clients the result is a myriad of barriers to receiving support, perhaps more so than for other survivors who are more socially enabled to navigate such systems.

Therefore, there is a risk of not being fully accommodated by a service as the person that they are, in addition to being someone who has experienced sexual violence. Relatedness between the facets of one's self becomes ever more elusive as personal identity is omitted from the process of making contact with a sense of self that lies within a client's control. This process of disconnection playing out externally within the mental health system can lead to disengagement and, at worst, a loss of hope of recovery.

As an example: a white, heterosexual, English woman may more easily access formal support whilst a bisexual asylum-seeking man with a basic understanding of English may not even know that such support exists. Compounding this is the former survivor's understanding that what happened was wrong, having words for their experiences, and an integrated cultural sense that it is okay to ask for mental health support. They are also assured by the fact that the person they see for support is also white and a woman.

The asylum-seeking man may also know that what happened was wrong, but is frightened to ask for help because contact with professionals in the United Kingdom has thus far been intrusive and hostile. Furthermore, he was forced to seek asylum in the United Kingdom because his bisexuality resulted in him being tortured in his country of origin. He is not ashamed of his sexual orientation, but often feels shame shutting him down when this comes up with professionals in relation to his asylum application.

Understanding this is important to psychotherapists because sexual violence is the disempowering injustice that has brought a client into the room and the process of accessing a support service can exacerbate disempowering injustice. Systemic barriers to disclosure and systemic barriers to accessing psychotherapy are in their most basic form relational injuries between persons. Therefore, contact with other selves within those systems can be re-traumatising.

In terms of how the past might influence the present in trauma work, psychotherapists may only take into account traumatic experiences, early attachment figures, and styles of relating. However, taking into account a client's previous experiences of systemic, societal disempowerment is just as important to consider in informing the work, understanding the client's current difficulties in relating within the facets of their self plus with other selves, and treatment planning.

To enhance our understanding of the above, it is worth considering the role of trust in the complex dynamics of a global society where sexual violence happens to so many people. Trust between persons is violated in the act of sexual violence. Through this process a survivor is thoroughly denied the boundaries of their own mind and body as they are intruded upon by another person. For many survivors the lack of control and disconnection felt on a reoccurring basis mirrors trust being violated, which becomes housed within their selves.

A way to decrease this impact stems from individuals and the spaces they offer where survivors can be fully attended to. Psychotherapy is one of these spaces. Very often the emotional traps of blame, shame, and guilt represent a fundamentally isolating feeling of 'I'm alone with this.' For those who fall outside of the aforementioned demographic categories in any configuration, these feelings pre-exist sexual violence as an underlying experience of everyday life whenever micro- or macro-injustices are experienced.

In practice such communal isolation from others can be observed as a lack of diversity in clients seen in psychotherapy services, non-attendance of appointments, and ultimately disengagement from a service. Simply put, barriers within the mental health system are disconnecting rather than encouraging of relatedness, especially when a client is already oppressed or disempowered by societal injustices.

The reparative nature of psychotherapy aims to counter relational injuries and disempowerment by offering interventions to promote recovery within a safe relationship characterised by clear boundaries. It proposes to achieve this by offering more freedom of speech and autonomy around the issue of sexual violence within a wider world that is invested in keeping the narrative around the matter very narrow. Narratives of this kind enable sexual violence to continue as an act surrounded by societal myths and collective silences.

However, the freedoms of psychotherapy are negated by long waiting lists and time-limited work. They are also negated by a lack of services specialising in sexual violence and a lack of services that are tailored specifically to protected characteristics such as gender. Psychotherapy as a healthcare intervention then becomes a privilege rather than a right and the humanity of it is lost.

The accessibility of psychotherapy services is similarly negated by the challenges of the structure of the mental health system. One of the most severe consequences here is that survivors continue to struggle to be seen, heard, and adequately responded to:

> The idea of being on a waiting list meant I felt like I was in limbo. It was intimidating to wait and not be in control. Disclosing to my male GP felt like a barrier to support ... I decided to go private and seeing my psychotherapist's photo before I met them was reassuring along with not having to wait.
>
> *Amanda*

Not being seen, heard, nor adequately responded to reinforces the relentless isolation of 'I'm alone with this' and means disconnection from one's self as well as the wider world. At times this disconnection at every turn can feed into a client's dependency on a service, as it may feel like psychotherapy is the only space beyond their selves they can bear to occupy within the wider world. This is counter to the aim of psychotherapy as a space to learn how to inhabit one's self, relationships, and other spaces in one's personal world more effectively.

From a relational perspective we can empathise with the human need to connect safely and get in touch with the overwhelming need for help in a dangerous world. For Amanda safety was signalled in working with a psychotherapist of a specific gender, seeing her face before they met, having a choice on who to disclose to, and not having to wait to receive psychological support. This is an example of how closely safety sits to being in control of the recovery process.

Consequently, the separation of safety from being in control by the mental health system because of its structure translates to personal challenges for the survivor to navigate alone on top of the impact of trauma. This is an injustice in itself, particularly because it reinforces a hierarchy of power rather than choice. The answer is to distribute power and define what constitutes power in a different way throughout the entire system.

Within a world where sexual violence exists, the truths of those affected by it should be placed at the centre of the mental health system. Spaces should be made for survivors by those currently in power so that their truths can **influence the shaping, management, delivery, and evaluation of psychotherapy** services.

Furthermore, power should be available to all so there is choice in utilising it rather than it being withheld, or distributed at the will of those who are at the top of the hierarchical chain. As a practice this reflects the integration of those with lived experience of sexual violence and their allies in more spaces within the wider world.

Psychotherapy should be one supportive intervention amongst many within a survivor's community so that help is found in many places, rather than being centralised within a largely inaccessible system. It should also be amended and delivered in ways that reflect the diversity of the people that want to benefit from it. Regulatory organisations for talking therapy, training providers, and funders of mental health services should also prioritise actions to diversify the profession.

This will ensure that the intersectionality of lived experience encompasses not only sexual violence, but also the varied combination of protected characteristics that psychotherapy needs to take into account to effectively work with every kind of survivor:

> As a Muslim woman I really struggled to find the right person at first. Most statutory and charitable organisations had very western values,

which excluded me. I felt they weren't accessible or could give me what I needed. I needed someone who could accommodate my ethnicity, culture, and faith but couldn't approach someone Muslim in case my confidentiality would be compromised. I looked for a private therapist who was Christian and she turned my life around.

Tayba

A part of this can include going out into communities to work as a psychotherapist outside of traditional appointments. A psychotherapist is no longer simply an individual within a hidden space, which too closely mirrors the preferred position of many in the wider world for sexual violence to remain a hidden issue. We cannot maintain our status as professionals who fully know the truth of sexual violence and have it remain with us, as on a wider scale this is denial or inaction of the issue.

There are three levels of privilege which need to be deconstructed and removed from the process of accessing psychotherapy. First, there is the assumption that every client has the language, practical resources, and theoretical understanding of psychotherapy as a form of healthcare. Second, privilege is founded on racist, heteronormative, binary theoretical frameworks as well as human-made systems. As a last point, myths operate in the same manner which reinforces barriers to support in many ways.

There is no social justice for sexual violence as a wider issue if the ways we consider it and treat its impact are narrowed by these limiting frameworks. The human construction of psychotherapy as a practice and the space it takes up within the wider world needs to be occupied and actioned differently in order to maximise its efficacy. Further directions on these ideas are outlined in Chapters four and five.

Practical barriers

The process of seeking any kind of support following sexual violence is practically challenging. The fact that its impact can manifest in many facets of the client's self means that multiple domains of the client's life suffer as a result. There may be difficulties in everyday tasks such as getting out of bed, washing, sleeping, and eating. Other responsibilities may be harder to take care of, for example: parenting, work, and handling personal finances. Trying to cope with distress can include withdrawal from others, self-harming behaviours, and excessive substance use.

Altogether daily life can feel much harder to manage and when this happens each survivor will try to find a way through somehow. When it comes to asking for professional help, those with multiple support needs are commonly expected to navigate a corresponding number of multiple services unassisted (Agenda et al., 2019). Furthermore, each service can be in different locations, each will have its own terminology, and each will have its own internal procedures that the survivor needs to learn quickly to get help. The isolation mentioned in the previous section can increase incrementally in the process.

The domino effect of sexual violence can reach into many places within the client's life and the provision of support (if it is available) may not exactly line up with what is needed, or when. One's attempts to secure basic, but essential support can therefore be repeatedly impeded. The longer this continues the more survivors are left behind by the denial of their experiences as they are not fully heard nor responded to with support. Lives paused by trauma without supportive interventions means that survivors are therefore denied access to their own lives, relationships, and communities.

Underlying a significant proportion of the above issues is the inconsistency in accessibility caused by funding within the field of talking therapy, including services specialising in the mental health needs of people affected by sexual violence. This is true whether such funding is national, local, or personal as each makes a significant difference as to when a client can access psychotherapy, as well as whether the psychotherapy they are provided with is specialised for survivors.

Therefore, clients often reach a point where they feel ready to ask for help with their mental health, but it is not guaranteed that they will have this need met at the point when it is requested. Knowing which professional or service to ask for, what kinds of psychotherapy are available or appropriate to one's presenting concerns, or even what training qualifications or registrations to look out for in a psychotherapist, is intimidating. Sometimes this is to the **point of being too difficult to navigate, so the survivor remains alone in their** struggle.

In public services a client is usually allocated to a psychotherapist on the basis of who is available, their level of experience, and their professional competency in working with the issues a client presents with. This is the best that can be done to ensure that clients are seen as quickly as possible by a practitioner who can appropriately meet their needs.

These aren't issues in themselves and in fact are ethically valid practices, but they can be problematic in practice. For example: a client may feel more comfortable with a psychotherapist of a certain gender, age, faith, or ethnicity. A client's comfort level is their sense of feeling safe and understood, which can more easily facilitate the process of talking therapy as a form of recovery from sexual violence.

As a contrast, if the survivor has personal funding for private services they can more freely choose who they want to work with. This choice is informed by anything that signals safety such as a list of the psychotherapist's specific qualifications or working experience, seeing their face in a photograph, knowing their name, noticing how the psychotherapist talks about their own style of working, and the option of open-ended psychotherapy.

There is more of an introduction to the person behind the professional persona at an earlier stage, whereas who a client will see remains faceless, nameless, and voiceless for a long time if they cannot afford private services. In the former instance the meeting of personal qualities and professional credentials is more transparent, which can better encourage safe relatedness in a psychotherapy appointment.

Given the overwhelming requirement for specialist talking therapy for survivors in public services, there are always waiting lists to ensure everyone asking for help is offered this opportunity. In some areas there are no such services, usually because of a lack of public funding. The delay in time between asking for help and receiving it becomes wider in the absence of personal funding. Relationally, there is no co-regulation of affect via human contact when being left alone to navigate multiple services and sit on waiting lists. Such human contact is essential to offer and mediate when the self is disconnected via trauma.

A lack of choice due to the aforementioned practicalities is another way that freedom of movement, speech, and autonomy are diminished on the part of the client. There is nowhere to go, what needs to be voiced remains unsaid, and a survivor's framing of their experiences comes up against the societal misconceptions surrounding them. Again, the impact of sexual violence can be exacerbated, as is the sense of isolation in having to deal with them in a victim-blaming society.

When mental health support is accessed, psychotherapists are sometimes the only professional a survivor trusts enough to open up to because they offer a private space to speak relatively freely and do not turn away from the significance of what is being said. The result is being in position where psychotherapists are often asked implicitly and explicitly to accommodate intersecting needs so that any kind of survivor is adequately supported. The weight of what needs to be attended to, and how this is a challenge, can thus be felt by all involved.

Psychotherapy can feel interrupted by requests to attend to other basic needs such as housing, income, asylum applications, physical health care, and child care. However, this is a form of direct contact with the domino effect of sexual violence in addition to any other form of disempowerments the client is subject to in their life. When formulating interventions all of these as practical and relational factors feed into the clinical material to be worked with to promote recovery from sexual violence. These also point to the practical need for wrap-around services which are few and far between.

Sadly, there are often discrepancies between what a client needs and what psychotherapists can offer even with regards to mental health care. This is primarily evidenced in practical factors such as how many appointments each client can have and working towards specialising within a generic service. If there are restrictions on talking therapy or intrusions into the confidentiality of the process placed by other human-made systems (the criminal justice system being one example), further practical amendments are put in place.

It is accurate to say that clients understand these as additional obstacles to receiving adequate mental health care. The fact that so many people disempowered by sexual violence and other societal inequalities come up against multiple barriers in order to simply receive mental care is inhumane. It is not unusual at all for psychotherapists to also experience disempowerment via the challenge of working with the traumatic impact of sexual violence, as well as empathically feeling the weight of these barriers their clients face. Progress in psychotherapy can be extremely slow and disengagement can occur as a result.

Psychotherapy is a profession saturated with volunteers, which creates a system whereby both parties are afforded (literally and figuratively) less value by capitalist societal standards. This is a double-edged sword as survivors seek out the safe space of psychotherapy because they are suddenly marginalised by a society that is unsafe and doesn't always want to respond to their needs. Survivors are undervalued in the act of sexual violence and continue to be undervalued when there are so many restrictions on accessing support in its aftermath.

For our profession, not having consistent funding for one of the most prevalent issues we will encounter in any setting we work in is fundamentally illogical. The result for services dependent on funding is that they are forced to severely amend what is available, sometimes to the point of missing a client's needs. In the meantime, survivors wait and deteriorate on waiting lists when they don't have personal funding because the need for specialist public services is always far higher than what can be provided.

> **I see funding coming with the implicit message that 'you are worthy of investment.'** There is a positive statement attached to funding therapy services both for the therapy services being accessed and for the individual accessing the service.
>
> *Crystal*

Many services are required to take on unpaid practitioners as volunteers to meet the demand for service provision in the perpetual absence of funding. The fact that many survivors in public services are sat across from an unpaid psychotherapist, whether they know this to be the case or not, is an offence to the value of their humanity having been violated and their subsequent suffering. Whilst money is not the sole indicator of value, it is another way that people become disadvantaged within a society that does highly value this factor.

Survivors are consequently pushed to the edges of another space in their lives and are dismissed as unimportant to the wider running of a community. Simultaneously, psychotherapists are required to undertake specialist work whilst not officially being part of a workforce due to their unpaid status. The invisibility of the prolific issue of sexual violence via its societal side-lining continues to be reinforced from all angles, which is fundamentally nonsensical. Its disruptive impact means that many people cannot participate in lives nor communities as they otherwise would be able to in the absence of trauma and disempowerment.

Here psychotherapy's focus on empowerment counters this dynamic, given that it invites people into a mutually agreed person-to-person process where a person is seen. Empowerment within a psychotherapeutic approach is interested in all facets of a client, even if such facets are too distressing for a client to make contact with at any given point. In this way humanity and relatedness are solidified as important values for navigating all spaces in the wider world.

Disclosing sexual violence, a pressured personal choice, can be the difference between accessing one service or another. For many survivors the element of choice is removed in simply feeling unable to do so whether for practical, emotional, or personal safety reasons. Wanting to report to the police with the understanding that therapy notes are routinely requested by the criminal justice system can be the difference between accessing a service, or not at all.

The decision to access a psychotherapy service can be taken out of a survivor's hands for many reasons. This can include instances where disclosure of sexual violence partway through talking therapy leads to discharge from a generic service, even if that service is able to offer treatment that can alleviate elements of the client's psychological distress such as depression or anxiety.

Although suitability of a service is an ethical dilemma to be taken seriously by practitioners, the outcome of these deliberations often risks disempowering survivors who find accessing suitable services already difficult. The answer, to ensure that training on the traumatic impact of sexual violence is mandatorily provided within talking therapy courses and becomes a part of retaining one's professional registration, is a starting point.

Using one's voice, only to be shut down, as a human experience is far too close to the injurious responses of the wider world. Further complicating this is the degree to which a survivor can verbalise past experiences along with their current impact upon bodies and minds. This can occur whilst knowing that doing so can be re-traumatising, hence the conscious or unconscious inclination to turn away from the full force of these. Simply put, a person may find asking for help too overwhelming to achieve it.

The myth that one absolutely has to talk about what happened in order to recover from it is not only incorrect, it is an unnecessary barrier to gaining support. It is possible to address the presenting issues caused by sexual violence without exploring the details of the incidents. If a survivor believes this myth but isn't ready to speak about their experiences, they cannot even consider talking therapy as an option. Therefore, perceptions of the mental health system can risk compounding already complex issues.

It is not necessary that all survivors receive open-ended or long-term psychotherapy, as brief work can be effective too. However, a lack of choice in what support one receives, and therefore personal freedom, is removed from the process of accessibility. Setting up a lack of choice in the early stages of engagement including once appointments are offered can affect the reparative efficacy of psychotherapy as an intervention.

Policy, procedure, and process are vital in delivering consistent and ethical services to clients. Equally, they can be barriers to the reparative elements of what psychotherapy offers, which is a human relationship. Contact with any psychotherapy service is an opportunity for human contact and a lack of this can be relationally injurious, in part manifested by disengagement from services.

For example: within services with long waiting lists, having no contact between referral and being offered an appointment risks damaging the relational baseline for undertaking what can be distressing and challenging work. Advising a survivor that they can contact a service to enquire about their referral, as well as confirming they will receive a regular notification to advise them of their place on it, can assist in mediating distress.

Giving clients the option to visit the premises before their first appointment, including a brief in-person introduction to their psychotherapist, can similarly mitigate any wariness or fear in each step taken towards engaging in psychotherapy. A pre-appointment phone call where the client can hear their psychotherapist's voice before they meet can likewise be effective in promoting relatedness.

As professionals we should continue to offer psychotherapeutic spaces to process traumatic experiences and recover as required. Additional consideration in service delivery is vital when a survivor already suffers from forced marginalisation due to protected characteristics, such as requiring a gender-specific or ethnicity-specific service.

The resultant pushing of both survivors and psychotherapists into private, quiet spaces means that societal marginalisation as an act is reinforced. This does not enable anyone to use psychotherapy as an effective bridge back into the wider world and everyday life. It also de-values the person and the ways in which they identify, alongside their status as a survivor.

The privacy and quiet offered in a benign way by psychotherapists sits closely to the oppressive silence forced by a society that does not want to hear the reality of the matter. Outside of psychotherapy appointments the survivor may feel less able to use their personal power including their voice (characterised within this book as freedom of speech) because of societal barriers and threats to their safety. A calling into question of how effective psychotherapy can be if change is only fully facilitated in the closed-off rooms we work from is discussed in Chapter three.

Dialogic barriers

Another barrier to accessing psychotherapy is the nature of the global dialogue regarding sexual violence. There are common themes on how sexual

Sexual violence in context 17

violence is spoken about and influenced at times by all the things that make people diverse, such as: cultural practices, sexuality, and the relationships we have with others. The commonalities that are modified a little by diversity include blaming the survivor, a contradictory emphasis on speaking out to the authorities combined with keeping sexual violence otherwise unsaid, and a gendered view on this phenomenon from a binary lens.

There are limits on how and how much sexual violence can be discussed in the wider world given that there is an investment in the mass disempowerment of people via this means. Such disempowerment reinforces the entitlement of bodies and sexual contact to many in the global community at the significant expense of the owners of those bodies. What is reinforced in these acts are the ways we all understand how the world, people, and relationships can operate even if these include human rights infringements.

The translation of these understandings permeates every layer of the wider world, our relationships, and our selves. It is these translations that are communicated in words, thoughts, actions, and inactions by every person across the globe. These translations can be the vital difference between taking in the fact that what happened was violating and brushing it off as nothing to worry about even though harm was definitely done. The tension between these two states frequently arises in psychotherapeutic dialogues, including when both of them hold equal weight.

A client's frame of reference for sexual violence is often put in place well before incidences of this kind occur, if they occur at all. For some people the chances that it will are higher than for others and this is reflective of the unequal distribution of power across persons within the wider world. As an example related to gender: it is more likely that those who are assigned female at birth will be subjected to sexual violence more often than those who are assigned male at birth (World Health Organization, 2016; Office for National Statistics, 2017). Male, female, and non-binary adults who identify as transgender are, in some research, more likely to have experienced sexual violence than both of these groups (National Center for Transgender Equality, 2015).

The oft-used term of the working relationship in psychotherapy being 'co-created' is as valid in the wider world as it is within this formalised space. This term refers to the collaborative process of relational work, including acknowledgement that the nature of this relationship is reflective of the collective processes that each individual brings to it. The co-created societal frame of reference for sexual violence is the same for all involved so care must be taken to unpick the problematic elements of this frame in psychotherapy.

Therefore, all of us can easily misunderstand the phenomenon as well as misunderstand the person and their identity at the centre of it. Problematising this further are myths about sexual violence which can be misconstrued as the truth and represent yet another barrier to accessing psychotherapy.

As an example, forced sexual contact by a partner in amongst other consensual contact might be rationalised as an overall part of sex with that person. In the context of an otherwise positive relationship the magnitude of thinking differently about intimacy, sex, and the relationship are enormous let alone seeking help for it. This in part stems from the myth that sexual violence only occurs between strangers where one simply seeks to attack another at random.

Dialogic distinctions between sex and different types of sexual violence such as rape can complicate a survivor's process of coming to terms with their experiences. These words exist, but a survivor's right to them is inhibited by a society that frames them in a certain way in colloquial language, whether amongst peers or in formally organised institutions. In practice sex can be assumed to occur by virtue of the physical act. In the application of language any kind of 'sex' can be seen in the same way, although in doing so the act of consent is overlooked. It is this gap where sexual violence occurs in practice and as a linguistic term.

Psychotherapy being a form of talking therapy can be an unhelpful misnomer for survivors who do not want to, or cannot, talk about their history of sexual violence. For some this is re-triggering of post-trauma symptoms and emotional experiences such as shame, all of which must be avoided given their ability to overwhelm the multi-faceted self which precipitates disconnection.

It can be helpful to ask clients to pick their own words, which the psychotherapist will also use, as a reference point for the focus of their work. Being clear with a client from the outset that they can say as much, or as little, as they wish on any element of their experiences (including sexual violence) can ease the pressure for a client on two levels. The first is providing an opportunity for informed consent, where the client can choose to participate in a type of psychotherapy that may or may not include detailed recall of traumatic experiences.

Second, there is more choice in what a shared conversation about sexual violence looks like on the terms of the person who has survived it. This is counter to narratives found in most other spaces between other selves within the wider world. There is more opportunity for a client to be immediately understood, on their own terms, rather than having what happened to them dictated to them by other selves or disempowering systems.

The nature of the chosen words is also reflective of a client's subjective process of making sense of the events and may differ from formalised language used in professional settings. As an example, a lesbian woman may refer to non-consensual sexual contact with her female partner as 'rape' as it reflects the degree of violation experienced. This is contradictory to British law where 'rape' can only occur from a person with a penis to another person.

Building an understanding of how different communities may conceptualise sex, relationships, sexual violence, and mental health is helpful in appropriately amending one's approach in conversation with clients. Within communities where sex is an especially private act perhaps due to religious beliefs on its meaning and purpose, clients may not be used to speaking about this type of physical contact (consensual or otherwise) without feeling inhibited. Additionally, within communities where mental health isn't a societally-understood nor accepted term, clients may refer more to physical ailments than psychological distress.

Myths contribute to our gendered misunderstanding of sexual violence, and are therefore misinformative, on two counts. First, people involved in sexual violence are categorised into cisgender male/female only. Second, stereotypical characteristics are applied to narrow understandings of those two genders. Such narrow definitions of gender make it difficult for many people to even consider accessing psychotherapy because this also narrows the configurations in which we believe sexual violence occurs. If the existence of sexual violence is called into question, then how can one confidently request help for it?

In many myths about sexual violence, men (using the definition of people who are assigned male at birth based on their genitals) are always seen as perpetrators and women (using the definition of people who are assigned female at birth based on their genitals) are always victims. The inclusion of stereotypes about both of these genders augments this limited view. Men are viewed as strong and women are weak. This makes people impacted by sexual violence doubly weak as in: if you are affected by this, you're not coping well enough. It also means that men have a particular experience of shame due to this perceived weakness, projected onto them via being in a typically female role.

A survivor's feeling unsure of what happened, whether it was sexual violence, and whether it can be disclosed, is often as complex as the circumstances by which they were placed in such a position. Conversely societal myths tend to categorise all perpetrators, survivors, and situations where sexual violence occurs, into seemingly straightforward narratives. The reality is that sexual violence is embedded into all layers of society between many different types of people, from impulsive violating interactions to prolonged and organised large-scale abuse.

Once a survivor enters psychotherapy there can be limits on how and how much sexual violence can be discussed there. This is particularly true for clients who need a lot of time to forge trust with their psychotherapist and build faith in the security of the working relationship, who have this process cut short by time-limited work or a lack of funding. In such cases it can feel as though the work has only just begun and the opportunity to fully resolve the issues is thwarted.

Guidelines set by the criminal justice system on talking therapy in the United Kingdom have restricted accessibility to it. For almost two decades a person with an active report, investigation, or trial has been unable to speak to anyone personally or professionally about the details of their experiences of sexual violence. Such clients are termed 'pre-trial' by these guidelines. They are unable to speak about their experiences because their account of what happened, seen as their oral evidence by the legal system, needs to be protected.

Speaking about this with a psychotherapist is seen to risk influencing their memory of the events and potentially change how they are recalled in legal settings such as court. Talking therapy services have either reduced the number of appointments on offer for those who were pre-trial, delivered more structured work that steered away from opportunities to recall spontaneously, or not offered anything until the criminal justice process had concluded. Many survivors have been forced to keep looking for help, choose whether to have talking therapy but not speak freely, or decline it completely themselves due to having this essential constituent of the process removed.

Media can have a huge effect on how conceptualisations of perpetrators, survivors, and support systems are internalised by all of us. Examples are television, print media, digital media, and social media. Specialist services for survivors, including psychotherapy, often see an increase in requests for support following contributions to the ongoing dialogue on sexual violence in these public formats.

Versions of these include well-known figures being investigated for sexual offences, famous people talking about their experiences of sexual violence, and storylines on television programmes depicting sexual violence in ways that might not otherwise be available. Consistent public visibility is required to widen our collective understanding of the details related to what constitutes the many types of sexual violence a person can experience.

In psychotherapy clients hope to have the following responses from speaking out: to be heard, listened to, and responded to appropriately in line with what has been said. This kind of dialogue is certainly reparative. Survivors have justifiably demanded the same take place in other spaces where they were prevented from being safe from sexual violence, or prevented from receiving help when it was disclosed.

One of the biggest examples of this in the United Kingdom is the formation of the Independent Inquiry into Child Sexual Abuse (IICSA). This represents a statutory effort to better understand past institutional failures to protect children and how to better protect them in the future. Reports from the Inquiry have been heavily led by interviews with adults who were sexually abused during childhood in places such as schools and the care system.

On a much wider scale on social media, the #MeToo movement has done the same primarily for women who have come forward to let the world know how powerful men have subjected them to sexual violence in the workplace, including the film industry.

It is not surprising that there is a continuous upsurge in contributions from survivors to the worldwide dialogue on sexual violence and its impact. Such contributions also occur in psychotherapy where it is becoming more common for survivors, particularly younger survivors, to want to integrate their personal understanding of their experiences alongside the voices of other survivors. This is part of the search for truth on the matter, becoming empowered, and creating safer spaces for all in the wider world.

As a last point on dialogic barriers, psychotherapists should acknowledge how the clinical language of their profession can be a help or a hindrance to accessing their services. For some clients talking about having chest pain makes more sense than saying they feel anxious. An understanding of cultural differences can be sensitively applied here as some clients from non-white, non-western cultures may not have as much ease in using clinical terms in conversational encounters. Mental health may also not be a commonly understood nor accepted concept in some communities.

Depression, disturbed sleep, and physical pain, for example, are outlined differently by each person that experiences them. The subjective nature of how these are verbalised should be mirrored in psychotherapeutic work by way of keeping the process as individually tailored to the client as possible and respecting them as the authority of the impact of their own traumatic incidences. The ways our bodies and minds react to sexual violence can provide useful insights into how the self of the individual client has been forcibly re-configured, including how their identity may feel compromised. Alleviation of post-trauma symptoms should not be 'one size fits all,' as this can miss the person amongst the trauma.

Diagnosis is not only a precursor to administering appropriate treatment. From a relational perspective it is also an opportunity to re-frame the presenting concerns of the client, ideally in conjunction with them. The emergence of various mental health difficulties in addition to post-trauma symptoms can further blur a survivor's understanding of what they've been through, what is happening now, and what can be done about it. Making any clinical formulation and treatment a collaborative process cements at an early stage a process of re-empowerment of the survivor, rather than the diagnostic system simply becoming yet another space in the world that is oppressive.

As psychotherapists our response can include learning a language each time we meet a survivor, as part of the basis of working together. Our traditional understandings of a theoretical framework should literally and figuratively translate into carefully considered words in conjunction with each client. This forms part of the shared process of psychotherapy and is supportive in meeting a survivor where they are to further empower them as the owner of their experiences and recovery.

Barriers due to the impact of sexual violence

A significant barrier to disclosure and seeking support are post-trauma symptoms. These represent the psychological, somatic, and behavioural manifestations of the impact of sexual violence. Such impacts can be heightened by anything associated with the traumatic events, such as: contact from the perpetrators, being in the same physical spaces where the sexual violence happened, various kinds of physical touch in consenting relationships, and anniversaries of the events.

The result is that clients are pulled back despite attempts to move forward. These symptoms are acutely felt as an inner experience within the multi-faceted self and can prevent disclosure and accessibility to support just as much as external factors. One way in which the former occurs is traumatic recall, where sexual violence is fully re-experienced in the body and mind as if it is happening again now. Examples are flashbacks, nightmares, and intrusive memories.

Traumatic recall can take place at any point, including when the survivor is going about their everyday life and there is no immediate threat to their safety from the wider world. For further information on the underlying physiological and neurobiological mechanisms underlying this, please refer to Chapter two. Recall of this nature arising in an uncontrolled way can lead some clients to question whether psychotherapy, as a place to work through this, is beyond their capacity or being unsure as to whether someone can help.

Understandably the isolation of this position in experiencing, re-living, and overcoming sexual violence on a regular basis can also instil a sense of hopelessness. For some, the only conclusion that can be reached is that they have gone mad, or that there is something inherently at fault within them. The longer this is the case, the more disconnected a client becomes from facets of their self as well as from others in relationship. This is on top of the disconnection from the present moment when being pulled back into the past where sexual violence took place.

Similar effects can be seen when clients struggle with affect regulation, another post-trauma symptom. Not being in control of one's emotions widens the gap of understanding and power in a survivor's personal world. Emotions are accompanied by changes in physical sensations in the body which may also be out of one's control and therefore disempowering. Survivors risk these being visible every time contact with others is made, including professionals such as psychotherapists.

Not knowing how one will feel at any given moment, what this means, if it can be controlled, and if it will be understood by another self are all precursors to a set of emotional experiences specific to sexual violence: blame, shame, and guilt. The result is a cycle of overwhelming physical and psychological stresses followed by a distancing or shutting down. Within one's multi-faceted self there is an intense, forced relatedness between these facets that needs to be mitigated by disconnection to alleviate the accompanying distress.

Client example: Jamie

Jamie had been repeatedly sexually assaulted by her step-father in the family home between the ages of ten and thirteen. At age eighteen when the stress of the nightmares and memories became overwhelming, Jamie decided to tell her mother what had happened. Her mother's response was to not believe her and to say that Jamie had brought shame on the family for having made up such a lie.

Feeling unable to stay at home any longer, Jamie fled to a refuge where she was offered short-term accommodation. During her stay she saw a leaflet for a local text support service in a women's organisation and decided to reach out. Aside from her mother, Jamie had never spoken to anyone before about what had happened and felt strongly that texting through her phone was the most she could manage without becoming overwhelmed.

Over the course of two months Jamie felt more ready to see someone face-to-face and asked to be referred to the organisation's psychotherapy service. She waited for an assessment appointment and was glad it was offered at a time when the nightmares were less frequent so that she was not as easily stressed. Jamie felt nervous, but comfortable enough with the psychotherapist she met with, who offered her appointments to start in a week's time.

As this approached Jamie's nightmares increased once more, as did the freeze response to them in her body. This was followed by huge feelings of shame, which shut her mind and body down further. On the day of her appointment Jamie struggled to get out of bed and got dressed very slowly as her body felt heavy. But she was unable to leave her room as the freeze response happened again, which meant she missed her appointment.

Although the organisation contacted her, Jamie felt unable to reply as she no longer felt ready to start psychotherapy. Six months went by, Jamie was relocated to a permanent address and in general felt more stable in herself. Whilst in her local town one day Jamie recognised the organisation's building and thought she would try speaking to them again. Jamie explained to the receptionist that she had been too scared to come to her psychotherapy appointment and wanted to try again now.

As a relational template shaped by sexual violence, survivors can have limited periods of being able to relate to facets of their self as an internal experience, as well as with others. For psychotherapists this pattern is the additional challenge of offering a safe space that can potentially create barriers to recovery even with the best intentions. Working relationally assumes that clients can engage in a relationship relatively securely, but this is often impaired by the very reason clients are asking for help in the first place.

Tangible safety in the psychotherapeutic relationship is key, as is the safety of the physical space in which the work is undertaken. The privacy of a closed door may also represent a lack of exit, thereby changing the freedoms of psychotherapy into yet another space in the wider world where the survivor is trapped.

Care should be taken to ensure that comfort is negotiated with the survivor at all stages of the process. This becomes a shared practice of feeling able to consistently manage responsibility for implementing what is needed to feel safe. As a fundamental baseline for everyday living, safety is a principle practised in relationship before being extended to the wider world.

When control of one's personal safety is removed in the act of sexual violence hypervigilance can set in thereafter at an unconscious, somatic level to prevent a survivor coming into harm's way. If a client is conscious of this it may be verbalised as a sense of feeling wary or scared of other people and places. An excessive mis-firing of this neurophysiological safety mechanism initiated by the amygdala can be triggered even when others are offering supportive communications and opportunities.

Hypervigilance may lead to difficulties in accessing a psychotherapy service from the point of picking up the phone, travelling to the organisation, and sitting in front of one's psychotherapist for the duration of the appointment. At a surface level it may appear that a client is displaying avoidant behaviour, also a post-trauma symptom, such as limited eye contact, not speaking, and non-attendance. This can be understood as the limits of a client's capacity to comfortably make contact with other selves, as well as the limits of their inner experience when distressing physical facets of their self emerge to the forefront of the person-to-person encounter.

A typical impact of sexual violence is difficulties in relationships, which is influenced by many of the factors discussed thus far. What is not listed in any diagnostic criteria, but is usually referenced by survivors, is how trust is destroyed when sexual violence happens. Once more this includes trust within one's self, as well as with other selves. As a basic principle of relatedness, how is trust now possible when the worst of human contact has been experienced?

In the case of disclosure and accessibility a psychotherapist can at least be trusted as a mental health professional with the training and expertise on working with the impact of sexual violence. What is just as important in the relational experience is the trust that a survivor will be understood, respected, and cared for. For many survivors this is more valuable and memorable than single interventions made based on theory. As psychotherapists we understand that both need to be delivered hand-in-hand to maximise efficacy of the services we provide:

> I found statutory services too clinical, as the process of sitting in a GP surgery waiting area didn't seem right.
>
> *Amanda*

The alienation of positive human contact from support services can reinforce mistrust not only in individual practitioners or services, but also the wider process of recovery. For survivors such as Amanda who are ready to receive support and to try relating to another in a sensitive way to do so, the procedural aspects of service provision can be another step further away from what is needed: the safety of another self.

Amanda's experience after the aforementioned moment was to disclose to the GP, which led to a referral, further disclosure within other services, and ultimately withdrawing from any support offered. On each occasion the circumstances didn't feel comfortable enough for Amanda as the provision of safe human contact was lacking, until she sought out her own therapist privately herself. As such, the relational experience of accessing support is an excercise in building trust via taking steps into the wider world as a person with sexual violence in one's history.

References

Agenda, Against Violence and Abuse and Lloyds Bank Foundation England and Wales, 2019: *Findings of the National Commission on Domestic and Sexual Violence and Multiple Disadvantage*. London: Agenda, Against Violence and Abuse and Lloyds Bank Foundation England and Wales.

National Center for Transgender Equality, 2015: *The Report of the U.S. Transgender Survey*. Washington, D.C.: National Center for Transgender Equality.

Office for National Statistics, 2017: *Sexual Offences in England and Wales: Year Ending March 2017*. London: Office for National Statistics.

World Health Organization, Department of Reproductive Health and Research, London School of Hygiene and Tropical Medicine, and South African Medical Research Council, 2016: *Global and Regional Estimates of Violence Against Women: Prevalence and Health Effects of Intimate Partner Violence and Non-Partner Sexual Violence*. London: World Health Organization.

Chapter 2

The personal impact of sexual violence

How we survive traumatic experiences

Survival of traumatic experiences happens during the events as well as afterwards as they come to life in the present despite being a past occurrence. There are multiple elements to each aspect of survival due to the complexity of this phenomenon, as well as the multi-faceted complexity of human beings in general. As such, clinical presentations can be as unique as the survivor themselves.

These unique presentations are often the places a survivor automatically and unwillingly returns to when everything else in their internal experience becomes difficult to grasp. Although these internal places can house the trauma, they can also hold aspects of a sense of self. The degree to which either can be experienced varies client to client and can evolve throughout the shared psychotherapeutic endeavour.

Humans are multi-faceted beings with conscious and unconscious processes comprising part of the general human experience. These can become apparent via the physical and psychological facets of the self which themselves can be communicated via the body, thoughts, words, or emotions. Thus far we have four primary facets of the self: conscious/unconscious and physical/psychological. The totality of these create: an individual's specific experience of relating to the different facets of their self (self-experience), relating to other selves, and relating to the wider world. The same can be said for disconnection in each of these ways.

Clients who are survivors of sexual violence report experiencing their selves in ways that are jarring, confusing, and alienating. We can primarily conceptualise this as a disconnected sense of self, as there is discomfort in relating to the different facets of one's self. Much of this stems from the body and brain becoming over- or under-activated as they respond to a self under threat in the moments that sexual violence is experienced. This is re-experienced afterwards as if the threat is still present even when it isn't and is a normal response to violation of the overall self.

Simultaneously, personal worlds become much smaller, sometimes to a point when survivors are unable to physically live in their communities or

DOI: 10.4324/9781003202943-2

their own bodies in a comfortable way. It is worth beginning with the body and brain in an effort to understand the physical chronology of surviving traumatic experiences.

The physical facet of the self, or the body, was of course involved in the traumatic experiences in a way that is particular to survivors of sexual violence compared to other forms of traumatic experience. This is the case even if the nature of the incident did not involve physical contact, such as witnessing sexualised behaviour. Paying attention to this facet of the self is important for psychotherapists in bearing witness to the impact of sexual violence, and provides valuable information on what needs to change during the psychotherapeutic process to alleviate this physical impact.

Specifically, the body barrier was crossed in a violating manner at the time of the traumatic experiences. Even from this basic notion we can understand why survivors often re-experience trauma via somatic symptoms that often feel out of their control. Examples can include muscle tension and physical pain whether this is housed in the part of the body associated with the specifics of their experiences of sexual violence or otherwise.

A secondary effect are the emotions and thoughts associated with these physical symptoms which can be considered as a part of one's psychological response to surviving post-sexual violence. Here is where these two facets have a relationship between them and create another useful arena for exploration within the psychotherapeutic work. These are often the places where blame, shame, and guilt arise which have a root in internalised societal myths about sex and sexual violence.

The nature of re-experiencing past trauma in the present is specific to the individual survivor and psychotherapists can notice commonalities in symptom presentations within this client group. However, part of re-empowering a client includes attending to their individual account, emotional process, embodied experience, and psychological perspective on what they have been through. Our own ability to be present in the present involves a theoretical understanding of the impact of trauma which helps us avoid getting lost in the client's powerful somatic and psychological experiences.

In this way, we begin with the resources they already have in place for surviving day-to-day as a base by which to build further skills to live in a re-configured self and world. Being a survivor means having gone through life using whatever resources available (however limited) upon the point of meeting their psychotherapist, in between appointments, during appointments, and continuing with life once the psychotherapy work has ended. The value of these to the client's survival, and any personal meaning that can be used to inform the work, should always be respected even if they are seemingly maladaptive.

This is important to note given that practitioners meet survivors at various points in their lives and are present for relatively brief periods overall within these lifetimes. The consequence of this is to take on the clinical responsibility of alleviating post-trauma symptoms as psychotherapists, and simultaneously the human responsibility of appropriately responding to injustice and distress at the point at which we meet them.

From a physical perspective, the use of the term 'survive' is apt as it points to a primal response to life-threatening situations. An event is traumatic because of this significant factor and demonstrates how an event is terrifying rather than simply scary. In this way, a client becomes automatically immersed in a particular kind of experience that makes use of biological processes that don't come into motion in our everyday lives if we are generally safe.

The human brain is comprised of three layers which have evolved into existence over time, making it a triune brain (MacLean, 1990). The oldest layer, found at the base of the brain, is called the reptilian brain. On top of this is the second-oldest layer, the paleo-mammalian brain, followed by the outermost layer which is the neo-mammalian brain. Only humans have this third layer, which allows for higher levels of processing such as language, conscious thought, and self-awareness.

What is specific to the survival of trauma is that the two older layers house the neural pathway associated with the fight, flight, or freeze response. As the entire nervous system runs throughout the human body an activation of this particular pathway within it means that, experientially, there is a whole-body response to being under threat. An overview of what happens here is helpful in broadening our understanding of somatic post-trauma symptoms. It can also assist in providing a base by which to understand psychological post-trauma symptoms as humans try to make sense of traumatic experiences with higher-level cognitive processes.

The nervous system is divided into the central and peripheral nervous systems (CNS and PNS, respectively). Both of these are concerned with either regulating homeostasis or surviving a threatening experience, both of which

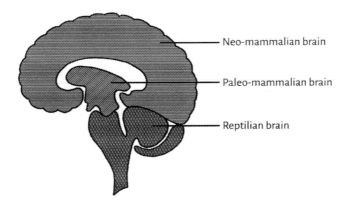

Figure 2.1

keep humans alive. Within the PNS, there is a further division into the sympathetic nervous system and the parasympathetic nervous system. Both are active at all times, although one can be more active than another during the process of survival.

Broadly speaking, if the sympathetic nervous system is more active when a person is under threat, a person will experience a state of hyper-arousal. This is more aligned with the fight or flight response and is possible due to increased blood flow to the muscles which allows for quick movement.

Conversely, if the parasympathetic nervous system is more active a person experiences hypo-arousal, which is aligned with the freeze response. Decreased blood flow to the muscles is a feature of this, which underpins immobility. An example of both these sub-systems being active is having an increased heart rate whilst responding to threat by becoming immobile (freezing).

The other part of the nervous system, the CNS, is responsible for activity in the brain and spinal cord. Here we can note the important role of the vagus nerve in trauma, as it represents yet another way that humans have evolved over time to survive threats to the self. The vagus nerve runs from the cranial stem to the colon, is the main parasympathetic nerve in the body, and reaches into various organs for direct autonomic influence.

It is a neural pathway that carries sensory and temperature information as well as holding the ability to heighten or lessen many functions of the body. In this way, the vagus nerve underlies some of the somatic symptoms which characterise hyper- and hypo-aroused states. Porges' polyvagal theory (2009) highlights the ways that humans can visibly witness a change in others who are under extreme stress.

Importantly, the vagus nerve is concerned with communication and socialisation, as well as mobilisation and immobilisation. It plays a role in management of the muscles within the face and head, thus we can literally see in conversation with another how they may be unconsciously responding to actual or perceived threat to the self. For example, changes in: facial expressions, the ability to speak, and the ability to take in information outside of one's self via listening can change as the client comes into contact with self-experiences and/or external stimuli that are distressing.

There are specific hormones and regions of the brain that initiate and maintain this whole-body response. Initiation at a subconscious level includes the amygdala as the alarm system for the brain being stimulated. Cells within the neuroendocrine system (present almost everywhere in the body) allow for messages to be sent to the hypothalamus, also in the brain. These cells are also involved in the creation of hormones. All are involved in the aforementioned process of keeping humans alive either through regulating homeostasis or surviving a threatening experience.

Where the endocrine system and CNS interact is via the hypothalamic-pituitary-adrenal (HPA) axis. The HPA axis regulates humans' responses to stress, traumatic stress being the most acute version of this. When this response is triggered, the HPA sends signals to the hypothalamus for release of corticotropin-releasing hormone, which binds to receptors on the pituitary gland in the brain.

When this occurs, adrenocorticotropic hormone (ACTH) is released, which in turn binds to receptors on the adrenal cortex as a way to stimulate adrenal release of cortisol. Should cortisol levels reach a certain level, higher functioning is suppressed within the brain, thus facilitating the momentary dominance of older parts of the brain. Accompanying this is an increase in norepinephrine/noradrenaline and epinephrine/adrenaline, which promote the fight-flight-freeze responses that are housed within these more primal areas of the brain.

Two brain regions involved in automatic responses to stress are flooded with these hormones: the hippocampus and amygdala. Both of these are integral in understanding why traumatic experiences are processed, stored, and recalled differently to memories created in states of homeostasis. The hippocampus' role in memory is partly concerned with placing them in context, including when they occurred. The amygdala in part manages sensory memories, making recollection of them rich and nuanced.

Hormonal flooding of these areas of the brain during traumatic experiences results in the amygdala becoming unable to place a date on the memory. Simultaneously the amygdala becomes too good at its job, meaning that traumatic memories can be extremely detailed. The combination of these lends itself to traumatic recall which is characterised by psychologically and/or somatically re-experiencing the past as if it is occurring in the present in a way that is out of the individual's control.

Recalling elements of a traumatic memory can occur at a primarily somatic level, as the survivor physically re-experiences the past in the present. When this traumatic recall occurs, the survivor typically responds in the same hyper- or hypo-aroused way in the body as they did at the time of the incident in order to try and survive it once more. Therefore, historical sexual violence can be re-experienced as if it is happening now via flashbacks, intrusive memories, and nightmares. Alternatively, memories created during traumatic incidences can present clinically as the difficulty, or impossibility, of explicit recall.

In both humans and animals this chain of responses to threat is automatic. Human bodies will do what is needed to survive what is happening at the time and for as many times afterwards as this is re-experienced. Any psychological or physical responses that occur are not in a person's control during sexual violence and this means there is no 'right' way to survive during or after the events.

For humans, the neo-mammalian layer of the brain struggles to make conscious sense of this. Most often, this understandably translates to a sense of loss of control over one's self during the experience of sexual violence, as there is no choice in how one reacts to such an event. Any meaning that is then inferred from not being in control and how their body reacted (or not) can become part of the individual survivor's material to work through in psychotherapy.

For clients the level of detail needed about these neurophysiological processes from a psychotherapist varies from person to person. Primarily, psychotherapists should be concerned with normalising the client's somatic and psychological responses to trauma as this is part of addressing the client's internalisations of blame, shame, and guilt. We should also hold firm to the knowledge that different parts of the brain, nervous system, and hormones are more or less active depending on actual threat at the time, or perceived threat thereafter. Doing so can be helpful in sensitively encouraging relatedness with different facets of the self, re-engaging with others via relationships, and re-engaging with the world.

The chances of finding somewhere solid to land within our internal landscape is impaired given that the physical and psychological facets of the self become dysregulated and forcibly re-organised. This is further extended to attempts to find a safe place in relationships, and a society which is full of potential threats such as the one survivors have already experienced.

As such, psychotherapy for survivors of sexual violence is a practice in increasing relatedness with the following domains: different parts of the brain, the mind with body, along with other facets of the client's self and personal identity. Our role is to start from the co-created space of psychotherapy as a way to facilitate movement into the wider world in a way that feels safe following forced re-organisation of the self, relationships, and the world.

An understanding of the parts of the brain, nervous system, neural pathway, and hormones involved in the automatic survival of threats to the self also allows clients to begin to place language on their experiences. This in itself makes use of higher levels of functioning within the neo-mammalian brain. In this way, clients are offered opportunities to practise having control of access to this part of the brain by using words to be as present as possible in the present, when the traumatic past feels as though it is taking hold of the self.

Since sexual violence is a phenomenon perpetrated by people to other people we must consider this as a contextual factor relevant to survival of such experiences. It is true that sexual violence occurs between strangers, as well as those who have some sort of pre-existing relationship to each other, however casual or close. Regardless of the nature of the relationship psychotherapists should not at all dismiss the psychological and physical presence of perpetrators in the survivor's life because the impact of sexual violence is such that they are often not far away in their minds, bodies, and communities.

It is not simply the threat of further violations to the self, and potentially re-experiencing the original violation at psychological and physical levels, that survivors repeatedly come into contact with. This can occur regardless of the perpetrator's actual presence. What also happens is holding the weight of knowing what occurred which, to varying degrees, is ignored or acknowledged by the perpetrator, others surrounding them, and professionals within various contexts to whom disclosures are made.

Therefore, survival of sexual violence repeatedly re-occurs by virtue of existing within society and relationships, as this was the context in which it originally occurred. For survivors this has psychological, somatic, and practical consequences that the psychotherapist must take into account in order to work effectively with this client group.

Being forced to re-organise multi-faceted selves and lives

It is difficult to overstate the impact of a survivor's traumatic experience of being forced into a situation between persons they did not consent to and having entry to their bodies and minds similarly forced into. This remains the case despite increased vocalisation and visibility of this issue worldwide from survivors themselves in the age of globalisation via the internet, plus civil disobedience or resistance activity such as public protests. We are all repeatedly exposed to the matter of sexual violence as told by those both within and outside the confines of our own community.

The facets of our selves operate on unconscious/conscious, psychological/physical, and related/disconnected levels. The nature of these is evidenced in the client's experiences of the following: their internal psychological world, the physical body as the primary place where they live, other people via relationships, and interactions with the wider world. What sexual violence primarily does is force re-organisation of all of these in the attempt to keep surviving, so we can expect to see varying configurations of difficulties in multiple areas in psychotherapy.

As a standalone divide, parts of the brain and nervous system being activated during traumatic experiences means the physical facet of the self is simultaneously less activated. A person's ability to put explicit thoughts and conscious awareness to these states of physical being is dependent on their window of tolerance (Siegel, 1999) which denotes a physiological state of calm, regulated homeostasis rather than the hyper- or hypo-arousal which is characteristic of survival. Within this window we are able to take in and process information optimally.

By its very composition the mind has less ability to think when a client is trying to survive actual or perceived threat because the older parts of the brain override the neo-mammalian capacity for conscious reflection. Not knowing what to think about what happened is exacerbated by societal myths around sexual violence and how this translates into forced responsibility for sexual contact that was not consented to. Thus, space is provided within the psychological self for internalised blame, shame, and guilt.

There are many conscious and unconscious processes taking place within all of our selves at any one time. What is in our awareness can ebb and flow depending on the demands of the present moment and what is being evoked from our past. This can move us in ways that are consistent with regular behavioural patterns, or can be completely unexpected. We also wouldn't be able to complete even basic tasks if all of our conscious attention held the totality of our lives in a focused way, although there is a lot going on at any given moment.

Any unconscious processes such as these can be brought to conscious awareness via reflection and psychoeducation on the part of the psychotherapist. Bridging the gap between the unconscious and conscious forms part of the process of relatedness within the self at large.

Making a distinction between physical and psychological processes that occur, and creating the therapeutic space within which the survivor is able to reflect on them, is an act of moving the person closer to their own personal processes of survival. Unlike other spaces within the wider world, psychotherapy can provide this as a way to facilitate re-empowerment of the self, starting with increasing a sense of comfortable relatedness.

The quality of relatedness or disconnection of each facet of the survivor's self points to areas that require attention during the psychotherapeutic work. The psychotherapist should respond to and eventually anticipate in advance which facets are at the forefront within every moment of the therapeutic dialogue. Equal attention should be paid to a client's range of affect, physical expressions, and verbalisations of their material as each offers insight into the particular presentation of the impact of sexual violence on an individual client.

Degrees of relatedness can in part be conceptualised as contact with facets of the self, which can be limited following sexual violence. Similarly, survivors can experience differing levels of comfortable and uncomfortable contact over time with all the different recollections of their lived experiences. As with any client, one of the aims of psychotherapeutic work is to increase an ability to more tolerably come into contact with anything that brings distress so that it is not overwhelming, particularly not (in the case of survivors) to the extent of being re-traumatising.

In order to begin understanding the multi-faceted self, raising awareness of the client's movement within their internal landscape is a helpful first step. This creates an enhanced consciousness of their relationship with their self overall and each of the different facets that constitute its totality. Doing so evolves into a practice ground for movement within the psychotherapeutic space in relationship with another, with the final step being autonomous movement in the world. Ultimately, we are seeking relatedness as much as possible between numerous domains in collaboration with the client.

For survivors, this therapeutic context is essential to facilitate recovery as it is part of the framework of psychotherapy within which any other specific aims can be achieved. The dichotomy of relatedness and disconnectedness is worth further dissecting, as this is one of the primary challenges for survivors in navigating a re-configured external world via a re-configured internal sense of self.

As an example in reference to diagnostic criteria, dissociation can be considered as a pronounced form of disconnection which has roots in both the physical and psychological domains of the self. However, I encourage psychotherapists to widen their definition of disconnection between facets of the self, in relationships, and the wider world in line with their particular theoretical orientation. Including other forms of psychological processes that protect against intolerable facets of our selves, and the experiences that survivors have been forced to internalise, means you are able to stay true to the way you practise.

As a last point on where disconnection originates within the self we can call on the neurophysiology of trauma to once again understand that memories are processed differently during states of extreme stress and recall is impaired thereafter. In doing so we return to an embodied response to traumatic experiences and how disconnection is a survival strategy.

Specifically, dissociation is a way to not be fully present during the horror of being subjected to sexual violence and this is life-saving. Additionally, it is absolutely normal to have gaps in memory, or no memory at all, of such experiences because they are not processed in the same way as other memories are when we happen to be in a state of homeostasis.

Having a lack of chronology contributes to degrees of disconnection within one's sense of self, as experiences of sexual violence do not sit within the psychological facet of the self in the same way that other life events do. Understanding disconnection as a spectrum of symptoms that can manifest assists in viewing the impact of sexual violence from a relational and compassionate lens, rather than simple cause and effect. To do the latter would risk losing sight of the **self amongst the trauma, which is not our role as psychotherapists** even if the survivor's everyday experience is that they are nothing but an abused person.

Difficulties in having comfortable contact between all facets of the self widens our understanding of a survivor's experiences of living in forcibly re-configured spaces. These are a series of literal and figurative worlds that change because of the impact of sexual violence. These are: physical body, psychological mind, home, local community, wider society, personal relationships, human-made support systems constructed within society, and the world at large. This type of re-configuration is especially felt in terms of size, as the worlds of survivors of sexual violence often suddenly become very small.

Experientially this is felt as disempowerment which is characterised by reduced freedom of: autonomy, speech, and movement. This is especially true when the distressed physical facet of the self dominates a survivor's ability to exist comfortably, as (at worst) this means the world can only extend as far as the limits of the body. For one thing, a decreased ability to comfortably occupy one's body, including freely commanding movement of its parts, comes when the fight-flight-freeze response is activated. When disconnection takes place to manage distress here in the aftermath of sexual violence, the physical place where the client primarily lives feels unsafe, uncomfortable, and out of control.

It is worth being explicit about when the physical facet of the self needs safety amongst other selves. This is relevant to the realm of sleep where, primally, we need to be off-guard from predators in order to rest and restore. It also extends to being in the world at large, including personal relationships and sexual relationships.

The potential for connection with the physical facet of our self and relating to the multi-faceted selves of others, is dependent on this baseline of safety. As every survivor is different, the degree to which an individual can be amongst other selves, including being sat in a room with a psychotherapist, varies considerably in the aftermath of sexual violence.

A tangible lack of autonomy, restricted freedom of movement, and decreased freedom of speech (disempowerment) has the potential to be replicated in the series of spaces the multi-faceted self occupies. Therefore, the ripple effect of forced experiences of sexual violence amounts to repeated violations of multiple facets of the self at conscious and unconscious levels within all of these spaces.

In this way survivors re-experience the impact of sexual violence in multiple spaces in their selves and lives long after the original incidents have occurred. For survivors that need to request psychotherapy after having coped with the impact of sexual violence for some time, it can be confusing to suddenly feel less themselves in all of these ways.

In order to appreciate this forced re-configuration of the self following sexual violence, psychotherapists should consider the particular spaces in the world they occupy as they extend support to survivors. Mental health practitioners exist within our respective societies' mental health systems (even if we practise independently) and this is one of many systems that humans create to organise aspects of their world. Other examples include: personal networks, professional networks, and education, religious, health, asylum/refugee, housing, and legal systems.

Each of these human-made systems has the potential to be impacted by the reverberating effect of sexual violence in some way and are spaces that clients must navigate to gain reparative support. Contact with support services is a forum where autonomy, movement, and speech can be compromised. These three factors are present by virtue of the human condition. As an immediate example relevant to our field: if the client doesn't have the personal or financial resources to access private psychotherapy, they immediately have less power over when they can access specialist support and who the specific person they want to support them is.

Another example is the inconsistent way in which survivors have been offered talking therapy in the United Kingdom during the process of engaging with the criminal justice system, known as 'pre-trial therapy.' Guidance from the Crown Prosecution Service has long stated that a victim of a crime could not discuss the details of it with anyone, including providers of talking therapy. The concern was that a victim's evidence, primarily their oral account of what happened, might be influenced in the process, which would undermine its credibility.

Some of the consequences included survivors of sexual violence being turned away from services, declining support themselves, or being offered short-term structured work only. Psychotherapists continue to come into contact with the ripple effect of forced restrictions on survivors in this area via navigating the ethical dilemmas and misunderstandings of what we can offer to meet the needs of this client group. Details of pre-trial therapy are provided in Chapter seven.

These two examples alone demonstrate how contact with human-made systems can increase the length of time a survivor is forced to address the impact of trauma as they move around various mental health and practical support services within their society. Another factor to be taken into account is an individual's personal ability and motivation to disclose their experiences of sexual violence. This comes with its own internal and external barriers, as described in the previous chapter.

Accessing therapeutic support services is rarely linear for many reasons. This is the case no matter which stage the survivor is at within that particular system: the point of enquiry, referral, being on a waiting list, attendance, and how the survivor presents in appointments. The individual survivor's pattern of engagement should be part of understanding what is manageable for their multi-faceted self within all of these opportunities for contact with support systems and the individual professionals within them. Working from this principle is part of offering psychotherapy in a trauma-informed way.

The issue of sexual violence as a global fact means that a survivor's position cannot be considered without the wider context that placed them in it. Forced re-organisation of the self is fixed around the structure of victim-blaming societies, with myths about sexual violence playing a central role in misleading us all. These are part of communal communications on the matter and such communications often hinder the progress of psychotherapeutic work. Further comments on myths, and how to manage their impact effectively, are discussed in Chapter four.

It is extremely common for survivors to have some sort of relationship with the perpetrators prior to their experiences of sexual violence and it is also true that often people are sexually violated by strangers. The term 'relationship' here is used lightly, as sexual violence is not an act of one self fully relating to the whole self of the other at all.

It is used simply to denote that perpetrators are often known to an individual before sexual violence occurs and that sexual violence occurs within the context of otherwise consensual relationships too. This includes consensual sexual contact between the same persons at any point, whether this be years or moments beforehand. Just as anyone can be affected by sexual violence, perpetrators can be of any gender, gender expression, sexual orientation, faith group, community, race, ethnicity, profession, and relation to the survivor.

Given this, we have to take into account the additional impact for survivors whose external worlds mean that continued contact with perpetrators is possible or actual. We have considered threats to the self in the moment sexual violence occurs, and those threats remain more real if proximity to perpetrators remains.

In instances where there are multiple perpetrators, and/or where sexual violence is used within the context of other systems such as trafficking or war, this threat expands evermore. As a consequence, the prospect of recovery is similarly threatened.

Within psychotherapy this can be seen as interruptions to the progress of the work and can be felt as such for all involved. However, this is the reality of working with sexual violence as a live issue regardless of whether this aliveness is due to somatic re-experiencing, psychological distress, or contact with perpetrators. In any case a survivor's relationship to their multi-faceted self, their relationships with others, and ability to fully be in the world are impacted.

Here we can better understand how the impact of sexual violence manifests in forced re-configuration of attachment styles plus ways of relating to the self and others. For survivors who have traumatic experiences that originate in childhood, those who have experienced repeated sexual violence at any point in their lifetimes, and those who are sexually violated alongside other forms of abuse, adaptive ways of relating to survive can become a deeply embedded relational system in itself that has been forced upon the individual.

Versions of this also exist for survivors that have experienced a single incident of sexual violence in adulthood. It is not a case of more or less than, but is instead a consideration of the quality of attachment and relating. For survivors who fall into any combination of the aforementioned three categories of sexual violence, disconnection is more enabled than connection as a way of being, experiencing, and relating.

In 2019, difficulties in managing relationships as a feature of Complex Post-Traumatic Stress Disorder was formally recognised in the ICD-11 (World Health Organization, 2019). Diagnostic acknowledgement of how somatic symptoms and protective strategies that manifest as avoidant behaviour can evolve into noticeable difficulties in relating to others is significant. It opens up the possibility of furthering understanding and professional interest in how humans as relational beings are impacted by traumatic events.

Regardless of whether an individual psychotherapist includes diagnostic criteria in working with survivors, it is useful to hold this within the context of supporting this client group as it is part of the wider mental health system in which we operate. As with every system considered thus far there is potential for forced re-organisation of the self, and diagnostic criteria being placed on a survivor can make them fall on either side of re- or dis-empowered.

Practical considerations for psychotherapeutic work

The psychotherapeutic relationship between selves is a vital channel and context for information on the client's presenting concerns. Additionally, addressing the impact of sexual violence within relational psychotherapy means its impact cannot be treated as an isolated clinical matter. When post-traumatic recall is alleviated there is still the question of how to consistently promote safe, comfortable relatedness within and between selves as a survivor navigates the spaces comprising their personal world. This is part of rebuilding not only a sense of self, but a wider life.

Within this sub-chapter several areas regarding the relational experience of working with survivors are outlined. The aim is to enhance a psychotherapist's understanding of the individual's re-configured self in relationship and options on how to respond accordingly. Steps on how to begin promoting relatedness between the body and mind when disconnection is prevalent are also outlined.

We understand that the physical facet of the self can easily dominate a person's overall experience as a post-traumatic stress response, including to promote survival even when there is no threat present. Care must be taken at all times to monitor whether a client is placed within their window of tolerance (Siegel, 1999). Concurrent attention is required to identify what promotes controlled homeostatic regulation, so that any contact with traumatic material within the client's self does not necessarily include re-living the events.

Disconnection between facets of the client's self will occur when traumatic recall is a feature of the impact of sexual violence. The body takes over and a client's ability to think enough to engage with the talking side of psychotherapy is halted. A psychotherapist's responsibility here is to promote regulation of the physical facet so that it can relate more effectively with other facets of the self.

Body-based interventions are primarily for the benefit of clients and the psychotherapist is assisted to regulate their self too. When achieved on all sides, co-regulation can take place which enables clients to safely relate to the psychotherapist as another multi-faceted self. Examples of body-based techniques to promote staying in one's window of tolerance are based on whether a client is hyper- or hypo-aroused:

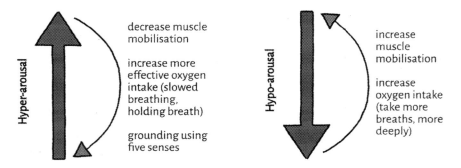

Figure 2.2

Upon first meeting a client we are not fully aware of the degree of traumatic recall, nor any other related mental health difficulty, that indicates being outside of one's window of tolerance. Any worry or anxiety the client holds in meeting their psychotherapist for the first time and the hopes they bring to the work may decrease the size of their window along with the body's automatic responses to stress.

An individual client's personal need, or wish to recall whatever they remember about the sexual violence they have experienced varies significantly. Some survivors are relieved at the opportunity to speak freely and do so with ease including at their first appointment. Others may require a lot of support to feel safe enough to do so. A psychotherapist may complete an entire piece of work without knowing any specifics about what happened. In any case, it is possible to treat the impact of sexual violence without going into the details of the events.

Psychotherapists can assure clients of this as a way to ease stress, plus add a sense of control over the process. In this way choice and consent are promoted for the individual client from the outset. Also asking 'What happens when you think or talk about your experiences?' is a neutral way to gain information about stress responses within the multi-faceted self. If a client has more specific language, including naming types of sexual violence experienced, the psychotherapist can mirror this accordingly to respect where they are in their process of recovery.

There may be a need to offer more than one assessment appointment for clients who present with significant degrees of disconnection between facets of their selves, to the point where it is similarly difficult to engage in the work being facilitated by the psychotherapist. Being unable to control use of the neo-mammalian brain associated more with cognitive processing because the older parts of the brain have taken over, means a client is unable to think. Working within a client's window of tolerance includes appreciating that more appointments than may be usually offered are required, in order to fully meet their needs.

As per the automatic responses of the survivor during and after sexual violence, whatever the psychotherapist's response is to the relational contact with its impact comes without judgement. This is the case regardless of which facet of our selves that responds, as a second-hand witness to a survivor's truths. What moments like this teach us as psychotherapists is the insidious nature of sexual violence and its ability to forcibly take up space within or between selves, a dynamic we should always be interested in.

Disconnection between facets of the client's self may also occur when repeated sexual violence is part of the fabric of living and is embedded in regular human interactions. Such incidences are violating regardless of whether actual physical contact was made. This can include, but is not limited to, a survivor's personal history where childhood sexual abuse, domestic violence, ritualised abuse, and/or human trafficking took place.

Many survivors grew up in environments where there were no boundaries around bodies. It may have been the case that different types of sexualised behaviour around them took place with neither consent nor control. A lack of privacy and excessive interest in a survivor's body may also have been a feature of growing up. For example: nudity or masturbation throughout the home or wider community from others as a regular occurrence, no lock on bathroom or bedroom doors, and children sleeping in the same room or bed with adults beyond an appropriate age.

How these histories translate to the present experience of being bodies together within a room in psychotherapy is not only a reflection of the client's lived experiences. It is also a reflection of how such experiences have informed their understanding of how relationships work and any emotional responses attached to this. A survivor may express worry at how the psychotherapist will cope with what they have to say, only be able to speak with the door open as a visible exit, or feel ashamed at taking up space in the room.

There are many things we can experience within the physical facet of our selves as we come into contact with knowing how a survivor has been shaped by sexual violence, whether verbalised or embodied on their part during appointments. Questions to reflect on can be 'Does my body feel manipulated into an uncomfortable position as we sit in the same room?' 'Can I breathe right now?' and 'Do I feel unable to move as freely as usual?'

Psychotherapists can be assisted by the information their body is providing whilst they work with survivors and come into contact with traumatic material. Usually any responses here represent the minutiae of the physicality of survival, or embodied countertransference. In part this is how we form enough understanding of the impact of someone else's experiences in order to use empathy as a vehicle for psychotherapeutic change.

The force of what survivors bring into the room can be extremely powerful regardless of whether it is overtly present in the moment, or quietly clings to us. Sometimes psychotherapists can feel the quality of this force before it is consciously named or described. Staying within our own window of tolerance in a way that is in our control provides a balance between being empathic to provide reparative interventions and becoming overwhelmed. Further information on managing vicarious trauma is outlined in the final chapter to assist in this area.

Alleviating disconnection via continued negotiation of the co-created baseline of the physical space (the room, our bodies) is vital to challenging the inherent power imbalance of psychotherapy. In this way we promote empowerment of the client via the working relationship. It is incorrect to assume that every client will be able to straightforwardly engage in relationships in order to benefit from the trust and safety that psychotherapy offers as part of its efficacy.

Therefore, for clients that have experienced sexual violence building trust can be a slow process that is easily derailed. This is because being in any kind of contact with another self puts them at risk of being overwhelmed by them, which is at one level a replication of the original trauma. Any experience of this can be a barrier to accessibility of support services well before the survivor even discloses why they have requested such services.

Practical strategies can include pacing the dialogue in accordance with the client's triggers related to traumatic recall, such as specific words. Identifying these assists in creating a tracking system between psychotherapist and client so that there is a shared understanding of where the dialogue can go verbally. Doing so also creates a hypothetical map of what a survivor navigates in daily life to get by, which can be helpful in beginning to understand what causes distress rather than it feeling completely random.

Structuring appointments in agreement with clients creates a sense of control over the process, just as planning in advance fosters consistency in what to expect. The opportunity to think and come to an agreement before acting on the consensus together is simultaneously a mark of requesting consent from the client so that they can exercise autonomy safely.

Psychological contact with others is required in psychotherapy, as is sitting in a room together, which is a challenge when disconnection is safer. Learning to be in a space with another person that won't hurt you, even if the client cognitively knows this won't happen, is also a significant challenge which may at times prevent the work from moving forward.

A hyper-vigilant survivor may take time to feel comfortable in the room and in relationship with their psychotherapist. Such hypervigilance is a safety mechanism originating in the amygdala and represents a lack of trust in the safety of other selves (including their bodies) as a result of sexual violence. Establishing trust, consistency, and safety may involve repeated negotiation over time until it is a felt experience rather than simply a cognitive task.

Psychotherapists ask a lot of questions from the outset as a part of fully assessing, understanding, and responding to clients. Explaining why a certain question is being asked is helpful in making the relationship a space where hyper-vigilance isn't required. Letting clients know that they can ask questions at any point about anything throughout the work is useful in repeated establishment of the relationship as a two-way process.

References

MacLean, P.D., 1990: *The Triune Brain in Evolution: Role in Paleocerebral Functions*. New York: Springer Publishing.
Porges, S.W., 2009: *The Polyvagal Theory: Neurophysiological Foundations of Emotions, Attachment, Communication, Self-Regulation*. New York: W.W. Norton.
Siegel, D.J., 1999: *The Developing Mind: How Relationships and the Brain Interact to Shape Who We Are*. New York: Guilford Press.
World Health Organization, 2019: *International Classification of Diseases for Mortality and Morbidity Statistics (11th Revision)*. Geneva: World Health Organization.

Chapter 3

Psychotherapy as activism

Psychotherapy is primarily concerned with improving people's mental health. Achieving this comes with the assumption that positive changes can occur in related areas such as the client's relationships and daily functioning. This is seen as a successful outcome for all involved and enables a client to move on with their life.

The notion of social responsibility extends the role of psychotherapists into a wider remit by acknowledging that the totality of our work can create shifts in culture, via the ripple effect of effecting change in individuals or groups that can spread further outwards.

Responsibility as a clinical term does extend to the general public, but is usually only exercised in relation to risk management. Otherwise the work undertaken, including the truths disclosed within it, are retained in private rooms. Psychotherapists are already practised in sharing information with others as required in some cases, and yet we largely withhold what we know about sexual violence, including the necessary reparative responses to it.

One common example of how psychotherapy effects social change is with clients who initially report scepticism about the benefits of being open about their mental health with a professional, but through psychotherapy learn that talking can be beneficial in not only staying well but relating with others. This person will take what they've learned to better participate in their life and the wider world in a new way. They may also participate more in their community, which results in influencing the shape of the world around them and the people within it.

Theoretically speaking this illustrates the active back and forth process between selves that slowly reaches into numerous psychological and physical spaces in clients' lives. Psychotherapy, therefore, has the power to influence change well beyond client appointments and even our profession if we intentionally direct our work in this manner.

Sexual violence as a devastatingly routine occurrence on a global scale leads to all kinds of people asking for help. Ideally this would happen when they are provided with the circumstances in which to safely disclose to someone what they've been through. As facilitators of such circumstances, psychotherapists

DOI: 10.4324/9781003202943-3

should not underestimate the value of being available, wanting to hear (not just listen), and wanting to sensitively step towards a survivor rather than turn away from the horror of what they are disclosing in the way others may do. Services and appointments in themselves therefore provide vital opportunities to promote recovery when a survivor can access them.

However, the scale of sexual violence means it is all around us in many different forms, some more overtly life threatening than others. The collaborative back and forth of the psychotherapeutic dialogue creates an arena in which the psychotherapist is entrusted with truthful information about this issue. Holding the weight of this responsibly initially feeds into treatment planning at an individual level and keeping clients at the heart of the process to ensure they get what is required on the basis of informed consent as much as possible.

Usually psychotherapists, services, and the organisations that regulate them stop at this point. We consider our jobs as completed from the perspective that clients are more effectively able to traverse their personal worlds from a stance of safe relatedness following psychotherapeutic interventions and collaborative work. This is usually all that everyone has implicitly and explicitly contracted for.

But how can psychotherapists be justified in collectively considering that action to only this extent is all that is required from us as professionals? The weight of the information we are entrusted with does not necessarily need to be put down as soon as contracted work ends and we welcome another client into the time slot where a survivor used to be. This information can be ethically shared in order to tackle sexual violence on a scale bigger than the psychotherapeutic relationship, which simultaneously creates a more understanding world for survivors to re-emerge into when the time is right for them to do so.

As a global issue sexual violence and the factors feeding into its perpetration touches everyone's lives to some degree. The mistake in seeing sexual violence as a matter only affecting a few people is not only statistically incorrect. It also overlooks the fact that it is the wider world that needs to change in order to stop this issue from taking place in the first instance, as well as needing to change to more successfully support those affected by it.

The client's self is re-configured as a matter of course because of sexual violence, often severely so, but this should not be pathologised as a purely medical or mental health problem located only within survivors accessing services. For psychotherapy to be fully effective the mental health system also needs to be re-configured to better accommodate the multiple needs that arise from this issue.

Here the psychotherapist can begin to think carefully about becoming visible in spaces other than appointments and with their peers, in order to educate the wider public about the truth of the matter. We can concurrently transfer our skills, knowledge, and experiences to advocate for change at a societal or global level, which feeds into the ways we can assist individual survivors. In doing so collective and collaborative efforts to help survivors are beneficially expanded.

In this way the value of the back and forth of psychotherapeutic dialogues is not reserved simply for those who have been able to access psychotherapy. A survivor can more easily make contact with information, support materials, and mental health professionals at a time that feels right for them. Psychotherapists being engaged in a societal dialogue creates a metaphorical door that can be opened at the time of a survivor's choosing, rather than their finding a closed door that needs to be pushed on their own to find resources on the other side.

A psychotherapist being visible in public spaces on the topic of sexual violence is especially important in pushing back against myths and misconceptions about it. These tend to be as prevalent as the phenomenon itself no matter where they are found. Myths have the power to prevent accessibility to support and justice, leaving survivors unsure of where they can go outside of themselves to find resolution. At worst myths and misconceptions only serve to create a context in which sexual violence can continue to be perpetrated, thus perpetuating hopelessness long after the incident has occurred.

The back and forth of what psychotherapists offer via the working relationship is simultaneously a space for clients to practise opportunities for relatedness within their selves, relationships with others, and the wider world. When psychotherapy offers a boundaried space where a client can exercise **freedom of movement, speech, and autonomy** in relative safety, violations of the self can sit outside of these boundaries.

However, the truth of sexual violence as it is told by survivors remains within the boundaries of psychological and physical spaces as offered by psychotherapists. Without making these truths more known in some way, there is no chance of successfully challenging society alongside promoting good mental health for those living in the world. Any reparative work achieved in psychotherapy is thus quickly contradicted by having to continually survive trauma, given that it continues to exist in multiple spaces in the wider world.

Within this chapter there is an explicit imperative that psychotherapists explore the ways in which our profession needs to evolve in response to the truth of sexual violence. The process of evolving should include how we can better deliver specialist psychotherapy services to directly meet the needs of clients, in acknowledging the reality of sexual violence not only as series of incidents, but as a recurring social phenomenon too. In this way, we maximise our ability to effect lasting change for clients who ask for our help.

The need for psychotherapy to evolve

In practice, psychotherapy is traditionally undertaken within the privacy of confidential spaces. Many training courses only extend so far as to prepare practitioners for self-contained, inward-facing work. This work extends into more spaces of a similar nature: conversations amongst colleagues, clinical supervision, and written pieces circulated within our own profession. A problematic dichotomy manifests in that we literally come face-to-face with the spoken truth of real people's lives and yet we tend to only echo what we hear in spaces within the mental health system.

It is of note that conversations such as these occur within limited parameters, despite the prolific prevalence of sexual violence. Psychotherapy is one of the very few spaces where survivors are given time, space, and attention to traverse the nuances of traumatic impact in supportive collaboration with another self.

Sadly, this is because responses to hearing a disclosure include ignorance, dismissal, minimisation, or silence. Such responses can be found as close to home as the survivor's personal network, including the perpetrator who can use them to prolong the abuse. They can also be found in the law, culture, and practices of everyday life so that the resulting oppressions are contextually solidified. As such, disempowerment is reinforced in both explicit and implicit ways wherever the survivor may turn.

The potential for disempowerment increases the further a survivor falls outside the categories of white, non-disabled, cisgender, and heterosexual. This is because there are less spaces, groups, and other individual selves that are readily available to validate a sense of personal identity along with one's traumatic experiences. There may already have been a sense of not belonging, or having to fight to belong, in the wider world before sexual violence occurred. Existing as a self with any number of potential gaps in human-made systems to fall through as a result is significant.

Sexual violence is found despite variations in societal class and personal finances. Institutions where the power of an authority is enshrined in rules specific to that institution also allows for opportunities to oppress those who find themselves at the lower ends of a hierarchy. We can recognise this in a world governed by patriarchal structures that only benefit the powerful few at the human expense of the majority in order to retain that power at the top of the hierarchy.

The psychological and physical spaces psychotherapists extend to clients should of course be protected in boundaried ways, as they form a context by which a reparative relationship is thoughtfully and ethically offered. These spaces are also essential for survivors to feel safe enough to trust their psychotherapist as a facilitator of their recovery along with the latter's skills and professional experience. Similarly, a client's wish to speak openly about sexual violence is in part assured by the psychotherapist's agreement to remain silent outside of their appointments via the principles of confidentiality and anonymity.

However, an unequivocal fact remains on all sides. Survivors and psychotherapists live in the same world. Both are exposed to the nature of sexual violence, including its misunderstood variations, to similar degrees. Many psychotherapists have lived experience. Empathically viewing the world from the forcibly re-configured lens of survivors in appointments means psychotherapists experience the world differently as a result of doing this work.

Being shown the reality of the world and being asked to respond to this reality when working with survivors is a serious matter for psychotherapists to consider. This is especially the case in considering exactly how much one responds outside of appointments, as this will vary between practitioners.

To be clear, simply providing psychotherapy is to provide a space where survivors can speak the truth of their experiences within a society that would prefer them to remain disempowered in speech, autonomy, and movement. Therefore, psychotherapy as a form of pushing back against this status quo is aligned with the wider cause for one's right to power in personal and wider worlds.

We cannot consider our shared world without including a consideration of the realities of the mental health system. The prevalence of sexual violence means that every service and lone practitioner will meet survivors no matter where they themselves as professionals are placed within this system. In every setting, demand always outweighs provision, which only serves to exacerbate the challenge of extending psychotherapy specialised to the needs of survivors.

Usually the only options are to turn individuals away, refer them on to other services, or offer less appointments than is therapeutically appropriate in order to ensure everyone gets something rather than nothing. Specialist services are available but subject to narrow funding cycles that debilitate their ability to create change in the face of traumatic circumstances. Clients who have funds to access psychotherapy privately gain the ability to bypass waiting lists and a restricted number of appointments, and can personally choose who they work with.

Practitioners in non-specialist services are asked to meet the need for specialist support without knowing exactly how, or perhaps not being trained to do so. Clients who fall out of the category of what a survivor is stereotypically understood to be feel the force of multiple barriers to not only having their circumstances made visible, but also miss out on having services extended to them appropriately.

On the survivor's part it may be difficult to believe that receiving non-judgemental support is possible because of internalised blame, shame, and guilt about having gone through sexual violence. Overall, there is a struggle to occupy spaces in personal worlds, which is worsened by post-trauma symptoms. The urge to seek support is therefore not always aligned with the internal resources to accept it when offered. A common result for survivors is that it is extremely difficult to find a professional who will provide them with what they need, when they need it, and for as long as they need it.

There can be a palpable process of having to sift through an enormous amount of misunderstanding, misdiagnosis, and missed opportunities to be emotionally and practically met in the ways that are required to facilitate recovery. The multi-dimensional impact of sexual violence means this occurs in many different professional services, alongside people in the client's personal life. As a consequence, the process of accessing services is rarely linear and can literally take decades.

A concurrent result within the mental health system is that psychotherapists are trapped in a professional survival process where services are offered in an emotionally, physiologically, and practically dysregulated manner. How then are we able to provide an experience, and therefore role model, the principles of consistent care in all senses of the word within this context? For the psychotherapist, the process of delivering a service is rarely linear and not just because of the varied material clients present with in appointments.

One answer is to extend our professional responsibility to individual clients within a wider remit of outward-facing social responsibility, the aim being to increase empowerment for all tackling the issue of sexual violence, regardless of whether one is a client or psychotherapist. This process can include advocating for changes in the mental health system, rather than complying with the demand for increased delivery with conversely diminishing resources.

Collective professional correspondence to local and national governments requesting ring-fenced funding may be part of being enabled to fully respond to the impact of sexual violence. On the ground it may be pushing for more appointments on a case-by-case basis when the severity of traumatic impact requires it.

The detriment caused by waiting lists and navigating multiple support systems to find the right kind of help cannot be underestimated in contributing to declines in the mental health of all clients. Psychotherapists must also take responsibility to look after one's self and each other's selves to avoid vicarious trauma so we are ready to meet survivors. This topic is further discussed in Chapter eight in the knowledge that it is common to struggle when working in pressured mental health systems as well as with traumatic material.

Meeting survivors and hearing their truths is an extremely privileged professional position that must be handled carefully. If we evaluate once more the notion that frank discussions about sexual violence are only echoed amongst those who have a prior interest, we are left with a limited version of the positive impact that psychotherapy could create in the wider world. When psychotherapists hear a survivor's truth, we are not only handed the responsibility of changing that individual's life alongside them, we are also tasked with taking on information that can be used to create social change.

Witnessing and responding to sexual violence as professionals within the limited parameters of appointments can risk increasing marginalisation of survivors in a global society which carries on regardless of the scale and impact of the issue. It seems illogical, and therefore unreasonable, to ask survivors to go out into the wider world as if it is safe and as if it will respond appropriately to them when they are re-traumatised. Unfortunately, this is rarely the case.

Furthermore, it is the client that is tasked with the responsibility to think, feel, and act differently based on what they have learned in psychotherapy. There are far less spaces in the wider world, including on an individual basis, where perpetrators are held to account or instructed to change their behaviour. Asking only survivors to change does not absolutely solve their personal concerns discussed in psychotherapy, nor address surrounding factors that continue to make them more vulnerable to having to take on such concerns. Even if recovery is achieved, disempowerment continues in other ways.

Here, psychotherapists can begin to wonder whether there is a point at which professional silence becomes unhelpful to survivors. Why place the responsibility of recovery from sexual violence solely on those who experience it and those who suddenly find themselves searching for support in unexpected circumstances? Professionally contributing to alleviating the wider issue of sexual violence, rather than simply its impact on individuals who make it into formal services, is where psychotherapists can effect societal change in service of clients, thus solidifying the remit of their work.

As a profession, and indeed the wider world, we request that survivors fully step towards what we offer so that we can fulfil our professional roles with them. This is often only done in line with the process of engagement with psychotherapy, the earliest point of which is making an enquiry or referral. At this stage a client's request for support and the distress motivating it becomes visible to psychotherapists.

However, there are many spaces where the impact of sexual violence is visible and psychotherapists or psychotherapeutic information are not. We wait for survivors to appear in rooms in order to respect their wish to undertake psychotherapy, but there is a process of engagement that could occur on our side well before this point to encourage accessibility through our visibility.

Again, barriers to requesting or accessing support are as intricate as the individual themselves and should be taken into active account when providing psychotherapeutic services. The information gained from evaluating barriers should also translate into evolving the ways that psychotherapists and the support we offer can be delivered to survivors in our communities. Further information on how to step towards survivors in these ways is detailed in Chapter six.

We generally ask clients of any kind to trust us even before they sit in front of us. In relational work trust is often viewed as a sign of effective and ethical psychotherapy, especially given that trust in other selves is one of the first elements to evaporate following sexual violence. We may even ask this at times when the client cannot trust what is happening within the psychological and physical facets of their selves. Relatedness with others can be impossible when disconnectedness characterises self-experience, so the possibility of trust needs to be demonstrated well before a client is sat opposite their psychotherapist for the work to be truly successful.

There are many cases where a survivor will tell their psychotherapist how difficult it was to initially disclose their traumatic experiences, including people's negative reactions that resulted in not being able to speak about it further. It may also be the case that a client will access psychotherapy for one reason and then only disclose sexual violence when trust has been established with their psychotherapist. In this way, work to address the impact of sexual violence can truly begin.

Another common experience of psychotherapists is that they can often be the only professional, or maybe even the only person, that a client is engaging with on a regular basis. This may be the result of many factors including the impact of a client's mental health on their ability to sustain contact with a professional or personal network, or how difficult it is to access services for other needs. Much of the time it is a matter of trust. A psychotherapist may then be aware of significant needs additional to a client's mental health that the former may practically or ethically be unable to address.

A lack of trust in other selves, systems, and other spaces a survivor can inhabit is a reality expressed in psychotherapy. As such psychotherapists learn how each of these are deficient forms of contact and therefore what needs to change across society so that survivors are not alone in their recovery. Some survivors can be vocal and societally active about this themselves. However, this is a personal decision to make, seeing as a significant amount of energy is required to create change on top of managing the impact of sexual violence.

If clients affected by sexual violence heard their realities expressed more often by psychotherapists, especially in response to attempts to restrict their personal freedoms, then trust can begin to be fostered at this early stage as a path to more easily step towards what we offer. There are myths about what happens in psychotherapy, and who this support is suitable or available for, just as there are myths about sexual violence. Part of the field's social responsibility therefore also includes a duty to be transparent about what happens in psychotherapy within public spaces, as well as with clients who make it into the room.

Being vocal in the face of silencing, however this is done, is another way of effecting societal change within a remit wider than the practitioner's room. It also means that the psychological spaces we offer can have psychotherapeutic benefits that extend further than those who are able to sit in front of us, having navigated internal and external barriers to accessibility. In incremental ways, psychotherapists can extend support into many more spaces than the ones we currently occupy.

Above all, psychotherapists should consider an important question in beginning to incorporate an activist stance in accepting the challenge of social responsibility: why limit change to the individual survivor? Many of us were brought to the field because we wanted to support others and facilitate change.

In empowering our selves as practitioners to do this work, we enable empowerment of survivors to change their lives, as well as mutually changing the face of a society that is violating. Maintaining the position of survivors at the centre of this includes taking action to effect change across a wide spectrum so that the possibility of recovery is an enabling process, and individual survivors do not bear the whole weight of change in a disempowering world.

Activism defined

The psychotherapist's responsibility to each of their clients can be extended to a responsibility to wider society, as professionals working with a societal phenomenon that negatively impacts a significant proportion of its members. This can be referred to as our social responsibility, which is achieved through participating in activism as psychotherapists.

Activism as a response to inequality is a well-practised phenomenon in human history. This is more stereotypically understood in collective actions such as protests, picketing, and petitions. Individual actions also fall into the category of activism in that everyday practices and decisions can be an expression of support or opposition to what is happening around us in personal, or wider worlds. In doing we are saying and vice-versa.

Dynamically, activism is a form of pushing back against something. This pushing can create space for people, ideas, and facts to become more visible. Thus, raising awareness on a subject to increase its visibility is an act of doing or saying in order for it to take up more space. Above all, activism is concerned with change at individual and societal levels so that there is better alignment with principles set by those participating in the activism.

Silencing, invisibility, and oppression are some of the results produced by societal inequality for those who find themselves at the narrow end of this power dynamic. Repetition of these power dynamics in many different spaces, often between selves, feeds the increasing scale of inequalities which manifests as disempowerment. As such these become embedded in human-made systems as implicit and explicit ways that people are treated negatively by those who hold more power in order to maintain, and gain from, this imbalance.

For those impacted by sexual violence, the forced re-configuration of personal worlds by perpetrators en masse equates to literally millions of people who are forced into this narrow end of personal and societal power. The human-made systems and humans themselves that survivors come into contact with thereafter can reinforce multiple inequalities, often increasing societal marginalisation.

Marginalisation occurs even when such systems and the humans that made them aim to address inequalities. One result is a translation into barriers that cordon off things that constitute a person's right to a private life such as relationships, citizenship, support, justice, health care, and safe housing. Also increased is the weight of internalised myths about sexual violence the longer such inequalities are left unaddressed.

With little to no spaces one can firmly occupy in a personal or wider world, survivors risk becoming ever more invisible. When those with more power see survivors edging visibly into action to push back against inequality, ways to perpetuate violence against them increase so as to maintain a one-up position. One can refer to how often online sexual violence activists with lived experience on social media are responded to with threats of rape as one way of understanding what form this can take.

Survivor's lives are recurrently interrupted by sexual violence and its impact, sometimes to the point of non-participation in that life. Activism can turn this interruption back onto a society that enables sexual violence to happen in forms such as strikes, marches, or online movements that bring regular life to a periodic standstill. In this way activism forces others to witness the impact of the issue, thus experientially raising awareness of the truth of it.

Doing so also makes visible the scale of the issue as a societal phenomenon when survivors within communities do not participate in the status quo. The stepping out of spaces that constitute regular life (for example: going to work) and stepping into another space with other survivors forces the public to witness the size of this community. Whether individual or collective actions, activism is disruptive in that it attempts to change the way an existing system operates in order to distribute power more equally.

These definitions of activism can be incorporated into psychotherapy both within and outside of appointments with clients. In Chapter six the concept of empowerment in psychotherapy is dissected to consider its three components: freedom of speech, freedom of autonomy, and freedom of movement. Activism, as a form of distributing power, can therefore be defined as any action or activity that promotes these principles. Therefore, psychotherapy itself can be considered a form of activism in the face of sexual violence when these principles are embedded into the work.

The notion of using one's voice to speak personal truths and having this responded to by others is already present within the tradition of psychotherapy. Including an activist stance is a way of amplifying speaking and truth-telling to enhance client work. Potentially activism can happen in additional spaces outside of psychotherapy appointments, where it can assist in positive change for survivors at multiple levels in the wider world.

Effective role modelling occurs when clients are able to witness a psychotherapist's embodiment of freedom of speech, autonomy, and movement. In this way the possibility of empowerment becomes live as part of the work. The psychotherapist may be seen to be doing this within the psychotherapeutic relationship, or outside of it. Assisting clients to find and use their voices is a first priority, cemented by collaboratively defending their right to speak freely.

Psychotherapists primarily do this by being available to hear what might be said via providing a professional service. Clients may be very clear in what they want to say and how they want to say it, which of course should be imitated by a psychotherapist who responds just as emphatically. The echoing of survivor's truths is valuable and powerful no matter whether they are uttered, including in the privacy of psychotherapy or in a public space.

Complementing this is the act of writing, speaking, and occupying spaces in order to push back against systems that oppress, silence, and disempower survivors. It may be the case that all parties engaging in psychotherapy are involved in activism of these kinds. This can occur within and outside the field of psychotherapy to the same collective end. As examples: responding to a myth about sexual violence with the truth when it is expressed in society, and making dedicated links with specialist service providers to increase accessibility of multiple services.

Psychotherapists can have a direct influence on the development of specialist services by getting involved as a trustee or board member at local, regional, or national level. Approaching organisations that regulate psychotherapy to conduct research, write, or speak raises awareness not only within that organisation but also the wider field.

In terms of influencing systems plus the rules that govern them, a psychotherapist may be motivated to challenge laws or guidelines from a top-down approach. Statements, testimonies, and reports (anonymised or not) can be collated as an individual or collective act in order to directly push for positive change in service of survivors.

The use of technology such as the internet to deliver psychotherapy services is evidence of the field's ability to effectively evolve into more spaces. Online is also a space where activism can take place and already does. Therefore, a psychotherapist's wish to evolve their work to include activism can include doing so online using the above ethos. One example is having a social media account to support and promote action related to supportive change for survivors (events, petitions, and local organising).

Safety is of paramount importance when engaging in any kind of activism, especially when an individual person, group, or organisation can be recognised. This is discussed in Chapter four in respect of confronting myths in public spaces. With regards to use of social media this can be moderated in the carefully considered use of a pseudonym or an umbrella term, as well as being attentive to one's digital footprint in general.

Action taken in other physical spaces should include agreements within groups on how to prepare for and manage unsafe situations should they arise prior to activist work. How to implement care-taking of each other and who will take responsibility for this in the instance that anyone is affected must also be agreed in advance. This can include how to exit from, or de-escalate, confrontations from those who push back against the actions taken in support of survivors, such as cat-calling or verbal threats during a protest march.

Dynamic loops

Psychotherapy is a profession that explicitly necessitates a consideration of ethical principles at every stage of the process. There cannot be a discussion about making truths known, or passing on information that psychotherapists

Psychotherapy as activism 53

are being entrusted with, without considering ethical principles that are pertinent when reflecting on the outward-facing elements of social responsibility. These principles are: confidentiality and upholding the professionalism of psychotherapy as a field.

A related topic (arguably also an ethical principle) to be explored is the psychotherapist's level of self-disclosure, which includes their right to a private life. As a psychotherapist becomes more outwardly participatory in shouldering social responsibility around sexual violence, their own confidentiality requires clearly defined terms to continue to prioritise reparative space for survivors. This is especially the case at times when psychotherapists directly co-exist with their clients in the same public spaces, including online.

Wherever and however a psychotherapist's activist role is exercised all three of the above factors can be extended as far as one's individual reach on the issue of sexual violence. In line with psychotherapy as we traditionally understand it, these three points ensure an ethical centrality of focus upon clients at all times.

In order to understand the bringing in of personal worlds in person-to person contact, and how to uphold professional ethics to appropriately engage with them, it is helpful to outline the concept of dynamic loops. Each person has their own dynamic loop that is comprised of all the spaces they traverse in life where information and experiences are consciously and unconsciously collected along the way. When applied to psychotherapy the client's dynamic loop begins and ends at a literal point where contact is made with their psychotherapist (usually this is an appointment):

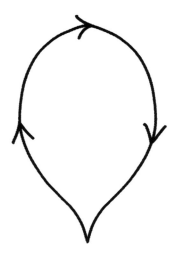

Figure 3.1

The survivor's dynamic loop is also therefore a channel by which such information and experiences from the spaces they occupy can feed into the material presented in psychotherapy. It is common for survivors to occupy less spaces along their dynamic loops following sexual violence, as their personal world becomes smaller. The nature and number of spaces that make up the totality of a dynamic loop is specific to each survivor. Curiosity about a client's dynamic loop in psychotherapy can reveal much about them as an individual self, as well as the impact of sexual violence on the multiple facets comprising this self.

A client's dynamic loop is representative of how one consciously and unconsciously brings their personal world into physical and psychological spaces upon contact with psychotherapists. It also cements the role of psychotherapy appointments as being integrated into the wider world as a space amongst many other spaces, rather than being completely separate from it. In this way, the task of facilitating effective change becomes increasingly possible as the gap between psychotherapy and the wider world is lessened.

Similarly, the psychotherapist also has their own dynamic loop along which they travel through multiple spaces in everyday life in a similar way. Continual acknowledgement of how the psychotherapist's experiences and information gleaned from the spaces they occupy outside of psychotherapy can feed back into appointments is relevant here. A benefit of doing so is being able to understand which elements of the psychotherapist's experience of a client originates from either person's material and when it is a combination of both in a co-created manner.

The psychotherapist is then more able to make interventions that appropriately respond to the facets of the client's self that are in need of attention moment-to-moment. If the psychotherapist is an activist outside of appointments, their dynamic loop is a channel by which to bring in useful information should it benefit individual clients, such as upcoming changes to other support systems they can access. The intersection of the loops of client and psychotherapist includes space readily available to hold any activism on the survivor's part within the work of psychotherapy.

Dynamic loops are the channel by which myths about sexual violence enter the psychological and physical spaces offered to clients. Myths can enter these spaces via the client and psychotherapist. It is also an existing opportunity for psychotherapists to take their work, fuelled by the truths of survivors, into spaces outside of consulting rooms. In any case, the loop always returns to the point where contact is made between client and psychotherapist, again typically in appointments.

One-to-one psychotherapy includes the two loops of client and psychotherapist:

Psychotherapy as activism 55

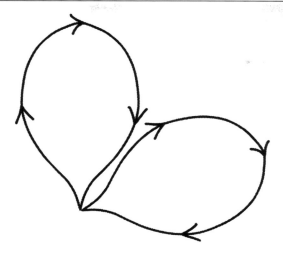

Figure 3.2

Group psychotherapy includes the loops of all participants:

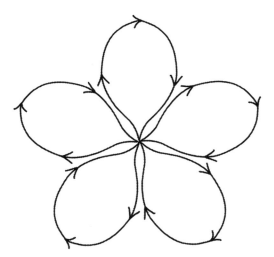

Figure 3.3

When such contact ends all will continue moving along their own loop, taking what they have learned from psychotherapeutic contact out into other spaces. As such this loop creates a dynamic, live feedback system where change occurs across several domains that have been forcibly re-configured as a result of sexual violence. These domains are the survivor's internal psychological world, physical body, relationships other selves, and the wider world.

The loop reinforces an explicit understanding that psychotherapists and clients move within a shared world increasingly contextualised by inequality when outside of the room where appointments take place. This is the case even though the psychotherapist may have a very different personal world to their client and can move along different spaces to each other. However, it is primarily the psychotherapist's responsibility to occupy spaces in the wider world in service of effective psychotherapeutic interventions aimed at survivors.

Finally, a loop of this kind means the boundaries of psychotherapy are upheld in accordance with a duty of care to clients and engaging with the wider issue of sexual violence in the world, as they co-exist with each other. Both are encompassed appropriately alongside the other as required to enhance the value of psychotherapy and social responsibility, at whichever point any survivor engages with it.

Therefore, the principles associated with empowerment within psychotherapy are offered as a part of the work a client can expect to benefit from. These are: freedom of speech, autonomy, and movement. Should a direct link between empowerment and activism be important to a client, then these principles can be explored more explicitly. Extending these principles also serve to minimise the inherent power imbalance in psychotherapy and promote collaboration.

In this way all are doing the same activist work even when they are not co-existing in the same spaces within each of their dynamic loops. Over time this work adds up to a collective pushing back against the perpetration and impact of sexual violence as something that is often deemed societally acceptable. This remains the case even if a client's personal world is very small at times, as finding a way to live in a violating wider world whilst retaining some form of personal power is a notable achievement in surviving.

Confidentiality

A psychotherapist's silence about what they are witnessing second-hand in conversations with survivors is the height of ethical practice, in that it upholds confidentiality. The privacy this affords is a part of what draws clients towards this kind of work. At the very least it is a condition that enables clients to make full use of psychotherapy as a space to think, move, and speak freely. This in itself can be a rarity in the client's life and offering something different psychotherapeutically can maximise the potential for change that is led by the survivor's wishes and needs.

In working with sexual violence, silence must be mediated carefully in the room to support and recognise a survivor's ability to use their own voice powerfully. Ideally, power is located as an internal resource the survivor is able to hold comfortably without fear of being overwhelmed to the point of silence within their selves. Common experiences of this are blame, shame, and guilt. To hear one's truths expressed internally, being able to respond in accordance with personal wishes, and to see this being applied effectively outwards, means power is extended beyond the self.

Such power is utilised to enhance relatedness with one's self, other selves, and the wider world. Facilitating a client's powerful use of their own voice is a priority in re-establishing trust between the facets of their selves that have experienced and survived trauma in various ways. Freedom of speech as a human value is highlighted here and is as much about a survivor's internal dialogue as it is about using voices externally amongst other selves to feel empowered.

Psychotherapy transforms the meaning of silence in allowing for a sensitively attentive holding space between persons when, in other spaces along one's loop, it can be an act of turning away from, which may reinforce internalised shame. In this way the appropriate limits of confidentiality, such as breaking it for the purposes of managing risk, can have a personal meaning to the survivor well beyond executing a practicality within the terms of a clinical contract to keep someone safe.

It is never the case that any survivor's account automatically becomes the psychotherapist's account to unreservedly re-tell upon hearing it. Doing so would be a direct violation of the ethical framework to which psychotherapists are accountable, the boundaries of psychotherapy, and the trust placed in them by survivors. However, coming face-to-face with the truth of sexual violence as told by clients affected by it means that the need for proactive social responsibility in response by psychotherapists grows and grows.

At some point, professional silence sits too closely to society's preferred silence on the wider issue of sexual violence, rather than simply being a professionally extended condition to enable survivors to recover within services. Given that psychotherapists offer a space in which to practise being in the wider world, our unwavering silence as a profession risks condoning one of the ways that sexual violence is able to be perpetuated. Therefore, how silence is handled outside of appointments has a direct link to how social responsibility, including activism, is carried out to support survivors in many ways.

Disrupting silence about sexual violence outside of psychotherapy appointments is primarily about educating and influencing others on the reality of the subject. Whether intentionally or otherwise, the psychotherapist in this instance is pushing back against factors that perpetuate the matter. Doing this is effective at a grassroots level, top-down approaches such as policy making, and every stage in between. Wherever it occurs the potential for change as allies with, and on behalf of, survivors is promoted.

The psychotherapist becomes a vehicle by which to pass on the powerful truths of lived experience of survivors without compromising confidentiality. A focus on identifying common themes, as well as the nuances that individual factors bring, are helpful in doing so. These can cover the impact of sexual violence, as well as what accessing support services is like.

Pushing back against the proverbial doors that are closed within a world to an individual who has been sexually violated, because they have been sexually violated, also creates a path by which to empower others to do the same. For the assurance of clients an explicit statement in writing and verbally about confidentiality being upheld whilst the psychotherapist completes work in public spaces is essential.

As an example: 'I hold my duty of care and confidentiality to my psychotherapy clients as fundamental principles at all times throughout my overall work. I consider my public-facing work regarding mental health and sexual violence to be related to but completely separate from my clinical work in appointments. This ensures you are kept as the focus of our work, for as long as we are working together.'

Survivor-led services can be properly established in this manner and denote one way in which formal psychotherapeutic spaces can benefit from the power of clients' voices. The profession should continue to be shaped by this influence if it is to fully meet the needs of this client group. Social responsibility takes this principle into the wider world and demands that more spaces should adjust to these needs rather than forcing survivors to adapt further.

In these ways psychotherapists empower survivors to take up space where it is denied and validates those who are already doing so. The societal impact of this is to re-open and maintain spaces in the world where survivors can move, speak, and think freely as part of their human rights to exist as such. Clients may wish to include how this looks to them as part of the psychotherapeutic dialogue, which opens up the possibility of relatedness to other selves where these human rights can be exercised.

When this occurs in psychotherapy, it is a great opportunity to practice inhabiting the spectrum of emotions, thoughts, embodiments, and words that resonate for individual survivors however loud or reserved they may be. The psychotherapist's ability and willingness to explore the audible volume of their own statements on the matter in public spaces is an opportunity for healthy role modelling and normalising the traumatic impact of sexual violence for the general public.

Upholding professional standards

Upholding the professionalism of psychotherapy as its remit extends further outwards is a weighty responsibility. Some psychotherapists may not feel comfortable with being visible along one's loop outside of the rooms in which they work as a general principle, whether this is their natural inclination or the result of careful deliberation. Working relationally involves considering how our visibility outside of appointments feels for clients regardless of whether we are occupying the same space at the same time.

If taken up, professional visibility outside of appointments as part of engaging in social responsibility has several points to take into consideration in order to do so effectively and ethically. First, a psychotherapist is a psychotherapist wherever they place themselves in the public domain in support of survivors. The first implication is that the same level of care is applied to one's behaviour, thoughts, and management of person-to-person interactions no matter which spaces one takes up in their dynamic loop.

The second implication is that psychotherapists should expect to have responses to their visible interactions with the issue from others and that this should be welcomed as a wider dialogue in support of survivors. This includes interactions such as speaking to an audience at an event, having an article published online, or marching in a protest.

Although all participants are addressing the same societal issue in various ways, the priority is addressing the client's mental health concerns, meaning that careful management of increased visibility is undertaken at all times. A client's curiosity and responses to their psychotherapist's work in spaces outside of appointments can be welcomed into the room. These are ways to further understand the nature of the psychotherapeutic relationship, including what the psychotherapist represents to their client at any time.

Being more visible as a psychotherapist in public-facing spaces requires an ongoing evaluation of our multi-faceted selves and therefore what we bring to working relationships with clients. This is a professional process to be maintained throughout one's career, in the same way that clinical work or supervision is undertaken as standard.

If more facets of a psychotherapist's self are visible and available to the public then it continues to be the psychotherapist's responsibility to manage these in line with creating change within and outside of contact with clients. This remains the case even if they are not offering psychotherapy to those members of the public that view them, thus reinforcing the principle of always being a psychotherapist before anything else.

For members of society who are in psychotherapy, the nature of engaging (or not) with a psychotherapist's public-facing work is potentially another helpful way to highlight specific needs and attend to them accordingly as appropriate. Using psychotherapy as activism effectively does not necessarily involve being explicit about all types of activism undertaken at any given time.

This falls under the category of disclosure, which can impact clients positively or negatively. Disclosure requires much personal and professional exploration on the part of the psychotherapist in order to ensure clients remain central to the process. What is most important is how work completed outside of psychotherapy appointments feeds back into benefitting individual clients and a multiplicity of needs.

Being the facilitator of any number of physical and psychological spaces that survivors can engage with means that such clients have the potential to consciously and unconsciously come into contact with various facets of the psychotherapist's self. This is where the psychotherapist's thorough understanding of their self is vital, as any area of disconnectedness between facets is a gap where they may struggle to adequately hold their client's material when making psychological contact with each other.

Many psychotherapists may feel hesitant about being visible outside of face-to-face client work for fear of jeopardising the value of their neutrality in the recovery process. There may be a related worry of jeopardising the value of consistency in the psychological and physical spaces offered as the client may have access to facets of the psychotherapist's self, professional opinions, lived experiences, and range of affect that may not have been visible within appointments before.

These are especially important points given that a survivor's self, relationships, and other elements of wider life become dysregulated because of what they've been through. Of course, this should not be replicated within psychotherapy if it is to be truly effective. It is at this point where the psychotherapist's decisions about what is publicly visible and directly attributable to them as professionals becomes vital.

This process should include thinking about how a psychotherapist personally and professionally feels about being visible outside of the rooms where appointments take place. How a psychotherapist would like to be seen inside and outside of such rooms, as well as noticing any differences between the two, informs the consistent quality of their movement within a dynamic loop where survivors are met at various points along the way.

Disclosures of the psychotherapist's self

Being a multi-faceted self means that certain facets may be more visible in some spaces rather than others. A psychotherapist undertaking activism outside of services should be personally comfortable and professionally sound about the fact that any of these facets are available for survivors to engage with at any given moment.

Anything visible about the psychotherapist wherever it occurs can be considered as self-disclosure, but it does not have to necessarily mean that the spaces provided to clients as a part of psychotherapy are compromised. Psychotherapists invite assumptions simply by being visible, even from one's name being on a letter to a client confirming their first appointment within a service. The core of managing this challenge well is how the psychotherapist's individual evaluations of their preferred level of visibility translate into consistent and coherent decisions.

This is because such evaluations become principles by which to work ethically with and for survivors. Being prepared to explore disclosures of the self as part of relational work adheres to the aforementioned principle of expecting to have responses to a psychotherapist's visibility whether this be actual interactions with others, or in the transference. In such instances it may be helpful to ask 'Is psychotherapy with me what you expected?' or 'Am I what you expected, from what you've heard/seen/read about me?'

Here, relatedness between facets of selves can be promoted between all parties moving towards shared goals in psychotherapy. Primarily this enables maintenance of trust through consistency, integrity, and transparency. The survivor can then more fully gain from the co-created, co-negotiated nature of psychotherapy as a consensual act. This in itself is reparative given its contrast to sexual violence, which is carried out against one's wishes.

Although it may not always be expressed, psychotherapists must be aware that there will be varying reactions to their visibility outside of appointments from different clients. This can include a client feeling uncomfortable about seeing their psychotherapist in public spaces, feeling reassured that they are allies for the same societal issue, and feeling anxious or concerned about their psychotherapist's welfare as an activist. Equally, a client may only expect (and want) to engage with a professional that is focused on helping them, which is absolutely reasonable and appropriate.

Any and all reactions are valid. In the spirit of relational psychotherapy, intersubjective dynamics or emotional experiences are sources of information on how our selves impact client's selves. These are reflective of attachment or relational styles where the degree and quality of reactions indicate how other selves are experienced in general. For example, a person with an internal template for secure attachments (Ainsworth, 1978) may feel comfortable knowing their psychotherapist does other work outside of their relationship, whereas a person with an insecure attachment pattern may feel threatened or angry by this.

Being prepared to manage this to offer consistency, integrity, and transparency with all clients can be taken in a few steps. Procedurally a psychotherapy contract can state that work is undertaken in the public arena (such as: writing, speaking, activism, community projects), which the client may come across. Should the client wish to discuss anything as a result of this, including personal reactions, they are welcome to bring it into the room so that it can be fully attended to.

Clients can also be made aware contractually that anything they do come across about their psychotherapist in other spaces will only reflect a limited aspect of their professional training, working experience, way of working with clients, and professional opinions. This includes content about their psychotherapist communicated by another platform or person.

Therefore, clients are repeatedly reminded of the reality of their psychotherapist as a multi-faceted self. The continual returning to the room to engage in the psychotherapeutic relationship is an act of giving resources and attention appropriate to the client's needs rather than them being overlooked.

Visibility of the psychotherapist in multiple spaces is not a case of taking up more space at the expense of the client, as to do so would take away from the latter's centrality to the work. Holding a balance between engaging with the truth of our clients as professionals, whilst largely not being personally known to them, is part of appropriately maintaining this.

What is offered when this balance is achieved are opportunities to healthily negotiate and manage the supportive spaces a psychotherapist holds for survivors in the world, with psychotherapy being one of those spaces. It is also an opportunity to practise healthy and meaningful relatedness between selves so as to re-establish lost trust in others. Other selves and relationships can then become safely tangible contact points over time.

The psychotherapist's offering of psychological and physical spaces are platforms to not only recover from the impact of sexual violence, but are also platforms by which to empower the activist in survivors who feel this is important to them. Including the client's activism within the shared work can simultaneously be a meaningful part of re-configuring the facets of the self following sexual violence, in re-establishing one's personal identity. In this way, we honour the person amongst the trauma if they identify as an activist.

Furthermore, visibility in multiple spaces is about being more explicitly allied with the larger goal of societal change so that the world is less of a place where sexual violence is enabled to happen or be acceptable. This will feed into being allied with a client's individual goals for psychotherapeutic work and vice versa. Should psychotherapists encounter potential, current, or past clients in spaces outside of appointments there are a few things to practise in accordance with extending ethical care in a boundaried manner.

The psychotherapist's self has the potential to become the embodiment, or psychological representation, of the client's link to the wider issue of sexual violence, including what is being done to push back against it. As such there are ways that one or all selves involved in psychotherapy can invite trauma and injustice into the room well beyond how they are specifically in contact with it.

Recognising the degree to which this may be jeopardising the client's process or use of psychotherapy can be done via being aware of any increases in disconnection between selves and significant movements away from the client's presenting concerns as the focus of the work. If there is attention on the wider issue to the degree that the client's self and their material become consistently less visible, then it is the psychotherapist's responsibility to sensitively encourage them back into the process.

There may already be a verbal or contractual agreement as to how seeing each other in spaces outside of appointments will be handled. Honesty about the potential, or actuality, of being in the same spaces outside of appointments should be modelled by the psychotherapist in being proactive wherever necessary. This enables an open conversation to maintain the various boundaries so that the client as a person and their respective wishes are appreciated rather than intruded upon.

The same can be in place for the psychotherapist given that we cannot be fully available for an individual client in public spaces, in the same way our attention is dedicated to them within appointments. Managing clients' expectations on how contact with each other is likely to be in action, and welcoming clients' experiences of these into the room, acknowledges the reality of living in a shared world whilst re-confirming the boundaries of ethical psychotherapeutic work.

As a collaborative and reflective process within psychotherapy this includes transparency and negotiating on both sides to ensure the client remains central to whatever is agreed or explored. An honouring of the client's activist contributions against sexual violence on an individual level and collectively for other survivors is part of honouring an individual's process of recovery in a re-traumatising world. When the psychotherapist is also an activist for the same cause, the allyship with survivors is solidified both within and outside of rooms.

Reference

Ainsworth, M.D.S., Blehar, M.C., Waters, E., and Wall, S., 1978: *Patterns of Attachment: A Psychological Study of the Strange Situation*. Hillsdale, NJ: Lawrence Erlbaum.

Chapter 4

The challenge of myths

Myths throughout the dynamic loop

The personal route of one's dynamic loop includes being confronted with truths and myths about sexual violence in the many spaces occupied along it. Both of these enter rooms where psychotherapy takes place and take up some of the psychological space offered here. Each sits alongside, between, and within the selves involved in this formal process of recovery. Attention to the needs of survivors within the context of social responsibility necessitates attention to how myths interact with other presenting material in contextualising and formulating a client's understanding of the impact of sexual violence upon them.

There is much to untangle about the specifics of sexual violence in order to treat its impact because there is much to un-learn along the way. Psychotherapists can deepen their understanding of the issue via exposure to the truth of it and at the same time this can be skewed by the intrusion of myths into the shared dialogue. Myths enter the room via each participant's dynamic loop and meet at the intersection of those loops in which psychotherapeutic contact occurs (usually scheduled appointments).

Myths present a dichotomy as they offer another avenue by which to better understand sexual violence as a societal occurrence, even though on the surface they divert our attention from the truth. This is because myths can illuminate how disempowerment plays out for individual survivors when truths attempt to be silenced. Such oppressions occur within each survivor's multifaceted self, with other selves, and within human-made systems along the spaces in their dynamic loops.

Being confronted with this dichotomy in each of our personal understandings of sexual violence presents one of the central challenges to recovery. All of us are challenged by myths about sexual violence regardless of whether or not one has direct lived experience. As psychotherapists aiming to treat a clinical population effectively, we as a profession are challenged on how to do so based on what we know (or think we know) about the issue.

The result of disempowerment is a societally-mandated creation, and its continual reinforcement, of barriers to living everyday life freely. This takes

DOI: 10.4324/9781003202943-4

place in addition to a client's post-trauma presentation that impairs an ability to exercise freedoms as they might normally do. Even the process of accessing psychotherapy services is one way in which myths interrupt the recovery of those impacted by sexual violence. As an example: a gay survivor wants to speak confidentially to a professional about his past experiences, but is unsure of approaching a rape crisis service as he has been taught that rape doesn't happen within same-sex relationships.

In psychotherapy truths are of significant value as they represent an element of meeting the person amongst the trauma, which is: the totality of one's self and their personal identity. At some stage in the overall process of recovery, whether it takes place in one piece of psychotherapeutic work or not, it is important for the client to make safe contact with the multiple facets of their self wherever possible. Doing so successfully is characterised by relatedness between facets of the self, such as the absence of psychological disconnection or bodily re-experiencing of the traumatic events. Relatedness between facets of the self is key in re-establishing a coherent identity that can include having survived sexual violence.

Part of what needs to be untangled about sexual violence includes the ways in which its truths are distorted and ignored. When repeated often enough such distortions and ignorance lead to the formation of myths that become shared amongst persons in the world as a misconceived frame of reference for this global phenomenon.

Giving space for truths is therefore part of responding in a humane, relational manner to the personal impact of sexual violence. Providing support with these qualities in place constitutes a reparative experience between selves, as it is counter to the violence and violation that brought a client to psychotherapy.

There is a level of concealment in individual acts of sexual violence to varying degrees, which fuels the existence of collective myths about it. The cognitive distortions placed on the individual survivor, achieved covertly or otherwise, grow to be reflected in how wider society is taught to think about sexual violence within the limited parameters of myths.

Such limited opportunities to talk and think thoroughly about the issue means these limited understandings continue. Furthermore, these limitations mutate into disempowerments via reduced freedom of speech and freedom of autonomy. Every time this occurs the concealment of the truth of sexual violence as a violation of multiple boundaries is reinforced, regardless of whether or not perpetrators are explicitly determined to hide what is happening from others.

To illustrate: it may be the case that a perpetrator intentionally wishes to conceal what they are doing and, to achieve this, will tell a child that they shouldn't tell anyone about the sexual touching taking place so as to not be a bad child. When sexual violence occurs in plain sight within institutions, in ritualised abuse, and in war, the concealment of the truth of sexual violence is that perpetrators are acting without shame nor consequence in a sub-section of the wider world where they powerfully set the rules for living.

In cases where a person's rights to dictate sexual contact on their own terms sits closely with religious beliefs, similar concealment of the truth of sexual violence occurs:

> In the community women are told to be patient with comments such as 'God loves patience.' In fact, in Islam women are to be honoured and respected which is evidenced by a chapter in the Quran that is dedicated to issues and laws regarding the rights of women called 'Surah Al-Nisaa.' There is also a chapter called 'She Who Disputes' ('Al-Mujadilah') referring to a woman who complained to the Prophet about her husband, so God sent this revelation in response to her predicament stating her prayer was heard.
>
> Women have many rights in Islam and can leave a marriage at any time for any reason from no longer being attracted to your partner to when abuse is happening. In fact, regardless of your gender it is your duty to leave an abusive relationship as much as this is possible.
>
> The Quran is a book of guidance and is open to mis-interpretation. One also has to look at the life and teachings of the Prophet Mohammed who was an embodiment of the Quran and thus gave context to the guidance of the Quran. The patriarchal and cultural lens through which Islam is taught and enacted means that women do not realise they have any power at all at so many levels.
>
> *Tayba*

Concealment of the truth of sexual violence is the disempowering silence survivors face in the moment and afterwards in many spaces along dynamic loops. Freedom of speech via interactions with other selves is denied in such spaces. Silence's power is to transfer responsibility for sexual violence onto survivors even in the moment, as the myth-fuelled accusation of 'You should have screamed or said no' makes clear. This misplaced responsibility is compounded every time client's disclosures are met with further silence or inaction from those they disclose to.

In any case, the survivor is left to hold the complex reality of the situation in their thoughts, feelings, behaviour, and embodied symptoms. Being in this situation whilst navigating spaces along their dynamic loop without chances to think and talk through myths increases the impact of sexual violence. By virtue of existing in society, everyone comes into contact with myths to the point where they risk being internalised as apparent truths if they are unchallenged. This type of internalisation is the first effect of myths.

A series of deflections happens when a myth is expressed so that the truth is distorted or ignored. These are deflections from the complexity of the survivor's account of: what happened in the moment, who was involved, how it happened, and what the consequences of what happened are. No matter what these look like in actuality, what it becomes in mythology are all the ways everyone tries not to believe the truth of the matter.

In this way myths are a failed attempt to societally organise a very nuanced issue to the point of being reductionist and incorrect. Part of this includes missing the individual person amongst what happened to them, in turn leaving them alone to be defined by the violating actions of another. Therefore, the second effect of myths is that sexual violence becomes justifiable because it can seemingly be explained in relatively simple terms to cover all people.

If for a survivor the circumstances in which they were sexually violated and/or the description of a perpetrator happen to fall outside of these explanations then society states that sexual violence is not possible:

> If there's anything out there about sexual violence I can tell you that none of the victims look like me, a black man. That includes all these high-profile cases coming out. Racism sets up the idea that we can only be perpetrators, so how can we be affected by abuse? The same goes for my gender. It's even more difficult when you think about race and gender together.
>
> *Rob*

The third effect of myths is a psychological distancing of the issue of sexual violence. It is often considered to be something that only happens to other people, or to us, when one personally fails in some way. At the same time perpetrators are equally 'othered' as if they could never be someone we recognise or know. A simultaneous reinforcing of the 'otherness' of survivors occurs via the societal marginalisation of those who are unable to participate in daily life as usual because of the impact of trauma.

Examples are believing that a successful working professional always goes home to a caring partner and that it is only men from non-white communities that groom children for sexual purposes. The shift away from wanting to understand, nor wanting to believe, the reality of sexual violence is an avoidance of blame, shame, and guilt. Each of these are deeply uncomfortable internal experiences with the potential to create disconnection between facets of the self and disconnection between other selves, in order to manage the distress caused by these discomforts.

A collective ability to turn away from the reality of sexual violence is in part an attempt to psychologically tolerate the horror of it via minimisation and othering. One example is 'Only women are raped and only men are rapists.' Attempts to societally survive this horror takes place regardless of whether one is personally impacted by sexual violence or not. 'It's not safe to walk alone at night' as a protective caution tries to fulfil this purpose through the implicit message of 'You can and must prevent this from happening to you.'

The totality of individuals not believing survivors' truths means that the following happens on a global scale: people are enabled to become perpetrators of sexual violence, perpetrators are enabled to continue sexually violating others, all perpetrators learn there are no negative consequences to their behaviour, and survivors are repeatedly disempowered across multiple domains.

What is created from this is a global society where sexual violence occurs to a staggering degree in all sorts of circumstances and amongst all sorts of people. Without proper dissection and attention myths continue to live on as ways to pass on misplaced responsibility for the existence of sexual violence. Psychotherapists are able to provide collaborative opportunities to un-learn myths as well as reduce their negative impact within psychotherapy appointments and other spaces in the wider world.

Dysregulation

Dysregulation can tell us much about how sexual violence disrupts the usual order of operating within individual selves and collective living in wider society. Being primarily focused on a survivor's personal process by virtue of delivering psychotherapy does not mean that an understanding of the wider implications of sexual violence on society are excluded from our shared awareness as selves living in the same world. Therefore, dysregulation observed in a client's multi-faceted self should be considered in the context of societal dysregulation, as both are subject to the impact of sexual violence.

Within psychotherapy a survivor will present with their own version of having difficulty understanding and managing their multi-faceted self. There is likely to be disconnection between facets where there was none before and negative changes in how individual facets seem to them. These stem from a sense of intolerability when a facet holding distressing material emerges to the forefront of experience. This is underpinned by an over- or under-activation of the physical and psychological facets of the self to try to handle this distress.

Survivors often report a reduced ability to manage embodied and mental distress than prior to sexual violence occurring, or a generally low capacity to do so if subjected to repeated and/or early experiences of abuse. In any case there is a change or difficulty in one or more of the following areas: daily functioning, self-experience, and personal identity.

There are variations to be found here, especially as survival (adapting to manage severe distress) can take on many forms. Nonetheless, a difficulty in understanding and managing one's multi-faceted self is also usually voiced in psychotherapy as not feeling in control. Psychotherapists can explain that this is rooted in dysregulation of the body and mind which is a normal consequence of trauma.

A similar process arising in collective living as a result of sexual violence can be referred to as societal dysregulation. From a perspective that sits alongside the truth of survivors, society is dysregulated by sexual violence in two fundamental ways. First, something significant happens within society when one of its members is subjected to sexual violence, given the violating nature of the act.

However, the daily life of the group as a whole goes on relatively or completely unaffected. This can include the daily life of the perpetrator, even if they are a member of the same community or group of persons as the survivor. If sexual violence occurs within society, it is nonsensical for it to only be an individual's problem, thus dysregulation of a community or group is cemented.

Second, sexual violence is largely inadequately understood and inadequately responded to when it occurs within society. Clients describe being unable to speak about it even when they have tried, for example. Dysregulation as a result of these inadequacies sustains the power of myths within a society covertly and overtly set on relentlessly disempowering survivors for the most part. Survivors are therefore often left holding the truth on their own for significant periods of time and become dysregulated within multi-faceted selves.

The blame, shame, and guilt that arise from myths represent the human cost of societal dysregulation. It is this human cost to clients that psychotherapists are asked to work through each time they meet someone with sexual violence in their history. Repeated assertions of myths within the wider world, even when confronted with the truth of lived experience, are attempts of a victim-blaming society to resolve the problem of sexual violence by placing responsibility for it onto survivors.

Clients in psychotherapy may assert the same myths in relation to themselves, even when holding the truths of what they have been through. Contradictions are created to navigate one's self, relationships with other selves, and the wider world. Dynamic loops and selves metaphorically become less solid ground to walk on under such circumstances where they are repeatedly challenged internally and externally by such contradictions. As a result, dysregulation occurs in the psychological facet of the self.

The ways that blame, shame, and guilt are experienced internally are signifiers of dynamic attempts to cognitively and emotionally find resolution in order to alleviate distress and perhaps even solve why it happened. When myths are considered alongside truths clients and psychotherapists can feel the push-and-pull of a seemingly impossible process of trying to create a linear chronology with something so disruptive. Survivors may feel as though they are living inside an isolated, disconnected self that also doesn't make any logical sense.

If these psychological and emotional processes occur alongside dysregulation in the physical facet of the self, the entire self as a whole continues to be under threat. Remaining in survival mode and re-experiencing elements of the original incident characterises the client's multi-faceted self as one makes contact with traumatic material. When severe enough, this colours one's personal identity too.

Additional societal dysregulation is at risk of occurring in a survivor's personal world when others become aware of what has happened to them, perhaps in their shared societal group. When responded to supportively, dysregulation can be replicated in varying degrees with other selves who take on the truth of what happened. Work with families, partners, and friends of survivors are an insight into this manifestation of dysregulation. This manifestation can include vicarious trauma when a person experiences the impact of sexual violence as if it happened to them, which is something that psychotherapists are not immune to.

When the truth is met with disbelief, dysregulation can translate into how much a survivor is unable, by no longer being allowed, to be in relationships nor society anymore because of what has happened to them. Placing responsibility for sexual violence onto the survivor to resolve the distress of other group members can underlie the reason as to why disclosures increase risk. Examples include what is often referred to as 'honour killings' of a survivor following disclosure of sexual violence and instances where a survivor becomes estranged from their family when they state that someone in that family has abused them sexually.

Here, the humanity of a survivor is overlooked in active or passive favour of ensuring that the usual order of society, communities, and groups is maintained. The societal rule is that if you have been sexually violated, you can no longer participate in that society as you know it. In psychodynamic terms this is the process of psychological contact with a 'bad' part that fuels pre-existing anxiety (Klein, 1957), which exists alongside a 'good' part.

The Kleinian Mother's 'good breast' and 'bad breast' being two parts of the same person is the origin of a life-long psychological conflict that must be managed. This dynamic can manifest in many forms between persons throughout one's lifetime. Primitive anxiety of annihilation (a risk of contact with a 'bad' part) can be managed via psychological projection of these 'bad' parts onto others. This is an attempt to reduce one's anxiety as a form of psychological distress and have our self or another self remain 'good.'

Within a victim-blaming society this can be seen in the maintenance of a perpetrator as a good person in comparison to the bad behaviour or character of a survivor. News headlines can refer to male perpetrators by their profession (good) rather than their crime (bad) even if they have been convicted. One such example is: 'Chanel Miller's memoir of assault by athlete wins prestigious book award' (*Star Tribune*, 2020) which was published five years after the incident took place and Brock Turner was convicted. Experientially and conceptually survivors remain the object of violence and violations of their own self.

A common post-trauma symptom is an avoidance of activities, situations, or people associated with the traumatic events (World Health Organization, 2019). From neurophysiological survival perspectives we can understand this as a normal response to try and retain a sense of safety that continues to be impinged upon long after sexual violence has occurred.

One resolution is to create some regulation in an unsafe, unsupportive world by retreating from it or adapting to a new, limited way of life. From this there is a fundamental inability to participate freely in society as usual from a place of autonomy. The value of challenging myths in psychotherapy is to create a recognisable self that one can reside in. Its value is further cemented in creating a similar sense of familiarity (including safety) beyond the self so that participation in daily life and communities is a realistic option.

Blame, shame, and guilt

The repeated emergence of blame, shame, and guilt in psychotherapy impairs the ability of all involved to sustain the belief that overcoming the impact of sexual violence is possible. When these are experienced in whatever configuration within one's self or beyond, disempowerment is reinforced. Considering them in relation to the challenge of myths reinforces the notion that sexual violence is not simply an individual's problem to be privately addressed in psychotherapy, but a wider societal issue to be resolved. Psychotherapists can take up this challenge in exercising their social responsibility, as discussed in Chapter three.

Myths challenge recovery from sexual violence as they precipitate the powerful emotive reactions of blame, shame, and guilt. When this takes place a disconnect between facets of the self occurs as a protective safety mechanism. Such a disconnect takes away a client's ability to be comfortably in contact with their self, thus threatening one's personal baseline for living and self-experience. Within the self, disconnection underlies fluctuations in affect, feeling out of control, and not having conscious access to all facets of the self.

To clarify: blame is the painful re-centring of responsibility for what happened onto the survivor. This uncomfortably takes up space regardless of whether it is directed from society to the individual self, between persons, or within one's self. Shame serves to isolate an individual from others via tightly regulating movement in literal and figurative terms. Isolation of this kind occurs as disconnection between facets of the self, between other selves, and from spaces in the wider world. Guilt increases the weight of what is carried as a result of sexual violence, making it difficult for alternative ways of being to become possible.

A frame of reference for sexual violence as dictated by society becomes internalised, primarily impacting freedom of autonomy. Moreover, this frame of reference is acted upon as a behavioural code of conduct via impaired freedom of speech and movement. Blame, shame, and guilt as a result of myths are conscious and unconscious efforts to organise a sense of self that has some sort of coherency. This happens amongst and because of the distress they cause within the psychological and physical facets of the self as emotional experiences.

Sexual violence becomes a cognitively arranged sequence of events to be put into logical order, when the impact of such experiences is far more than a psychological task. Any survivor can tell you that the impact of sexual violence is not limited to one's thoughts but also to their feelings and bodies, in addition to changing the many spaces inhabited beyond these elements constituting a sense of self.

Simply thinking one's way out of the impact of sexual violence is an incomplete approach. A reliance on a cognitive process alone illustrates the reductionist function of myths and points to their inadequacy as societal narratives internalised by individuals. Furthermore, such reductionism enables sexual violence to continue within the wider world without consequences for individual perpetrators and systems that perpetrate violence.

Survivor's truths as psychological concepts are held up against a world that generally continues as if nothing of note has occurred. Some people a survivor discloses to may believe them and others may not. Here, the survivor's account does not consistently chime with the wider world nor the other selves within it. This very real aloneness with the issue relentlessly maintains an inability to move forward with recovery, as disconnect characterises internal and external experiences in the aftermath of sexual violence.

One result is that the survivor is forced out of spaces with only blame, shame, and guilt as answers. Very often this creates a strong barrier to not only disclosure, but also to seeking support, reinforcing this isolated position. Within psychotherapy this aloneness can be mitigated in the psychological and physical spaces offered. The practice of actually sitting with another self can combat this feeling, as well as having boundaried psychological contact from the supportive psychotherapist's self. At two levels trust may begin to grow as a way to try moving forward safely, however fleeting this can be at times, on the part of the client.

The physicality of truths is evidenced via the embodied impact of trauma which occurs via traumatic recall such as flashbacks and nightmares. It also occurs through similar symptoms linking the body back to the traumatic past, such as muscle tension, physical pain, and changes in levels of controlled mobility or movement. Whatever is recalled within the physical facet of the self forms elements of the wider truth of sexual violence for individual survivors, including when recall is impaired.

Being suddenly introduced to one's somatic ability to survive traumatic experiences is both a blessing and a curse. It has kept one alive, but makes living thereafter unbearable for as long as the impact of sexual violence fails to be adequately addressed at an embodied level. Not being in control because of inherent mechanisms that aid survival is hugely injurious to a client's sense of self, where they may usually feel in control of what their body does.

Within psychotherapy clients may express wanting to speak but not being able to, or knowing they are safe but sitting on the edge of a chair within bodies that want to escape a room. Blame, shame, and guilt are therefore not only emotions nor cognitive experiences, but are also are elements of one's mental health experienced within the body. Therefore, the physical facet of the self must be a part of what is addressed when clients express blame, shame, and guilt. The psychological and physical facets of the self being disconnected in this way may occur outside of a client's awareness.

What is a protective mechanism quickly creates a state of unrecognisability of the self and a loss of personal identity. Sexual violence casts out the bodies and minds of survivors in many spaces in their dynamic loops in the wider world, as well as being facets they do not consistently have safe access to themselves. In working with all the facets of the self at conscious and unconscious levels the psychotherapist introduces the possibility of making sensitive contact with these even when the client is unable to initiate this process.

All of us are societally taught what to expect with regards to sex and sexual behaviour, including how it is possible for someone to be subjected to non-consensual sexual contact. This comes with the reinforcement of what is correct, normal, and right by the terms of societies. A skewing of social conduct to reinforce disempowerment leads to the formation of the many myths that clients will be challenged by, even if a client is sure that what happened wasn't right or normal.

For survivors who are sexually violated repeatedly in their lifetimes, particularly in childhood, the normality of such incidences is also set within the myths of smaller groups such as families, institutions, or cults. Grooming children for sexual contact similarly skews a survivor's implicit and explicit understanding of how the world works, including who dictates access to one's body, and what one's body is for.

A point of tension in working with the internalisation of myths in psychotherapy comes from wrestling with the notion of responsibility. Although the psychotherapist easily begins from a place of believing the client need not hold onto blame, shame, and guilt because myths aren't truths, on the other side of the room a different process often takes place.

Conceptualisations of how one can prevent, or stop, sexual violence translate into ways to try to psychologically manage the fact that one has been treated in this way. In terms of what myth applies here, it could for example be: 'If I hadn't said yes to going on a date with them this wouldn't have happened, so I must have led them on somehow.'

It is normal to be psychologically, physically, and emotionally unable to bear the reality of not being in control of what happens when we are in danger. Being unable to bear the aftermath of sexual violence as the body and mind try to survive the experience again is also normal. Not being in control of the physical and psychological facets of the self contributes to the disconnection between these two parts, which many survivors describe as feeling there is a line of separation somewhere that they can locate physically. Remarkably, this is often the head separated from the rest of the body.

Every time sexual violence is experienced and re-experienced there is space uncontrollably prioritised for blame, shame, and guilt within the survivor's self. This also happens when others do not believe, or know but do not help.

Such powerful emotions combined with physical sensations and related thoughts create a hammering reinforcement of myth's power to de-centre the survivor from their own self and individual belief systems.

The psychotherapist may always reflexively approach manifestations of blame, shame, and guilt with criticism as they are so closely linked to internalised myths. Motivating this is the understanding that myths derail clients from their own constructions of what is true or not. When myths are left unattended to the client repeatedly loses their sense of self and we fail to invite them fully into the room for their truths to be known and validated.

However, it is also the case that the truth of the matter can give rise to blame, shame, and guilt, especially as emotions are experienced in the body along with being considered in psychological terms. For example: feeling ashamed that one felt physical arousal during non-consensual sexual contact, or guilty for staying with a partner after being subjected to sexual assault. In this way we can understand the specifics of how each client relates to, or becomes disconnected from, each facet of their self in assessing their experiences within psychotherapy.

The experiential and relational dichotomy that myths create reflects the dual position that psychotherapists are required to take up in navigating this conflicting aspect of recovery. Although it can be relief for a client to hear from someone else that what happened wasn't their fault, it may also reinforce the lonely position of distressing feelings being unmet.

Expressions such as this from the psychotherapist's side may only therefore address one part of the freedoms that are sought in untangling one's self from the impact of myths. Making sense of one's range of emotional reactions is part of untangling the complexity of human-to-human abuse. This is especially the case in instances where a survivor has a pre-existing relationship with the perpetrator before sexual violence occurs within the context of that relationship, as is more common than not.

Another sticking point in attending to the negative impact of societally-constructed myths is that they represent a tie to group practices and norms. Finding a way back to one's societal groups as a survivor of sexual violence involves re-configuring one's self in relation to other selves, regardless of whether these other selves are aware of the sexual violence that has taken place. Simply put, it can be the difference between belonging or not.

In this way restrictions on thinking, speaking, and moving freely are found in many spaces along a client's dynamic loop. Re-configuring myths as part of the work of re-configuring the self involves the psychotherapist in the process of enabling clients to make decisions centred on their truths and perspectives rather than defaulting to a forced position contextualised by myths.

A significant factor related to how myths compound blame, shame, and guilt for sexual violence is trust. If the spaces one traverses internally (minds, bodies) or externally (relationships, societies) do not operate as usual and something seems not quite right, the erosion of trust occurs in such spaces. At worst clients do not trust their selves and become lost under the insidious, isolating weight of these three states as disconnection takes hold. Without this baseline of trust within the self, survivors can remain in the early stages of recovery indefinitely.

Increasing a client's ability to psychologically and physically address the impact of myths as they internally arise is a helpful first step in working towards holding conflicting states of mind and body. The same applies when clients are faced with myths in spaces along their dynamic loops, including with other selves and systems.

To achieve this the psychotherapist can apply their understanding of how we all survive traumatic experiences within the physical facet of the self. Teaching clients the fundamentals of neurobiological and physiological processes normalises the impact of sexual violence. Normality as truths, when embedded in the framework of psychotherapy, pushes back against the notion of responsibility, given that these processes occur automatically.

Truth via normalisation can therefore assist in loosening the grip of blame, shame, and guilt held within the self. For example, survivors whose bodies went into a state of freezing during sexual violence can unlearn the myth that one has a responsibility to stop what happened by taking action in the moment. Similarly, the notion that one consented to sexual contact because they didn't fight back is re-framed with the truth of the matter.

Further to this teaching as being a directive (information giving) intervention, the psychotherapist can offer an inclusive (information sharing) experience by asking clients to be interested in what happens within the physical facet of the self at points throughout the dialogue wherever possible. Deciding and practising together what to do in response to somatic symptoms before they occur is vital in managing this re-experiencing of trauma. Again, the psychotherapist offers opportunities to try trusting one's self and other selves as they collaboratively make forward steps.

Regulating one's physical facet of the self becomes parallel to the process of regulating one's emotions and thoughts within the psychological facet of the self. A crossroads often encountered in psychotherapy is the survivor's wish to focus on facets of the self that are re-triggering at a somatic level. Where embodied symptoms are present, choice is often removed as the physical facet of a client's self makes the decision for them. Lack of trust, control, and the minimal opportunity to re-configure one's self with personal consent are reinforced.

An essential principle here is to know that cognitive processes such as reflection are less possible when the physical facet of the self is hyper- or hypo-aroused. Psychological work can only be undertaken when the neurobiology and physiology allows for it. Deciding and practising how to attend to this can include practical, body-based techniques agreed upon in negotiation with the client.

The physical facet of the self is always making an assessment of safety and, when this has been impaired because of traumatic experiences, results in hyper-vigilance. Although a process largely beyond awareness, clients can report a consciousness of it in stating they feel wary and unsafe. This can manifest in situations similar to the incidences of sexual violence experienced, such as with specific people and locations. It can also occur more broadly within a world at large that is threatening, and it is here that trust becomes out of one's reach.

Blame, shame, and guilt's ability to cause disconnect feed into a loss of understanding of what is happening. The continuous ups and downs of how one is psychologically and physically experiencing the impact of sexual violence significantly affect an ability to comfortably relate to any facets of the self. Clients may wish for calm, but feel completely unsafe when it is within reach as hyper-arousal is now the norm. In this instance another intervention to be made by psychotherapists is the sensitive promotion of stillness as part of the push back against blame, shame, and guilt perpetuated by myths.

With everyday survival and journeys within spaces along one's dynamic loop, there is not much time for stillness as a pause in pace. For some highly traumatised clients, pausing puts them at risk of being attacked by another self or another facet of their self. One's thoughts, behaviour, physical sensations, and emotions become a series of reactions rather than deliberate choices. Again, there is a loss of control which impairs relatedness amongst facets of the self and between other selves.

Sexual violence marks a significant pause in a client's life, a pause which can stretch for decades. Surviving in this way, within a world that doesn't want to stand still enough to know or help, is part of the societal damage. **Talking through myths and their impact in psychotherapy gently opposes this reactivity, as they can be dissected as required in order to re-configure or reject the information presented.** The psychotherapist's provision of pausing to think and process myths psychologically is an offer of something that doesn't always exist in the wider world.

Similarly, we can acknowledge that blame, shame, and guilt causes silencing. In spaces along one's dynamic loop silencing takes place whilst myths are communicated, however loudly this is done, because it is the truth that is muted. The psychotherapist can once more offer a different quality of experience here to survivors in order to repair the societal hurt caused by myths. Silence offered in the pauses of the dialogue by psychotherapists becomes a space to be heard, rather than drowned out or ignored.

A curiosity about what is happening for clients in moments of silence is a way of inviting them back into relatedness between selves, as well as relatedness with facets of their self that are about to be pushed aside by blame, shame, and guilt. Societal silence is just that: silence. Within psychotherapy there is an explicit understanding and explicit response to the truth of what is happening when on the surface nothing is being expressed.

Similarly, psychotherapists may notice a silencing of psychological processes but an activation in the physical facet of the self. Clients may become unable to think or find words in the psychotherapeutic dialogue, as well as struggle to make contact with the physical facet of their self comfortably. No matter how it manifests, the question to consider together is 'What is trying to be said?' and in the case of challenging myths 'Is there an alternative feeling or point of view here?'

The power of blame, shame, and guilt to force disconnection between facets of the self means that a psychotherapist is required to counter this with relatedness wherever possible. Maximising any recognition of communications from the self verbally, in writing, via artwork, or the via body is a start in returning to the truth of the matter as it is expressed within each survivor's self. Being seen and heard amongst the dysregulation that myths perpetuate is a way to sensitively enhance safe relatedness at multiple levels.

Making space for truths

As both psychotherapists and clients travel around their dynamic loops information about sexual violence is collected via occupying different spaces, which may be myths or truths. We can look to the bodies of survivors as another source of truth on sexual violence, given that its impact is apparent in this facet of the self. As selves living in the same wider world neither will be new to descriptive misconceptions of sexual violence, perhaps even to the point of believing them as internalised myths that have yet to be questioned.

This is not a phenomenon exclusive to psychotherapy, but rather a representation of what happens in the wider world when a complex societal issue characterised by multiple forms of disempowerment is systemically embedded in many spaces. The process of having to re-organise one's personal and wider worlds (including how they are understood at all points throughout the dynamic loop), is thus a task for all members of the wider world if space for truths is to be facilitated.

Survivors are tasked with holding the weight of being viewed through a narrow lens and forced to comply by misconceived standards, due to their lived traumatic experiences. A psychotherapist's repeated response throughout the work should be to hold this weight with them. Doing so increases the possibility of collaboratively exploring alternative ways of thinking, feeling, and living in personal worlds in attempts to increase relatedness. In this way the truth of sexual violence, as qualified by survivors, is widely known as well as personally utilised as an empowering force.

The potential for spaces along dynamic loops to become uninhabitable by survivors is determined by how much, or how little, the task of re-organisation is taken up by other selves. For example: when accessing support services, hearing a myth being expressed can result in a survivor's disengagement, as it becomes yet another place where they cannot speak their truths. In this instance, the hope of recovery is lost.

One contradiction that encapsulates the simultaneous seeing, but not seeing, of sexual violence in the wider world is summarised in the following statement: sexual violence is extremely common, but it should never be deduced that sexual violence is a part of normal life. Psychotherapists are open to seeing the truth of sexual violence because of the nature of services provided. We are also at risk of disconnecting when confronted with it at points because of the power of myths to dissuade us and because of our human responses to knowing the horror that these truths bring.

However, part of a psychotherapist's social responsibility includes actively addressing and reformulating these myths with the general public. Doing so on our own, with colleagues, and/or with survivors along our dynamic loops, ultimately assists in competently working with this in psychotherapy appointments too. In this way collusion with myths is bypassed via widening the narrow lens that leads all of us to globally misunderstand all the different elements of sexual violence and its multi-layered impact.

Furthermore, we open our understanding of how varied responses to sexual violence can be from self to self, even if there are commonalities across survivors as a group. In the place of restrictions there can be promotion of freedom of speech, autonomy, and movement. When promoted often enough truths create a power to push forward with recovery, push back against a victim-blaming society, and the client can use power to sustain their self rather than having power used against them again.

The cost of disempowerment is humanity and human life. Survivors, and psychotherapists that support them, are aware of this truth no matter where they are in their dynamic loops. Personal safety is of course an ongoing theme **to be explored for survivors of sexual violence in psychotherapy, and this can** include retaining a sense of safety when challenging myths as they are presented with them in daily life.

Similarly, personal safety is essential to consider in assessing whether it is safe for psychotherapists to act on our social responsibility as professionals every time we have the potential to do so. Acting outwards in various spaces in defence of the truth may also include considering the safety of others associated with us. Any facets of the self linked with personal identity such as gender, sexuality, religion, and ethnicity may automatically require protection in spaces where they may be under attack. Similar considerations of safety when taking action against sexual violence and related disempowerments are outlined in Chapter three.

Regarding safety in this broader sense simultaneously broadens our understanding of the additional ways that people are societally mistreated because of who they are, outside of or in addition to being a survivor. As an example: challenging the myth that all black women are hypersexual not only fetishises black women, but also assumes their sexual availability for the purposes of men specifically. Challenging this myth on the basis of racism and gender may feel precarious enough in relation to one's audience. If one aims to re-assert heteronormativity also, then they risk being the target of a hate crime if they are effectively stating their non-heterosexual orientation.

Finding ways to exercise freedom of speech, movement, and autonomy on the issue of sexual violence with other selves means sitting with the possible consequences of doing so. This includes personal and professional outcomes where mistreatment plays out. We may live in parts of the world that generally allow for these three freedoms, but they are likely to be challenged or even revoked in pushing back against a society that dictates them. The result can be any type of harm such as fatigue, hopelessness, or even forms of abuse or burnout for any person undertaking this task.

As such, psychotherapists cannot make space for truths alone all of the time. Just as we become allies to survivors in our work, we require allies ourselves to ensure that the impact of taking on social responsibility is supported by others. People of this kind can be found in both professional and personal settings, particularly as a motivation to work with sexual violence as a human rights violation rarely comes from a merely professional place. This can mark the beginning of reverberating the echoes of conversations about sexual violence into more spaces, which is a practice of extending one's professional remit outwards.

There are many ways that truths find a way to surface, including seeming to take on lives of their own at times. Psychotherapists can observe this in clients whose truth spills out of them in their verbal narrative, physical body, disconnection between facets of their self, and the saturation of trauma within personal worlds. Part of a survivor's feeling in control of all the facets of their self and life includes feeling more in control about decisions to bring the truth of sexual violence to light in ways that are empowering rather than disempowering.

A resolution can be found on a case-by-case basis, with the protection of human life and individual choice at the core of assessment each time. For some survivors the risk to personal safety is less harmful then staying silent, even if there is certainty of being harmed somehow. Psychotherapists may also feel this way in personal or professional spaces. One's choice to speak out can be respected insofar as it as an expression of powerfully pushing back against a status quo that relentlessly perpetuates harm towards survivors and those that are allied with them.

Psychotherapy offers a psychological and physical space to experience communicating one's truth, feeling more assured in doing so, and re-configuring one's self in alignment with this truthful assurance. The intentionally boundaried, regulated space of psychotherapy offers a way to experience this, bearing in mind that the impact of trauma is a constant threat to the self's ability to be in the present moment as the past comes back to life. When personal safety is threatened by post-trauma symptoms, or by other selves, concurrent explorations of practical risk management need to take place.

Within psychotherapy there are opportunities to dialogically and somatically practise pushing back without significantly compromising personal safety and increasing a client's ability to feel able to do so. This is especially important for clients who do not feel safe in their bodies and struggle to occupy even the boundaries of this physical facet of the self. In this instance it feels better to stay withdrawn from anything beyond that boundary, sometimes to the point where it becomes an essential position to avoid harm.

Practising a different way of relating to one's self and the psychotherapist's self in the context of a working relationship is achievable in several ways. These are: collaboratively considering options, negotiating what to try, and being clear on when to pause or stop practising completely. These stages of preparation further facilitate trust because they are carried out in a controlled manner, at the client's pace.

The psychotherapist is responsible for tracking and holding the client's material at each stage. When successful there is more relatedness between facets of the self as tolerable contact is made internally, which can be replicated in how one engages with other selves and their personal world as the truth is relayed further outwards.

Client example: Charlie

CHARLIE: I really struggle with the idea that it wasn't my fault on some days, because I had the option of going home. But I didn't, I went home with him instead.

ADAM: I can see you trying to make logical sense of the sequence of events and where that takes you emotionally. How do you feel on other days?

CHARLIE: Like today I'm angry because of what he did to me and that there was no way I saw it coming. So how could I have stopped it?

ADAM: Okay, you're angry. Where is that anger at this moment, as we're speaking about it?

CHARLIE: It's in my face. I've just noticed I'm clenching my jaw, actually.

ADAM: Right, it's in your jaw. Is it possible to make any small changes there right now?

[Charlie pauses, breathes, his face relaxes a little]

CHARLIE: A tiny bit. But I'm so mad about it. It makes it hard to speak. When I've tried to speak to people about it before I imagine they'll think it was my fault too, even if they don't say so. You're not supposed to go home with someone you've just met.

ADAM: You haven't had an opportunity to properly speak about it before coming here, of course it's going to be hard. You've said before you've written about the abuse and shown it to a friend, which is a huge step in voicing what happened. And not only that, the effect it's had on you personally.

CHARLIE: Yeah. It's been easier to write about me rather than speak sometimes. I see other people being really vocal about what they've been through and they're so up front about it not being their fault, but I'm not there yet. I feel like if I got there then I've not only gotten better myself, but I'd like to help other people too. It would be good to connect with other people like me eventually.

ADAM: The idea of it being your fault on some days is so tough. Today you seem to be in a little in touch with a part of you that has a different view: that you're angry about what he did.
CHARLIE: Yeah.
ADAM: Do you want to try writing down some of what you're trying to say that stops at your jaw? I'll check in with you every so often to ask about the physical feeling there and we can go slowly.
CHARLIE: Yeah, I'd like that.

The role of psychotherapists in public-facing spaces within their dynamic loops is to facilitate safety in the shared wider world via acts of pushing back against systems, people, and practices that perpetuate sexual violence. In this way we aim to empower survivors to take up space with their truths as a general principle in the act of everyday living, as well as offer platforms for their voices to reverberate further into society than perhaps would have been achievable on their own. This constitutes being an ally to survivors of sexual violence wherever we are placed in society and making space for truths within multiple spaces.

Relational psychotherapy is interested in the subjective and intersubjective encounter that allows clients to not only address personal material but to be the authority on it. For all persons such authority is moderated by society and its members even before sexual violence occurs as it dictates an apparent fact within limited parameters. Authority becomes lost once more in relationships when others are disbelieving, sceptical, or non-responsive following disclosure after the events.

In this instance power over one's narrative is also lost as the trajectory of one's chronology of their life is similarly interrupted. Here it is appropriate to state that it is possible to psychotherapeutically alleviate the impact of sexual violence without dissecting the narrative of the event, although at some stage this may feel necessary to the client in re-establishing empowerment within their self as a whole. Clients may feel that re-framing their chronology in relation to the impact of sexual violence is adequate to meet the goal of living as a survivor.

There may be a personal meaning for the client in knowing, or not knowing, some or all of what happened when sexual violence took place. Here elements of the truth of the event are not even known to the survivor and the truth of its impact is more familiar. This is due to the formation, storage, and recollection of memories being impacted when one is trying to survive something traumatic compared to when one is physiologically settled. At a neurophysiological level, brain structures involved in processing memory are unable to function as usual when under extreme stress. Further information on this is detailed in Chapter two.

Sexual violence being interwoven into the reality of a relationship, or family life, may make it harder to get into contact with what the survivor themselves truly thinks or emotionally feels about what happened. This is not to discount at all that many survivors are absolutely sure of what happened, how they felt about it then, and how it seems to them now. It is also the case that there may be fluctuations between these two states as the survivor moves through their life, which in part can change if they are brought back to the past in some way. One common example is one's children reaching the age a survivor was when they were abused, sparking a new phase of re-configuring the self through their personal perspective.

Variations in recollection is the antithesis to collective endeavours to condense the societal narrative on sexual violence into a more straightforward act, cemented into the perspective of victim-blaming. One myth that is relevant here is 'Since you can't remember all of what happened, your account can't be trusted.' Unfortunately, this appears in many places where a survivor discloses their experiences, from interactions with loved ones to the criminal justice system. Again, truth is pushed out of spaces along dynamic loops even when it is spoken.

Re-configuring one's self and life when one's narrative is disrupted by sexual violence is apparent in the subjectivity of the relational encounter whilst the narrative is articulated. A psychotherapist's experience of a survivor's self whilst placed in intersubjective relationship with them is a source of information in understanding what it is like to be that particular survivor. Therefore, an insight into the specific configuration of the client's self is available to be known, which is another place for truth to emerge in relatedness between selves.

Discrepancies between what the psychotherapist feels in their body plus the tone present in the room, compared with the client's words, is useful in attending to the multi-layered impact of sexual violence. This often points to unconscious material just outside of the client's awareness within disconnected facets of the self. When appropriately timed, it is helpful for a psychotherapist to sensitively bring this material into shared conscious awareness. This should be done upon assessment of the client's ability to remain in their window of tolerance (Siegel, 1999) where they are ready for social engagement with an ability to reflect rather than their body prioritising physical survival.

Re-configuring one's personal truths alongside re-configuring the self includes learning to have more freedom of autonomy. At times the psychotherapist holds the challenge of how and how much to confront a survivor's belief in a myth, because to do so might include shattering an already-shattered sense of self and the world. Even if one hasn't experienced sexual violence the consequence of myths being ingrained within the context of a shared world means an understanding of how the world works, and why, is heavily influenced. Many survivors want a place in the wider world, but cannot conceive of how to exist in it.

Alternating between holding on to the edges of one's truth about sexual violence and being pulled into believing a myth can sometimes result in internal conflict. This can be understood as facets of the self being unable to relate to each other, resulting in the overall self being out of consistent psychological and physical reach. One way this disconnection is experienced is feeling that one is going mad, which sits closely to the myth that those saying they have experienced sexual violence are somehow always making it up, or mistaken.

Psychotherapists can address this type of internal conflict by responding to truths as an act of much-needed validation of not only a survivor's experiences, but also an act of honouring their self. Being able to sensitively listen is an essential step in a client's wider world where disclosures are deliberately not heard by the majority. Being curious about the client's words or phrases that produce significant distress, sometimes to the point of disconnection from facets of the self, is helpful in supporting a client's expressions of freedom of speech.

Simultaneously supporting clients to understand and regulate this distress allows psychotherapists to model being able to meet facets of a client's self and elements of their experiences without becoming overwhelmed by blame, shame, or guilt. As such the psychological and physical facets of a client's self learn that emotion and being re-triggered are not always the same thing. More freedom of speech, autonomy, and movement occurs when emotions are safe to emerge in these facets, enabling truths to emerge in many spaces.

Finding selves amongst trauma

Working with the impact of myths in psychotherapy predominantly includes the task of learning to manage any conflict between what is true and what is false. Being caught up in this conflict is part of what causes disconnection between facets of an individual self and between selves in relationships. On a wider scale this includes disconnection from communities, groups, and the world at large.

Ultimately there is a process of not only re-evaluating but rejecting myths at individual and societal levels. This is work for the psychotherapist and client given that both come into contact with myths about sexual violence by virtue of living in a shared world. When myths enter the psychotherapeutic space as dynamic loops intersect, disconnection can take place in this working relationship if not handled carefully.

Personal identity is part of what can be lost when sexual violence forces re-configuration of the self to take place. The grieving process involved in divorcing one's self from myths may be replicated in the loss of relationships as well as membership of communal groups and spaces that one previously occupied. Experientially these may replicate loneliness or abandonment characterised by shame. Once more, a survivor can become isolated and stuck within their own self as disconnection takes hold.

Successful psychotherapy with survivors of sexual violence could end at the point where post-trauma symptoms are alleviated and, for some clients, this is more than adequate. However, true relational psychotherapy is also interested in finding the self amongst the trauma wherever possible. Doing so honours the individual survivor as a person and their individual process of recovery which is carried along all the spaces in their dynamic loop.

Living within a self characterised by relatedness, personal control, and empowerment assists the survivor to live by personal truths, rather than living within restrictive rules set by myths. Survivors can then create a life that is more aligned with the individual self as set out by them before and above anything else as an influence. As freedom of speech, movement, and autonomy is exercised the multi-faceted self is in turn more reflective of one's personal identity. Over time a tangible sense of self is established which is not only able to survive, but to thrive.

Psychotherapists can expand their understanding of widening a client's personal world, including support networks, to put the above into action. Collaborative considerations of other selves and spaces that would chime with personal truths and identities can be explored as part of this. This can include seeking spaces along their dynamic loop to be with others who think, feel, and identify in similar ways in order to be seen, heard, and validated.

The practice of learning how to hold truths in the face of myths is part of being able to tolerate existing in a wider world where one's lived experiences and views are repeatedly questioned. Making use of freedom of autonomy and speech in psychotherapy creates opportunities to make decisions on how **one aligns their self with their own truths. It can be a safe practice arena by** which to manifest these truths in many ways.

The creation of more spaces in the world where individuals freely live in accordance with the truth of sexual violence as survivors, as dictated by them, is possible. There is enough space in the world for the diversity of survivors and their lived experiences to exist even if seemingly impossible. Such spaces can be found in connecting with other survivors online or in face-to-face interactions. Allies of survivors can also be part of these spaces, increasing the numbers within this supportive community.

The process of finding selves amongst trauma in psychotherapy is characterised by relatedness, knowing that this can be impinged upon by disconnection. In many instances survivors hold on to the hope of consistently sitting comfortably within the totality of their facets at some point. Clients may phrase this as wanting to feel in control, wanting to feel normal, or wanting to feel like they did before the sexual violence happened. Psychotherapists can in part understand this as a willingness to establish and exercise relatedness within multi-faceted selves.

Establishing relatedness within one's self, with other selves, and the wider world constitutes the re-building of one's life. In psychotherapy re-configuring the self from an empowerment-based approach, in response to the forced re-configuration of the self due to sexual violence, is the goal at all times.

Achieving this within one's self as a starting point forms a client's template by which to replicate this in other spaces along dynamic loops.

Increasing empowerment reduces the need to adapt thoughts, emotions, and behaviour as survival strategies whilst one regains control overall within their realm of personal power. The configuration of one's self is specific to each survivor and includes a personal identity. Using this to create a life that has purpose, resonance, and meaning further re-establishes control and choice in line with who one is. Personal worlds become shaped by the survivor, rather than the other way around.

Myths about other elements of one's identity within society, as collective ways to dismiss the truths of many people's lives, may have fuelled disempowerment prior to experiences of sexual violence. If this is the case, psychotherapists should be actively curious about any number of myths that compound the impact of sexual violence on the multi-faceted self.

Often psychotherapeutic work includes a focused exploration of the self as the survivor knows it, the self they would like to be, and what it feels like undertaking living in the dissonance between those points. For clients who have more disconnection than relatedness between the facets of their self, this dissonance weakens the opportunity for a personal identity to coherently grow.

Disconnection pushes facets of the self apart, maintaining more room for trauma than anything else as a characterising feature of one's self-experience. A psychotherapist getting to know who their client is every time contact is made can be a slow process challenged by the impact of several intersecting myths, combined with post-trauma symptoms.

Myths in general have the ability to make people feel they are inherently problematic and being a survivor of sexual violence is no exception. The impact of this is rooted in misplaced blame, shame, and guilt. Ideally psychotherapy offers spaces within dynamic loops where survivors are not only welcomed but fully accommodated, thus removing the additional weight of simply existing alongside the challenge of surviving sexual violence.

However, interrelated myths that touch upon multiple elements of the client's identity or experiences increases the weight they bear in everyday living. Consideration of this includes acknowledgement of how psychotherapy services need to evolve to better meet the needs of all survivors, knowing that anyone can be affected. Acknowledgement of the need for psychotherapists to purposefully find each of their client's selves amongst their traumatic experiences is also key. Putting these acknowledgements into action appointment by appointment is possible and necessary for doing relational work.

To do so psychotherapists need to reflect on how the psychological spaces we offer can be limited by how we inadvertently contextualise them with myths, which are false homogenisations about groups of people. In this way a reinforcing of the notion that sexual violence only happens to certain people is at risk of taking place in the intersecting spaces in dynamic loops between selves where psychotherapy takes place. Related to this are internalised myths about how sexual violence happens and who perpetrators or survivors are likely to be.

As an example, a transgender woman using she/her pronouns may be forced to bear the weight of a multitude of myths within her self and surrounding wider world before she can feel allowed to access specialist psychotherapeutic support as a survivor. This weight continues to be momentarily palpable as she anticipates and pushes back against them.

This includes myths such as: those who are assigned male at birth do not face sexual abuse and that one is transgender because something bad happened to them (perhaps sexual violence). These are expressions of how it could never be the case that a person who discloses sexual violence is telling the truth, thus the individual person's identity as well as their traumatic experiences are negated.

Sitting very closely to myths about sexual violence is a discriminatory message: that psychotherapy is only available to certain people. For the transgender female survivor, this may be the case when women-only spaces seem to only invite contact from cisgender women. Knowing that there are many barriers to be crossed for many different types of client in order to access psychotherapeutic support maintains this narrow remit for how our profession is, or could be, supportive. If psychotherapists do not widen their lens conceptually nor in action, the spaces we offer remain closed off to many. An exploration of these barriers can be found in Chapter one.

Part of responding to the reality of sexual violence as a profession means evolving to incorporate the truths of many different types of survivor. When we are effective at doing so, we offer inclusive psychotherapy. The professional pushing back against interrelated myths is a move away from problematic stereotypes that cause harm, and invites more clients into the spaces we provide. Pushing back also improves quality of ongoing dialogues about sexual violence which seek to benefit all persons impacted by it, rather than perpetuating more disempowerment.

Automatic neurophysiological responses to trauma are inherent in all people as an existing survival mechanism but the multi-faceted self, including one's personal identity, is subject to much more diversity. Psychotherapists need to be interested in meeting all these different facets of the self along with clients however they are expressed in the working relationship, spaces in the community, and further into the wider world.

From an empowerment-based perspective the provision of spaces to speak, think, and move freely in relation to the topic of sexual violence results in more people being included in this global conversation. This occurs whether we are placed in formal psychotherapy appointments or outward-facing spaces.

Changing the nature of how sexual violence is discussed in public actively increases the possibility of recovery. The psychotherapist's supportive intentions towards all survivors is solidified, rather than being provided only to those who make it into formal services. Thus, psychotherapists can enable survivors to paint a true picture of sexual violence as an individual experience, societal occurrence, and global phenomenon.

There are some fundamental steps to be taken in maximising the three freedoms characterising empowerment as part of delivering psychotherapy so that individual selves and personal truths are validated. Understanding that there is no one set way to behave, appear, communicate, or interact as a survivor despite commonalities as a clinical population allows for this. Doing so means psychotherapists do not welcome myths about survivors and sexual violence into the room as an unhelpful starting point.

Myths explicitly and implicitly ask members of a community to comply with pre-determined behaviour no matter how they feel, thus removing the element of choice from one's power in reacting to sexual violence. If this occurs in the provision of psychotherapy the client's multi-faceted self and their personal identity are missed out from the process. This results in the impact of sexual violence continuing to be unaddressed:

> I was offered self-soothing sessions, which were not tailored to me nor allowed me to express my anger: which was my response to what had happened. I felt I had to comply with stereotypically feminine behaviour which was to be sad, or quiet.
>
> *Sam*

In this instance Sam's responses to sexual violence were limited to what the psychotherapist expected to see based on their assumptions of a survivor's typical responses and also of Sam as a female-presenting person.

Additionally, Sam felt her view of feminism (as a political movement of freedom to be who you are) was similarly limited in accessing a feminist service that did not meet her expectations via asking her to conform emotionally and behaviourally in a limited way. Therefore, Sam's emotions were not attended to therapeutically. At a much later date, working with a different practitioner was more effective because appointments were then personalised to her.

The double effect of this psychotherapeutic encounter was not only a failure to alleviate the impact of sexual violence, but also a failure to meet the self amongst the trauma. Both of these are opportunities for relatedness within and between selves, including tapping into sources of empowerment that are useful in encouraging such relatedness. Furthermore, for Sam:

> Empowerment means being able to take part in something bigger than me rather than it being an individual process.

This statement encompasses the relatedness between the self and wider world that is important especially if a client's identity demands it be the case. As a feminist Sam was a part of a community pre-dating the sexual violence within her personal world, with other selves that met this central part of who she is.

As such, Sam states that this was part of processing what happened immediately and long after the event outside of psychotherapy. In this way her personal world contains spaces to be met as a multi-faceted self that includes how sexual violence has shaped her understanding of her self and the wider world, as a survivor.

This example outlines opportunities for psychotherapists to be challenged by clients as we each review our own internalised myths, in being taught by those with lived experience. This in itself is a form of active respect for the client's process in psychotherapy, however it manifests, rather than making interventions based on misconceptions of sexual violence or pathologising facets that point to personal identity.

Being allies to survivors as psychotherapists does not mean a reliance on being taught by them, although taking in their truths is a valuable part of this process. Beyond formal training, clinical supervision, and peer learning, psychotherapists have a wealth of information available to them about sexual violence such as never before. Tapping into other spaces along one's dynamic loop where one can learn of survivors' lived experiences, including online spaces, offers uncensored insights into the truth of sexual violence. These can be used to adapt psychotherapeutic interventions and clinical thinking accordingly on an ever-evolving issue.

A continued development of thinking and action in the wider world as a psychotherapist is vital to maximising the efficacy of our interventions wherever they are made. There are endless opportunities for psychotherapists to be visible in presence, voice, and action so that anyone impacted by sexual violence is assured that recovery is possible.

Ongoing development in this way is achievable wherever a psychotherapist is placed in their own dynamic loop, including how and where this intersects with the dynamic loops of survivors. Combining this with re-configuring myths about sexual violence results in making psychotherapeutic support more accessible as we widen our professional lens to better understand who can be affected and its impact.

References

Associated Press, 2020. *Chanel Miller's Memoir of Assault by Athlete Wins Prestigious Book Award. Star Tribune* [online]. Available at: https://www.startribune.com/chanel-miller-s-memoir-wins-prestigious-book-award/573037811/ (accessed November 2020).

Klein, M., 1957: *Envy and Gratitude: A Study of Unconscious Sources.* New York: Basic Books.

Siegel, D.J., 1999. *The Developing Mind: How Relationships and the Brain Interact to Shape Who We Are.* New York: Guilford Press.

World Health Organization, 2019: *International Classification of Diseases for Mortality and Morbidity Statistics (11th Revision).* Geneva: World Health Organization.

Chapter 5

Working relationally with sexual violence in psychotherapy

Working relationally in psychotherapy requires revision when it comes to supporting survivors of sexual violence. Psychotherapists must be prepared to manage the dual responsibility of the global and individual matter of sexual violence wherever possible. It is a human rights violation and a live process both within and outside of the psychotherapeutic space. Furthermore, our profession is required to continue evolving to best respond to sexual violence given that the issue shape-shifts so frequently.

The additional factor of increasing numbers of survivors across the demographic scale requesting therapeutic help solidifies this requirement. We might be seeing, hearing, and experiencing the traumatic impact of sexual violence by virtue of our roles but that does not mean we know all there is to know. A careful balance between being client-led and guiding with our range of skills constitutes the allyship psychotherapists form in appointments in navigating recovery collaboratively.

Extending this to being an ally to survivors outside of appointments can be part of promoting societal change in response to trauma caused person-to-person. In any space we undertake such work with and for survivors their voices should be included as a priority to maximise efficacy. In this way the truths of sexual violence are utilised in appropriate resolution to the scale of the issue and disempowerment aims to be minimised.

Being immersed in this kind of work means seeing the wider world as it is rather than colluding with others that do not want to, or cannot, look for themselves. The survivor will have been forced to look and forced to react in the moment, followed by repeatedly thereafter as a survival mechanism. Simply being available to listen in any capacity is a key opportunity to offer something different and potentially reparative as an act of witnessing.

Supporting survivors will fall within a psychotherapist's remit many times throughout their career, simply due to the prevalence of this issue. As generation after generation grows up intertwined with the internet and technology there are ever more places in which people can be sexually exploited, thus multiplying this frequency of clinical contact. Psychotherapists will find this is the case regardless of the context in which they offer their services and

DOI: 10.4324/9781003202943-5

whether sexual violence is their specialist area. We should thus expect to engage with this subject repeatedly and be prepared to view the world through a survivor's eyes, many times.

Engaging with sexual violence as a phenomenon to best support clients doesn't end when the appointment does. Outside of this time, both parties re-enter a world where it occurs repeatedly in many ways. Each will then repeatedly be subject to knowing its truth in many spaces.

For the psychotherapist this might include immediately after an appointment in the shared office space, meeting other colleagues also working with survivors. Conversations with friends and overheard comments are linked to the latest media headline. The material explored in the appointment may linger within the psychotherapist's mind as thoughts or images, and their body as physical sensations, potentially because it hooked into their own personal experiences too.

In this way, it can be difficult to fully leave the content of an appointment within the boundaries of the psychotherapeutic space. Asking our clients to work on the areas we have addressed in between their appointments also applies to us via continuous practices of looking after our own physical and mental health. This is especially palpable given that the mental health system is a space where demand always outweighs provision. Such pressure on all involved in this context can further reduce accessibility to specialist services and ultimately reduce the chances of processing trauma.

Part of minimising the inherent power imbalance of constrained service provision comes from acknowledging that all bodies and minds react in similar ways to being exposed to sexual violence. As a starting point, we noted in Chapter two that the result of forced re-organisation of the self following sexual violence can multiply enough to make a survivor's personal world very small. A forced existence into smaller spaces often results in feeling unable or unwilling to relate with other selves on the part of the survivor.

Psychotherapists must therefore take on this challenge of working relationally when relationships are not safe spaces. The responsibility of being a part of a survivor's recovery from sexual violence is thus a serious undertaking. Simply being available and empathic to clients is rarely enough to facilitate lasting internal change when collaboratively rebuilding a life following sexual violence.

For psychotherapists working within services where there are a limited number of appointments available, plus the possibility of disengagement partway through the work wherever clients are seen, each appointment is an exclusive opportunity to offer something that is unlikely to be gained elsewhere. We may be the only professional a survivor is in contact with due to a lack of additional, accessible support services plus a potential lack of trust in others. We also therefore need to consider the fine line between empowerment and dependency on the psychotherapeutic relationship.

Sexual violence and its impact are hard to look at, especially when we see more of it the longer we hold our gaze in its direction. A natural consequence is oscillating between relatedness and disconnection ourselves, alongside our clients' own movements in these ways. This is a natural response to the horror of trauma. The psychotherapist's awareness of the limits of their capacity to know is an important factor to bear in mind, not only to work successfully, but to simultaneously avoid vicarious trauma (see Chapter eight).

To do this, it is necessary for psychotherapists to consider multi-faceted selves existing within multiple spaces, the latter of which contextualises contact with other selves. Understanding this within a relational perspective means we are enabled to understand how all of these facets interact with each other and therefore how they come to life as intersubjective experiences in the psychotherapeutic space.

Working relationally includes actively acknowledging a client's process at each point of contact from beginning to end, as this indicates any difficulties or possibilities in relating. Psychotherapists meet a survivor for a relatively brief period of time within the latter's overall lifetime so due respect and interest should be given to how they have survived thus far.

This can include accepting that the psychotherapist may only come into relational contact with some facets of the client's self during their work and that a premature disconnection from the mental health system (as part of the client's personal world) may indicate that further relatedness feels impossible at that point.

Ideally it is a client's choice as to when, with whom, and for how long they consider support is required. Powerful internal experiences such as shame can enter at any stage to force this disconnection, as does a client's relational pattern or attachment style. Questions to consider throughout the process of psychotherapy include: are we real, tangible, taken in small doses? Would the client relate in similar or different ways with another self?

With all of the above elements in flux, the psychotherapist is asked to work with the individual amongst all of these moving parts that manifest beyond the context of the psychotherapeutic relationship. Within this chapter the idea of working relationally with sexual violence is outlined, including how the facets of the survivor's and psychotherapist's selves interact throughout the process.

Relating within and between selves

Qualifying the nature of and need for relational work is vital in providing psychotherapy to those affected by sexual violence. Offering the working relationship as a context, frame, or vehicle that the work occurs in is commonplace within modern psychotherapy where we are asked to give more of our selves (not just learned skills or techniques) in order to advance the work and support our clients fully.

In Chapter two we established that a self is comprised of multiple facets, each of which has the potential to relate to or disconnect from each other.

The degree of this relatedness or disconnection characterises the relationship between each facet. These relationships are largely shaped by one's relationships and life experiences. We also cannot discount the influence of genetics, nor how a person identifies, in order to consolidate a sense of self. The forced re-organisation of relationships between facets and therefore the overall self is indicative of the traumatic impact of sexual violence on an individual person.

Relationships between facets of the self are worth paying attention to at a micro level so that our understanding of the client as an individual, their presenting concerns, plus their ability to engage with all stages of the psychotherapeutic work (including their psychotherapist as another self), is enhanced. The same applies to us as practitioners, as we are also multi-faceted selves in the process of relating to a client throughout the work in order to attend to what is needed at multiple levels.

Each person's experience of their self, as well as what is co-created within a shared relationship when multiple selves come together, should be given equal weight. The psychotherapist's understanding of their own internal landscape, including the places where the survivor's material is located within it, provides a map by which to navigate the work in creating a baseline for the therapeutic relationship.

This map comes under the psychotherapist's category of material to hold in service of the work, and their decision to make a specific intervention should be assessed in line with the following:

i   Is the client in a state of physiological homeostasis where they can comfortably relate to another self?
ii Is it therapeutically appropriate and useful for the client to hear this intervention right now?
iii Which facet of the client's self needs our attention in this moment?

In doing so, the psychotherapist is constantly evaluating whether their interventions are purely information giving (directive), or information sharing (inclusive). Both of these are beneficial in the privacy of psychotherapy to reduce distress, begin to facilitate trust between persons working together, and foster re-empowerment for clients. The psychotherapist's choice to act in a directive or inclusive way at each intervention is a careful one to make because psychotherapy should not replicate the forced experience of being done to.

Asking what a survivor thinks of any information provided enhances the collaborative nature of the work. It simultaneously moves the dialogue from directive to inclusive as the individual becomes the focus of the mental health system, rather than having psychotherapy fall into the trap of other societal systems that are de-humanising. This simple question encourages the development of a multi-faceted self that can better interact with other selves and human-made systems within the wider world, over time.

In providing psychoeducation, describing to clients that what they are experiencing is normal means that there is another person within their society who can facilitate an objective narrative about sexual violence and its consequences. When the psychotherapist can explicitly acknowledge how this intersects with factors such as gender, sexual orientation, ethnicity, and faith, the survivor has their self-experience contextualised in accordance with who they are. Over time, normalisation of post-trauma symptoms encourages comfortable relatedness within the self that can be built upon to further facilitate the recovery process.

Psychotherapists providing a space where talking about the truth of sexual violence is possible is a different human experience to that which survivors may come across in the wider world, within relationships. Creating a dialogue between selves can begin with co-formulation of the client's presenting concerns early on in the work, and enables ownership of a personal narrative which includes surviving sexual violence. Communicating this together, however it is done, is part of the reparative work within a relational context where previously contact with other humans were violating.

Attachment and relational styles

To say that working with survivors is an insight into a small part of the world is to compound the myth that sexual violence only happens to certain people, perpetrators fit into a set profile, and the circumstances under which sexual violence occurs are unique. As the actual scope of all of these is enormous and can transpire in any configuration, it is true to say that the experience of working with survivors on a consistent basis gives more onus to meeting the individual wherever possible rather than just their symptoms.

Working relationally includes finding ways to connect with the individual person and keeping the self alive under the fluctuating weight of their trauma which perpetuates disconnection between facets of their selves. Disconnection in its most severe form, wherever it is found, can sometimes manifest in a wish to not exist. Psychotherapists will likely be familiar with the pervasiveness of suicidal thoughts, intentions, and actions as expressions of this.

However, we cannot assume that our attempts to connect with clients or their material will be met with an equal level of ability, or positivity on their part. Offering a person-to-person relationship is challenging when human contact is part of the original trauma. A client therefore will not necessarily take up the offer of a safe, boundaried relationship when it is available. Having the space to talk can lead to silence. Clients can request a service, then refuse it once an appointment is offered. Where, then, do we start?

Working relationally involves treating every point of contact as an opportunity to understand the survivor's individual experience of their self, others, and the wider world. The same applies to each part of the survivor's engagement with what the psychotherapist offers, from: considering accessing a service, making an enquiry, being referred or referring themselves, being on a waiting list, and all the elements of engaging with a piece of contracted work including risk management.

The practicalities of delivering a psychotherapy service characterises it as a human-constructed system in its own right that the survivor comes into contact with. We can broadly name this as the mental health system and know that many survivors will have accessed (or tried to access) other support services before the point at which we meet them. By virtue of being a system it becomes a formalised process of relating that has set expectations and boundaries on both sides.

An observable relationship to the mental health system is a useful lens by which to understand the individual survivor within it. The information gained can then be used to appropriately adapt what we offer from a trauma-informed perspective, which is further discussed in Chapter six.

The question of what each client needs in order to engage, relate, and access a service is important. At each point of potential contact, the psychotherapist extends a psychological space which the survivor has the potential to command in any number of ways. Sometimes phone calls are frequently made with a different query each time, e-mails can be unanswered for weeks, clients are invisible behind a referrer that speaks for them, and some clients turn up at an organisation's door outside of set appointment times on a regular basis.

Whatever the nature of the contact, we are offered a view into the survivor's process of relating and the different facets of their self that require something from others. Individual attachment styles are repeatedly displayed in these instances as part of the presenting material that is helpful for us to know.

It is easy to read the nature of a client's attachment style as purely that, but consideration should also be paid to the fact that post-trauma symptoms include a lack of trust and safety in relationships. Diagnostic criteria at the time of writing states that 'difficulties in sustaining relationships and in feeling close to others' is a feature of Complex Post Traumatic Stress Disorder (World Health Organization, 2019). We can agree that this observation of how relationships and attachment styles are forcibly changed by sexual violence is correct, but it does not acknowledge why this occurs for a multi-faceted self.

The degree to which a survivor's level of relatedness and disconnectedness can be understood by a lack of safety and trust varies considerably from person to person. Repeated sexual violence, particularly that which is experienced in childhood, can more acutely shape a survivor's way of relating into an observable attachment style such as those defined by Ainsworth (1978).

Overall, a client's ability to securely attach embodies the knowledge that: they are a human being acceptable in their own right, they are allowed to take up space alongside others, that their personal boundaries are tangible, that their boundaries are likely to be respected, and an assurance that their needs will be met by specific others as required.

Systems, including the mental health system, expect persons within them to relate from a secure attachment style. What we are implicitly asking survivors to do when accessing our services is to consistently step forward with their whole self competently when, at various points specific to the survivor's self, it feels safer to shrink or push back.

When a survivor is clear on what factors should be in place to enable them to step forward, including what will support them to recover from sexual violence, it is important to honour them wherever possible:

> When I told people around me what had happened with my [male] partner and that I wanted a male therapist, I was repeatedly told I should work with a female therapist. This was frustrating as I knew what I needed to model a healthy relationship and I wasn't being listened to. I ended up looking for a therapist privately for these reasons.
>
> *Anna*

Concurring with these external communications was Anna's internal awareness that working with a female psychotherapist would have made her feel less secure in a relationship as a starting point. Anna could attribute this to the negative impact of some women she experienced as dominant in her family of origin, which she knew would have been a challenge to her recovery if experienced with her psychotherapist.

The overlap of the role of shame should not be dismissed here given its ability to force survivors to retreat into small spaces literally and figuratively. This includes not wanting to relate to our own self, let alone other selves, nor the wider world. Ideally, shame is a mediator for social conduct but, at worst, it is uncontrollable non-participation in daily life, regardless of whether we are alone or with others. In psychotherapy services, shame can decide whether engagement occurs more so than the survivor themselves.

At varying levels, the survivor will quite rightly anticipate that to engage in psychotherapy is to some degree making one's self known to another self. This also includes having to make their trauma known to another self, given the space it takes up within their physical and psychological self-facets. There may be concerns on the part of the client about how this will affect their psychotherapist, given that the survivor is all too aware of the intensity of knowing it themselves. Being visible in these ways can enhance shame, which is felt as psychologically and physically disempowering.

Difficulties in disclosing sexual violence are down to multiple, intersecting factors. As examples: whichever culture a survivor comes from will have its own set of expected practices regulating behaviour, including sexual behaviour. Further community rules such as those found in religious faiths can operate in the same manner. Expected practices are often limited by gender and binaried into cisgender male or cisgender female only. The internalisation of expected practices and language surrounding it feeds myths about sexual violence which, in turn, fuel a sense of blame, shame, and guilt around having experienced this.

In total, these create the many obstacles that a survivor navigates within their self, with others, and the external world, in order to access what they need with regards to professional support systems. It is extremely common for clients to step towards a service and then step back, repeating this process many times until they are ready to fully engage. We must bear in mind that much back and forth goes on before contact is made with the mental health system and that its physicality represents a psychological process.

The psychotherapist's response throughout is to sensitively raise awareness wherever appropriate so as to acknowledge the facets of the client's self that are surrounded by shame. This response adds to the collaborative baseline of the psychotherapeutic relationship within the mental health system, thus increasing a sense of safety as the client learns where in relation to them their counterpart will place themselves.

In order to promote choice for the client around how much is known about their self, including their trauma, the psychotherapist extends the psychological space in a consistent manner to facilitate the holding environment (Winnicott, 1960). This concept acknowledges the shared work as having a distinct life of its own that is attended to by separate persons, each with their own internal processes that periodically come together.

Choice comes from the continued negotiating and agreement of what the client needs to fully access a service. Practitioners can step towards clients in small ways to increase accessibility and facilitate trust. Prior to starting psychotherapy, a client could be offered an appointment to fill out a referral form together, or be shown around the premises to gain familiarity with a service.

For assessments, perhaps more than one is needed so the survivor gets used to their psychotherapist before further work commences, or having a family member in the room for part of the assessment appointment. Finally, agreeing that a section of the client's weekly appointment is dedicated to grounding techniques to attend to the physical self may help.

The aim is to demonstrate psychotherapy as a space to enable relating between facets of one's self, with other selves, and the wider world. In turn, this enables survivors to re-engage more fully with each of these aspects of living using the psychotherapeutic relationship as a practice ground.

Transference, countertransference, and projection

Our selves include facets that reflect elements of who we are at various stages of our lives, meaning that the totality of facets (when relatedly connected) represents all of who are we as individuals. These facets emerge into the consciousness of our self-experience in line with what is happening in the present moment as we interact with other selves and the wider world. Reminders of the past via transference (Freud, 1991) and somatic memories

(Rothschild, 2000) can unconsciously bring older facets of our selves to the foreground along with their experiences.

Working with states of relatedness and disconnection amongst each facet of the self leads us to question how this manifests within the therapeutic relationship. How do we experience our client's self and how do they experience our self? Just as the client can feel overwhelmed by their trauma, the psychotherapist can tangibly feel how much space it takes up in the room.

Opportunities to meet each other in the psychological space provided by the psychotherapist are challenging and both counterparts are forced to relate as best they can in ways that take them out of the present moment as the multi-faceted selves they are. At times what occurs within the relationship in this manner is transference and countertransference.

It is worth being clear that transference is not what happens when the survivor psychologically and physically re-experiences the instances where sexual violence took place. This is the normal impact of trauma. Transference in the psychotherapeutic working relationship occurs when facets of the psychotherapist's self make psychological contact with facets of the client's self. What results from this is a re-playing of internal dynamics within the client's psyche that is projected outward onto the psychotherapist (Freud, 1937). The psychotherapist's response to this is called countertransference (Maroda, 2004).

The psychotherapist can expect to engage with this powerful unconscious process as it provides an insight into how the client relates to and is psychologically moved by others. Fluctuating levels of relatedness and disconnection within facets of the client's own self are reflected in how much the psychotherapist is able to grasp a sense of the client's overall self as they work with them.

This is an extremely valuable way to learn about how the impact of sexual violence has influenced relationships with other selves, especially as most examples occur between people that are known to each other including to the point of having a categorised relationship such as: friendship, sibling, or marriage.

When working with survivors there are additional types of transference for the psychotherapist to manage within their clinical practice plus the psychological and physical facets of their self. Forming a relationship, and using it as a way to progress with treatment, opens the door to psychological contact. The internal world of the client's self becomes known to the psychotherapist's self, meaning the two can interact and interrelate.

Scrutiny of our relationship with the wider world as one where sexual violence occurs is essential when working with survivors given that it is almost impossible to engage with this issue and its impact solely within the therapeutic space. To do so is to deliver a disservice to our clients who are forced to engage with it within every domain of their lives and many (if not all) facets of their self. One example is how myths enter psychotherapeutic spaces, as outlined in Chapter four.

A survivor's personal world becoming smaller in the aftermath of sexual violence demonstrates a disconnection from the wider world. It is a disconnection we can empathise with as it comes from a lack of safety and trust. The psychotherapeutic space, as a pocket of the world the survivor has chosen to enter, has the potential to also feel very small as a relational exchange amongst one's week. This is largely dependent on the level of disconnection the client presents with and can be felt as acutely as moment-to-moment.

Conversely to the therapeutic process, the nature of sexual violence necessitates physical contact between bodies. In the case of survivors who grew up in houses where behaviour from adults was sexualised but no physical contact of this kind occurred, there is still contact between persons as the body of another violently encroaches on the survivor's personal space. This kind of forced participation in sexualised behaviour can create a need for disconnection, particularly for children for whom leaving the family home is not an option.

In any case, by psychological contact the psychotherapist is introduced second-hand to the persons and their bodies that violated the survivor. This can be felt in the psychological and physical facets of the self. There is a human response to being confronted with the reality of sexual violence, as well as a countertransference response, the latter of which is pertinent when witnessing how the survivor's self is overcome by their trauma.

Client example: Malik

Malik was an only child and had been brought up by his maternal grandfather from the age of five as his parents were unable to care for him due to their drug addictions. His grandfather had repeatedly subjected him to varying forms of sexual violence until the age of fifteen, when he passed away. Over the years Malik moved between the homes of various family and friends.

As an adult in his twenties Malik formed a relationship with a female partner who was sexually and psychologically abusive towards him for several years in their home. Malik had tried several times to leave the relationship and stated that moving to a different town was a big part of finally separating from his partner.

He had contacted the police once during the long process of leaving because his partner was showing up in his local area the friend's house where he was staying, and his place of work. Malik told the police he wanted her to leave him alone, although he did not disclose any information about the abuse because he felt ashamed.

He felt that the police's response was unhelpful, as they said it wasn't against the law for his partner to be in all of those places. Malik had little faith in support services and felt that he had to deal with what was happening on his own. His strong feelings of not trusting others meant he felt being left alone was best.

Two years after moving to a different town and with no contact from his ex-partner during that time Malik decided to see a psychotherapist. This was because the stress of his experiences made him constantly nauseous and he struggled to sleep at night because of nightmares that depicted his experiences of domestic violence including sexual abuse.

From the outset Malik spoke of the various memories of the different kinds of abuse he experienced in vivid detail and at times this made him nauseous enough to have to stop speaking. In response I explained why these memories and nightmares were making him nauseous via detailing how traumatic experiences can lead to the physical symptoms he was having. I then explained that our conversations would involve finding moments in amongst what he wanted to share to try to help him to learn how to manage these symptoms.

My aim was to both respect Malik's wish to use the psychological space in a way of his choosing in addition to also responding to his explicit wish to stop the nausea and nightmares. Although Malik verbally agreed this would be a useful focus, he spent much of our appointments repeating the content of these memories and nightmares, including talking over me or ignoring me when I tried to interject.

In this example of the earlier stages of a piece of work, the client's wish to use the psychological space as a way to simply re-tell what happened points to how stuck he felt and the hopelessness of his trauma being resolved. It also demonstrated how being alone was preferable, as I was pushed out of the dialogue at times. His assertion that he didn't want any other support meant he could retain the small limits of his personal world, so for a while our work could only go so far, in the same way that he could only go so far within the wider world because other people there could be abusive.

I hypothesise that, as another person in the world trying to connect with his self via a relationship, I was a potential perpetrator given that abuse occurred within relationships. This unconscious psychological process was replicated in his physical self where nausea, as a sign of his past trauma being re-experienced in the present, also served as a reminder for him to stay vigilant.

One of my countertransference responses was to feel as though I was being manipulated and abused, which placed the client in the role of perpetrator. This was absolutely an unconscious process that pointed to the extent of psychological trauma that accompanied his physical symptoms and not a conscious wish to hurt me. Above all, the client was making use of the systems available to them to make sense of their traumatic experiences and the mental health system was one place to speak freely rather than be ignored.

It made sense to me that my movement in the psychological space was unconsciously being restricted, because in that way he could be assured that I wouldn't unexpectedly appear in places in relation to him that might put him at risk. This fear had a root in his partner's behaviour, as well as his grandfather's, constituting people he couldn't get away from.

Here, Malik was bringing his unconscious organising principles (Stolorow and Atwood, 1996) of how he expected relationships to be in order to keep his self safe. In this way I could empathise with his central dilemma, which was: how to exist in a world where relationships and connection are required when other people are harmful? Mindfully selecting which facets of the client's self require empathy is part of responding to transference in a relational way. This also minimises the risk of vicarious trauma to the psychotherapist, when used carefully.

It is acceptable to empathise with a relational dynamic (a process), rather than a facet of the self. At times when there is disconnection between facets of the self this is the most psychological contact that can be had. The psychotherapist can extend this wherever possible to let the survivor know they are emotionally understood, which is a path to reaching specific facets linked to a relational dynamic in a sensitive way over time. It also brings an unconscious process into conscious awareness, so that it can be attended to as needed to facilitate change as per the client's wishes.

Projection as a form of transference Freud (1937) can also be experienced as part of working with survivors of sexual violence. Psychotherapists should make a practice of building awareness of their own bodies, in addition to their own minds, as part of this work. We can learn as much from our own bodies' responses to others and the world, in the same way that we encourage clients to learn from what their body is telling them.

Client example: Natalie

To illustrate this point, I refer to a female client called Natalie who had experienced sexual violence for several years during her childhood from an adult male in her community that she and her family had frequent contact with. Natalie felt that her father, who she lived with then, had an awareness of what was happening at the time because of things that he said about the perpetrator whilst she was growing up. However, it was never discussed further nor did he intervene to keep Natalie safe.

Several days after this disclosure, I was at the kitchen sink at home washing the dishes. I jumped as a male family member walked into the room unexpectedly and felt as though I didn't want to turn my back to him. This was, and never has been, my usual response to this family member. Moments afterwards I realised that I was holding my breath a little and that my shoulders were tense.

I understood this as the physical facets of my self bracing for something that felt threatening. If I were using diagnostic terms to understand this in Natalie, I would refer to this as hypervigilance (World Health Organization, 2019). This is an unconscious body-based response that many clients verbalise as being on edge, wary, not trusting people, or being scared of going out.

Upon further reflection of what else was disclosed within our psychological space, I remembered that Natalie had said that she had never worn a skirt or dress as an adult. Her reason for this was that it would be harder for someone to access her body against her will, especially if she was going to be walking home late at night. In addition to feeling physically secure in her clothing, Natalie's statement encompassed two common myths about sexual violence, first: that what one wears determines whether or not you will be raped. Second, that perpetrators are more likely to attack if you are walking alone at night. These are socially-influenced responses to sexual violence.

Where these two levels of my responses intersected was the internalising of Natalie's lived experienced to be wary of men, the weight of which was multiplied by societal messages around the socially acceptable behaviour of women. In both cases they are misled attempts to stop sexual violence occurring and misplace the responsibility for it onto potential survivors. Simply put, I had somatically internalised the message to be wary of men, to the extent that I felt it so strongly in my own home where I normally felt safe.

Lastly, re-framing projection is required so as to enhance a relational understanding of what occurred between our selves in her appointment. Projection as defined by Freud (1937) is a defence mechanism used to protect one part of the psyche called the ego from unwanted thoughts and feelings. Natalie was unconsciously passing on the burden of holding onto the bad things that had happened to her to the extent that I felt them in the psychological and physical facets of my self.

As per the previous client example this was not a conscious wish to hurt me in any way. The dynamics outlined represent what happens between two selves when the impact of sexual violence is re-experienced in the psychological space, including when the force of perpetrators enters the room. My transference response to Natalie's process can be further understood via Klein's (1946) extension of the previous psychodynamic idea, which is projective identification.

My self unconsciously took on the difficult elements of Natalie's experiences that had split off from her because they were understandably unwanted, to the extent that I momentarily embodied them. In doing so I could better understand Natalie's fear in everyday living which was known not only via her disclosures in appointments, but in the reverberation of physical sensations.

The combination of all three levels of coming into contact with Natalie's self allowed me to psychologically and physically understand the impact of sexual violence for her. This in turn led to greater co-creation of the psychological space, as I then relationally re-adjusted what I offered based on a greater understanding of what the most unbearable facets of her self needed in order to move on.

Alternating spaces

Working relationally involves setting aside specific interventions periodically to safely be open to the experience of being with another person. Each element is just as helpful to the process of recovery as the other, particularly as the client's presenting issues are due to traumatic human-to-human contact. The psychotherapist should practise alternating these elements just as much as their clients do by reflecting on their experiences of the work within their self and with others. For psychotherapists this includes clinical supervision, peer supervision, and personal psychotherapy.

Providing space for both being and doing has a psychotherapeutic impact on several levels. Its benefit largely comes from offering relational contact that empathically recognizes the survivor's experiences of person-to-person contact that resulted in trauma, as a contrast to being treated inhumanely. Space being given for the sole purpose of supporting the survivor is in itself converse to a society and people within it that do not respond to this matter in the wider world.

Traumatic recall in the physical facet of the self is an example of responding to threats to one's life and self. Post-trauma symptoms such as flashbacks, nightmares, sleep disturbance, and physical pain occur after such threats are no longer around. These represent a state of neurophysiological homeostasis that has been disrupted, coupled with the psychological facet of the self that is similarly disrupted.

Psychotherapists are therefore required to extend space of a certain quality to survivors in order to promote relatedness at implicit and explicit levels. This space has both physical and psychological components that are consistently offered to the client to achieve this, bearing in mind that each client will engage with what is offered differently at each point of person-to-person contact.

At this point it is worth noting that, as selves within the mental health system, we will not always be enabled as psychotherapists to physically offer what is needed. Perhaps this is due to the location of a service, internal processes that determine when/what/how communications are sent, when a client can be seen, how many appointments are offered, and any practical considerations in offering a gender- or culture-specific setting.

All of these factors are ways for the client to be met in relationship by a practitioner and the service they are placed in. Thus, they are opportunities to help or hinder the overall process of psychotherapeutic change. In any case having a consistent baseline of physical and psychological space available reinforces the baseline established between the psychotherapist and the survivor.

The psychotherapist is urged to more fully step into what they can offer as a psychological space, as this is more in their control as a tool by which to offer what the client needs at any given moment. The particular use of self that is required intentionally demonstrates to the client that the co-created baseline of the relationship is being upheld and protected by the psychotherapist.

Being available as contracted is part of consistently extending the psychological facet of the self to the client and this of course continues outside of the appointment too when the psychotherapist thinks about the work. The end result is being held in mind between bodies within a physical space, which fulfils a primary relational need for humans.

At psychological and physical levels for the survivor this is likely to feel counter-intuitive because of an impaired sense of safety. As such, an absence of safety to whatever degree means that the survivor will maintain a parameter of existing that is very small. Often this is out of the survivor's control and can become their preferred position because in some respects it feels better than the alternative.

Part of co-creating the psychotherapeutic relationship is to explain interventions, interpretations, and formulations as required. The purpose of being transparent in this matter is two-fold: first, the client has an insight into the psychological space and is encouraged to give informed consent to proceed. This can build a sense of safety as the client knows what will happen next and builds an internalised familiarity with relational acts that occur with consent.

Psychotherapy, as much as possible, becomes a combined effort rather than another act that is done to the survivor by another person in a position of higher power. Second, it provides the client with opportunities to step into the relationship, as well as retreat from it when necessary. Autonomy and freedom of movement can be respected here as principles to which each human has a right.

The ability for these two principles to manifest in the psychotherapy room aims to counter the extent to which they may be limited elsewhere. For those who have had sexual violence used against them as a part of human trafficking, or experienced this during the often-dangerous process of seeking asylum across countries, there is a literal restriction on movement and autonomy of the individual as placed on them by the state and its laws. When the impact of sexual violence occurs, this is replicated in how little a survivor can inhabit the physical and psychological facets of their selves.

A client's somatic responses to the physical space offered should sit alongside cognitive assertions from the psychotherapist, as they equally denote any internalised messages about its use, who can access it, and who can take it away. For survivors of childhood sexual abuse, moving freely in a space where there is a powerful other (originally a perpetrator) is something to be learned rather than continuing to operate from an adapted position where it is best to hide away or be silent.

The extension of opportunities possible within the two types of spaces offered relies on the psychotherapist's pacing of each appointment. The self's difficulty to be present in the present moment because it needs to keep surviving threat can manifest as either immobility, or moving faster than is required, uncontrollably even in the absence of the original threat.

To manage this the psychotherapist must quickly learn their client's indicators of traumatic re-experiencing and their precursors to it by monitoring the client's physical and psychological expressions. Clients are usually well aware of these within their selves as an experience, which may include exploring together which words are best to use to refer to what happened so as to avoid re-triggering.

This creates experiential examples of attending to a multitude of needs when combined with the alternating provision of directive and inclusive interventions. As a practice in itself, the psychotherapist is supporting the survivor to re-learn how to regulate all the different facets of their self. Over time, a sense of control over facets of the survivor's self is re-established in the place of forced doing created by their personal experiences of sexual violence.

Bringing the world into appointments

When the survivor brings their personal world into the room with them to each appointment, they also bring in the people that populate that world. We may meet the perpetrator to varying degrees, as well as the people that enabled the sexual violence to occur, or left its impact unaddressed. For some survivors the violation of the body is mirrored in a dominance within the mind by such persons. The echo of a perpetrator's judgements can feed into the disconnection between facets of the self, as the survivor was not allowed to be their own self whilst in a relationship with them. This is common (but not exclusive to) survivors of partner, family, and cult violence.

Many survivors struggle to voice what they have experienced in their own words, due to this dominance by another self. This can be reinforced when others have responded, or not responded, to their knowledge that sexual violence is happening. It can also be due to what is said to the survivor that keeps them silent and misplaces the responsibility for what is happening onto them, thus creating a relational environment where sexual violence is perpetuated.

For children, this can be messages that other family members will be upset if they speak out. For adults, particularly where coercive control is present, the survivor is told that what they're being put through is a punishment for not behaving in some way (such as being stupid, or failure to complete a task). For both, this can include threats to their own lives, or the lives of others, as emotional blackmail.

Within psychotherapy, the act of speaking honestly about experiences of sexual violence can bring the perpetrators to life. As such, they take up the physical space in the room as well as psychological space whilst the psychotherapist and client are forced to attend to their presence. It is common for the voices of the perpetrators and the meaning attached to these messages to introject the psychotherapeutic dialogue as an additional voice.

This impact is specific to humans given the nature of relationships we have and that the neo-mammalian layer of our brains allows for cognitive functioning that includes placing emotions and language onto our experiences (MacLean, 1990). As examples: survivors deducing that sexual violence is justified because they are weak, or that another person was saved from this mistreatment because they offered themselves instead.

Society's myths and misconceptions about sexual violence saturate the external world as we are confronted with them whether they be everyday comments, social behaviours, or news headlines. These can be sense- or crazy-making as they settle somewhere within the survivor's psychological facet of the self and find space within the psychotherapeutic dialogue. Given that myths and misconceptions present themselves to the psychotherapist too by virtue of living in the same world as their clients, both must actively work with these when they are apparent.

Bringing in a personal world includes practical matters such as cultural customs, faith or religious practices, accessibility arrangements, childcare, housing issues, and the asylum process. We are quickly introduced to all of these factors including at the point of enquiry or referral and are asked to respond as part of facilitating a psychotherapeutic relationship. Although we may adapt the physical space to accommodate a survivor, further adaptation is required throughout the process as all the moving parts of a client's life changes.

In this way we are repeatedly attending to each facet of the client's self as it relates with the wider world, including the systems within it, to sustain the co-created baseline of the working relationship. We may feel that the process of recovery is interrupted by the other parts of the client's life and there is some truth to this. The multiple needs of clients demonstrate the multiple challenges that many survivors within our world face, and part of our response when this occurs is to remain consistent in what we therapeutically offer.

Once more, every opportunity for contact with a survivor is an opportunity to understand and react in ways that strive to be reparative. The ultimate aim is to meet the individual person amongst the impact of trauma and the re-configuration of their personal worlds. This can of course feel challenging to a psychotherapist whose boundaries mean that the remit of supporting a client's mental health is all they can ethically and practically offer.

Re-negotiation of the co-created baseline can include consideration of managing practical matters if this feels appropriate and therapeutically beneficial. At the least it could include talking over a practical matter to be managed, so that the client can think the steps through before actioning them on their own. The underlying message is not that the psychotherapist will take over, or take care of, all elements of the client's personal world.

Rather, it is a sensitive and explicit acknowledgement of the related factors that exacerbate the impact of trauma that result in a survivor feeling unable to participate in regular life. It may also prevent such factors from turning into barriers to accessing any number of systems and services a survivor needs. For those who work with asylum seekers and refugees this is a familiar concept (Michaelson, 2017).

At all times, the psychotherapist should complement any assistance in practical matters with interventions that increase the client's ability to manage such tasks for themselves in the future. In this way we are minimising dependency on the mental health system and the individual psychotherapist within it, as this does not coincide with the longer-term goal of an increased ability to be in the world within their individual self as a survivor.

A system in the wider world that psychotherapists should be keenly aware of when working with survivors of sexual violence in the United Kingdom is the criminal justice system. This may be one way a survivor decides to respond to what they've experienced, which begins by reporting to the police. Within psychotherapy this can appear in several ways given that a client may have reported in the past, is thinking about reporting now, and/or has made a report which can be at any stage of the criminal justice process.

The provision of talking therapy to clients who are undertaking the criminal justice process whilst accessing any kind of talking therapy is known as pre-trial therapy (Crown Prosecution Service, 2002). In such cases the psychotherapist can reasonably expect the impact of navigating this system to exacerbate any existing mental health difficulties as the survivor is exposed to various stressors along the way.

Some of these stressors can replicate the dynamics of the original traumatic experience, not least because the process of recovery can feel intruded upon by the legal process (Waxman, 2019). Within the psychotherapeutic field, we can view this as a replication and extension of perpetrators intruding on the self of the client as per the original incidents. An overview of the criminal justice system, an exploration of the pre-trial therapy guidelines, survivors' experiences of pre-trial therapy, and ethical considerations for the psychotherapist to consider are further discussed in Chapter seven.

Safety and risk are elements of the wider world that show themselves within psychotherapy as part of the client's presenting material. Having experienced sexual violence means a lack of safety of varying degrees and therefore the characteristics of the physical space offered by psychotherapy (for example: privacy, confidentiality) can counter this. When services are specific to gender, culture, or sexuality this sense of safety can increase given the implied assurance that the psychotherapist will work from a shared world view in meeting an individual's particular needs.

It can be easy to view risk as another interruption to the process of recovery, especially as it can preclude the inclusion of additional systems such as safeguarding. However, this is another chance to understand the multi-faceted self including where relatedness and disconnection is occurring. It is entirely possible to work with a survivor who is currently at risk of harm from others and at risk of harm to themselves, from a relational perspective.

The fluidity of working relationally with clients is above all a lens by which to view the multi-faceted selves that enter the psychotherapeutic space. Their movements within the physical and psychological spaces provided feed into our understanding of presenting difficulties. The psychotherapist's role as another multi-faceted self is to model the safe back and forth of being in a relationship within the three domains of: the facets of individual self, other selves, and the wider world.

In doing so there is an ongoing live practice of enabling relating where disconnection exists, which also promotes affect regulation when the physical facet of the self re-experiences trauma. Psychotherapists are responsible for responding to whatever facets of the client's self are present at any given moment at conscious and unconscious levels. Working with a self that has been forced to change because of sexual violence means seeking consent within a co-created process that becomes ever more inclusive, rather than simply directive. Here, the re-configuration of the self via psychotherapy is achieved in ways that are out of choice wherever possible rather than perpetuating a sense of being forced.

References

Ainsworth, M.D.S., Blehar, M.C., Waters, E., and Wall, S., 1978: *Patterns of Attachment: A Psychological Study of the Strange Situation*. Hillsdale, NJ: Lawrence Erlbaum.

Crown Prosecution Service, 2002. 'The Provision of Therapy for Vulnerable and Intimidated Witnesses.' Available at: https://www.cps.gov.uk/legal-guidance/therapy-provision-therapy-vulnerable-or-intimidated-adult-witnesses (accessed November 2020).

Freud, A., 1937: *The Ego and the Mechanisms of Defence*. London: Hogarth Press and Institute of Psycho-Analysis.

Freud, S., 1991: *Introductory Lectures on Psychoanalysis*. London: Penguin.

Klein, M., 1946: 'Notes on Some Schizoid Mechanisms,' *International Journal of Psychoanalysis*, 27, pp. 99–110.

MacLean, P.D., 1990: *The Triune Brain in Evolution: Role in Paleocerebral Functions*. New York: Springer.

Maroda, K.J., 2004: *The Power of Countertransference: Innovations in Analytic Technique*. London: The Analytic Press.

Michaelson, J., 2017: Holding Hope: The Challenge for Therapists Working with Survivors of Torture, in Boyles, J. (ed.) *Psychological Therapies for Survivors of Torture: A Human-Rights Approach with People Seeking Asylum*. Monmouth: PCCS Books.

Rothschild, B., 2000: *The Body Remembers: The Psychophysiology of Trauma and Trauma Treatment*. New York: W.W Norton.

Stolorow, R.D. and Atwood, G.E., 1996: 'The Intersubjective Perspective,' *Psychoanalytic Review*, 83, pp. 181–94.

Waxman, C., 2019: *The London Rape Review: Reflections and Recommendations*. Available at: https://www.london.gov.uk/sites/default/files/vcl_rape_review_-_final_-_31st_july_2019.pdf (accessed November 2020).

Winnicott, D., 1960: 'The Theory of the Parent-Child Relationship,' *International Journal of Psychoanalysis*, 41, pp. 585–95.

World Health Organization, 2019: *International Classification of Diseases for Mortality and Morbidity Statistics (11th Revision)*. Geneva: World Health Organization.

Chapter 6

Promoting empowerment in psychotherapy

Trauma-informed services

Making service delivery trauma-informed requires psychotherapists to state what trauma means in relation to survivors of sexual violence and use this information to better adapt what is offered to such clients. In Chapter two the former is explored within the context of a multi-faceted self, noticing how far the impact of traumatic experiences can extend. Therefore, psychotherapists need to re-examine what is extended to potential and actual clients at every point of service delivery in order to maximise successful engagement and treatment efficacy.

One of the common impacts of sexual violence is re-configuration within the multi-faceted self. Externally relationships with other selves can become more difficult and the wider world has less spaces that can safely be occupied. Survivors therefore find limits where there were none before, whilst the usual demands of life continue.

Despite the ever-growing understanding of mental health within western society and positive shifts in the degree of public transparency about the truth of sexual violence, on the ground a survivor is still forced to act as though nothing has happened, for many reasons. Within private lives there is the understandably protective attempt to hang onto a sense of self and a routine that signals normalcy.

The impact of blame, shame, and guilt also keeps a survivor silent to varying degrees. Children are protected from their parents' struggle, employers know nothing behind requests for sick leave, and communities assume all is well. Wider society does not offer a consistency of understanding that makes it possible to feel fully supported to the extent that is required.

Overall there can be few points where a survivor can internally and externally return to in order to consistently see recovery as a realistic option. This means the process of vocalising one's traumatic experiences, the approach towards seeking support, and engagement with support, are rarely linear. At each point the client who has experienced sexual violence is faced with potential disempowerment and misunderstanding.

DOI: 10.4324/9781003202943-6

In offering a relationship through which to facilitate recovery, it may be the case that an individual psychotherapist finds referring to diagnostic criteria akin to de-humanising a client's personal experiences and presenting concerns. Psychotherapists are not trained to diagnose individuals, although through experience it may be helpful to recognise clusters of symptoms that enable us to inform treatment planning appropriately.

On the other side of the psychotherapeutic relationship, the client may or may not have received a diagnosis themselves at some point. If they have received one, there may then be any number of reactions to it. In addition to this, symptoms resulting from the traumatic impact of sexual violence often co-exist with other mental health issues such as depression and anxiety.

The result here is twofold. First, clients with a combination of symptoms navigate the mental health system to the best of their ability, which can result in misdiagnosis and being passed around services in attempts to meet their needs. Second, the survivor's ability to disclose any element of traumatic experiences and how these have been affecting them since is repeatedly challenged for many reasons (see Chapters one and two). All of these factors equate to ambiguity, rather than clarity, around diagnoses which occur for all selves involved in managing the impact of trauma.

Therefore, it is worth holding diagnostic criteria lightly as another lens by which to understand the needs of a client who has experienced sexual violence as we work with them. Any diagnosis can be a relief, or a further weight to bear, for such clients. Diagnostic criteria can allow psychotherapists to better understand behavioural, emotional, and cognitive symptoms so that we better respond to clients, rather than simply viewing symptoms as ways the client can't engage with what we offer. We can broadly refer to these as post-trauma symptoms.

Responding more sufficiently via trauma-informed service delivery is extremely important. This is because being met with a negative response to disclosure and post-trauma symptoms from anyone can prevent survivors from seeking further support as it reinforces disempowerment. At one end of the spectrum of possible outcomes, not being adequately responded to can equate to not being believed, which can feel worse than the original trauma.

In terms of a starting point, we return to the idea of meeting the person amongst their trauma, however much the latter dominates the multi-faceted self. Concurrently the psychological and physical spaces psychotherapists offer can be dominated by the impact of sexual violence more so than anything else. It can therefore be difficult to find ways to relate, rather than disconnect, between selves in the client–psychotherapist relationship when this occurs.

Sometimes all a psychotherapist can do in the absence of relatedness is name it as disengagement via non-attendance of appointments offered, or a service not being appropriate because there are multiple needs that cannot be addressed solely within a talking therapy service. The result is that a survivor is forced to start again, perhaps at a point where they feel ready to do psychotherapeutic work but are finding it hard to know how.

110 Promoting empowerment in psychotherapy

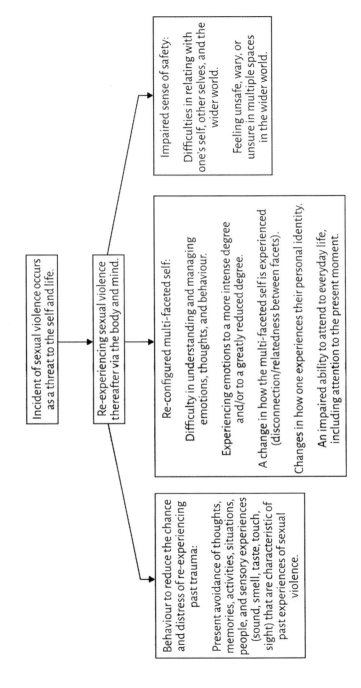

Figure 6.1

A trauma-informed response that can be applied throughout service delivery is to expect survivors to participate in varying ways with everything we offer. As such we meet all of the facets of a survivor's self to the best of our ability in a sensitive and empathic manner, including those that have been forced to change by the impact of trauma.

Re-framing post-trauma symptoms via use of the ICD-11 criteria (World Health Organization, 2019) for Complex Post-Traumatic Stress Disorder, along with commonly reported difficulties, can assist us in becoming more trauma-informed from a relational perspective.

In whatever combination they are experienced, the above points to a loss of control, combined with repeated instances of coming into contact with the feeling of disempowerment. With all of these elements at play psychotherapists need to step towards their clients' self when the latter are unable to step towards our self in relational, co-created work.

Although psychotherapists often begin from the point of 'What is wrong?' in order to help, a more empowerment-facilitating perspective is to include the questions 'What can you manage?' 'What keeps you going?' and 'How do you make sense of what you're experiencing?' We then attend to what each survivor needs in the knowledge that there are forced limitations on speech, movement, and autonomy that can impair one's ability to engage consistently.

Formulation can be reviewed and revised throughout as part of the collaborative process of psychotherapy. What can be verbalised, embodied, and thought in line with the survivor's truths is reparative within a mental health system with many barriers. Encouraging co-formulation is helpful in minimising any negative impact of diagnosis or informal labelling, which is often alienating as a way of misunderstanding the person and their problems.

Client example: Mark

Lisa managed a psychotherapy service for men affected by sexual violence and offered appointments herself too. One morning she received an enquiry from Mark, who was seeking help for the first time. He began to explain a little about his childhood experiences of sexual violence and that it had been hard to find support. Upon being informed that the waiting list was four months long, Mark began to raise his voice saying he was frustrated that there was no other specialist support for men in the area. Lisa explained that she understood how hard it must be but Mark said that wasn't good enough and hung up the phone.

Later that week Lisa was told by a colleague that a voice message had been left by Mark, who wanted to ask about referring himself to the psychotherapy service. Lisa felt hesitant because she didn't want to be shouted at again, but called him back to give him the relevant information.

In starting to explain how the organisation could help and what Mark could do to access what he needed, Mark once more raised his voice before hanging up the phone. Feeling that the situation wasn't resolved, Lisa started to feel nervous wondering whether Mark would call back again. When she later received his referral form via e-mail she felt a mix of being glad he had managed to do this for himself, as well as relieved to not have to repeat their previous conversations.

When Mark was allocated an appointment several months later, Lisa found herself waiting for him to arrive ten minutes after their start time. She received a message from reception saying Mark had called to ask for directions as he was struggling to find the building and that he had overslept due to the side-effects of his medication.

Lisa greeted him when he arrived to direct him to their room and was met with a stormy expression. Lisa once more felt nervous in anticipation of Mark's anger potentially escalating and a little annoyed that she was just trying to help but was only being met with rudeness. Lisa didn't understand how someone who had said they needed urgent support could be late for an appointment, either.

After a few weeks of working together, Lisa felt it would be an appropriate time to ask Mark about what it was like for him to speak to someone after having gone through his life alone with his problems. Mark said that he felt conflicted because he knew he couldn't go on as he was, but that pushing people away was his default as he couldn't trust others and that was the point when he decided to call the service.

Mark explained that he had hung up the phone when they had first spoken because he had forgotten the specific questions he wanted to ask about psychotherapy and that being forgetful was frustrating. Mark also explained that he had calmed himself down after a few minutes and that he often felt ashamed when becoming frustrated in front of people because he felt out of control of his own emotions. He said the shame was 'hard to shake off' afterwards. Lisa asked whether he found it hard to think in those moments, to which Mark responded 'Yes, always.'

They discussed how heightened emotions can make it harder to think and how shame can pull us away from other people. From this Mark was able to pinpoint examples of this in his early life and began naming where he felt shame in his body as an adult. Over two appointments they identified where anger tended to emerge along with other emotions and physical sensations. Mark said it was helpful to have these 'mapped out' because it had been confusing before and added to his sense of feeling out of control.

Lisa asked whether it would be helpful to have moments in appointments to pause to check in with how he was feeling, to which Mark agreed. He also asked whether Lisa could point out if she saw any change in his body language or emotions as they spoke, as he wasn't always clear on what was happening. Lisa agreed and felt that she better understood Mark too in the process of him trying to understand what he was experiencing.

Moving forward they used this 'map' as a benchmark for assessing together the progress being made in psychotherapy, as Mark gained more control of the impact of the sexual violence he had experienced. For Lisa this was a form of evolving co-formulation, which she felt became clearer over time alongside their developing working relationship.

There may be some instances where psychotherapists feel like stepping back from, rather than towards, their clients who are impacted by traumatic experiences. On the surface it can be easy to misunderstand a client's behaviour, particularly when it is acutely seen upon contact with a service. The use of a client's personal power is primarily forced to adapt as a result of sexual violence. Coming into contact with professionals and procedures in support services can reinforce the use of adapted power because relating triggers stress responses within the multi-faceted self.

In asking survivors to behave by following a set process in an expected manner to access a service, we only make deductions from their behaviour from a distance rather than creating a space to meet their multi-faceted self. Reflecting on patterns of engagement provides information on a survivor's ability to relate and how a service may need to change to better respond to trauma, including changes to internal procedures.

As practitioners concerned with psychological experiences, more understanding needs to be extended to the inner experience of survivors not only at the point when they are in psychotherapy, but throughout the process. This includes giving the same level of thought, time, and attention as we would do in an appointment to every point of contact made by a survivor.

This may include expecting clients to spend a little more time on the telephone if they become distressed, which is more about giving them time to regulate their affect enough to continue the conversation, rather than giving the impression that psychotherapeutic support is available via telephone. Psychotherapists can explicitly explain this during such phone calls to reinforce appropriate relational boundaries and reiterate which elements of accessibility are the client's responsibility whilst being supported by the service.

We are individuals and teams of practitioners who are ready to meet survivors to provide psychotherapeutic support. Within the mental health system we become practitioners who are equally ready to not meet survivors because of limited resources (time, funding, and available appointments). The result is being forced to ask survivors to stay out of sight and out of our minds, until they do what is needed to sit in a room with us. Limiting our understanding to observable behaviour is not in the spirit with which we aim to facilitate relatedness, nor does it assist us in widening our understanding of what a survivor 'looks like.'

In applying re-framed post-trauma symptoms to the physical and psychological spaces we extend to clients, psychotherapists can note that these categories are not restricted to gender, gender expression, sexuality, faith, spirituality, religion, disability, nor ethnicity. This is not to say that these individual factors do not hold value for the survivor, the psychotherapist, and their shared work in contextualising and respecting the personal impact of sexual violence. It means that they can be actively respected and included as required to meet the survivor where they are, knowing that contact with these facets of self-experience is important.

Power dynamics within the mental health system intrinsically stem from a psychotherapist's position of being more psychologically well than their clients. They are also more practised in managing the impact of sexual violence to whatever degree this is a result of personal and professional experience.

Psychotherapists also dictate how often contact takes place, what kind of contact there is available (talking therapy), and how long it is available for (the length of a session and contract). Lastly, there are greater states of relatedness rather than disconnection, and feeling safe rather than wary, in the psychotherapist's self.

From this position psychotherapists primarily offer our selves, psychological spaces, and physical spaces as part of the client's professional network of support along their dynamic loop. How much we step towards a client in offering these includes not fully losing such a position. This is not because we want to maintain power over the client, but because we should promote empowerment rather than a dependency in being available via a boundaried relationship.

Empowering clients means passing over the resources we have so that they can be internalised by the survivor to use on their own, in ways that align with their re-constructed self. When psychotherapists do this consistently, opportunities are offered to enable clients to use the psychological and physical spaces we offer as starting points for becoming more empowered in other ways. It also begins to put into practice an active respect for a survivor's personal process, personal boundaries, and their ways of communicating distress when it occurs.

Doing so supports re-creation of experiences of safe relatedness within and between multi-faceted selves. As an example, the emergence of risk as part of the survivor's material is an opportunity for misunderstanding and for disempowerment to occur when handled incorrectly:

> I much prefer a trauma-based model rather than a medical model when it comes to support services. Even when I have felt suicidal this is more helpful. In a trauma-informed therapy service I had a choice on whether to continue talking there. However, other professionals were worried that it was the talking that was putting me at risk so they said we should stop. Not being able to talk about it would have increased my feeling suicidal and led to a sense of powerlessness because my decision to speak would have been taken away from me.
>
> *M*

With all of this in mind, we move on to an exploration of how to promote empowerment via facilitating freedom of movement, autonomy, and speech in practical ways. Appropriate, ethically considered boundaries can be extended to increase a survivor's freedom in these areas so that the edges of their personal worlds are similarly extended.

Empowerment

Qualifying empowerment as a term is essential and, to do so, we can examine what is personally lost in the act of being sexually violated. Disempowerment stemming from sexual violence is in part characterised by a reduced freedom of movement. Within the self this psychological and/or embodied experience can either be impaired contact with certain facets (disconnection) or an excess of relatedness, which are out of the survivor's control. Beyond the self a survivor moves in a more restricted manner with other selves in relationships and within physical spaces in the wider world.

The impact of these alone pushes clients to places many others will never come close to in the name of survival and adds to the equally diminished experience of seeing their selves reflected back to them in other selves or the wider world. Psychologically this contributes to disconnection with one's personal identity and can be phrased as the questions: who am I now and where do I belong?

Empowerment can broadly be understood as the ability to move within physical and psychological spaces freely. It is the sense of being able and allowed to have consistent access to such spaces in addition to the possibility of expanding upon them as we wish to. Feeling empowered is both something that can be experienced within our selves on our own, can be facilitated by other selves, and is not only observable as a behaviour or action. It is known as an internal psychological experience, as well as experienced collectively between selves.

Dynamically, empowerment can be conceptualised as potential or actual movement which can take place within psychological and physical spaces. Such movements are confident, assertive, and validating in nature. Making movement an actuality stems from internal resources within an individual and external resources such as personal networks. Empowerment can act as a platform from which to 'be' or 'do' amongst states of relatedness and disconnection between the multiple facets of the survivor's self.

There are opportunities for psychotherapists to promote empowerment for survivors in the wider world, which extends the remit of this dynamic process beyond the consulting room. We are in a position to influence the wider world to better accommodate the needs of survivors, rather than colluding with the status quo of having such persons remain societally marginalised and unattended to. This translates into social responsibility, or more specifically psychotherapy as activism, which is explored further in Chapter three.

Promoting empowerment with survivors involves looking at how to effectively facilitate freedom of movement, autonomy, and speech. Maximising freedom in these three areas occurs in line with the client's individual psychotherapeutic goals as states to be achieved, and point to the beliefs surrounding them so that any goals are personally meaningful. At best, beliefs are one source of internal empowerment a survivor can keep protected for themselves at times when the self is under threat, so the value of goals should not be underestimated.

As an example: wanting to be able to leave the house without being scared could clinically be understood as increasing a sense of safety and reducing hypervigilance. For the client, achieving this goal would mean being able to pick up their children from school, or take them to the park. Being able to do these things would strengthen their identity as a parent, enable relatedness to their children, and provide a practice ground to replicate the skills around this goal in other spaces in their lives.

Reduced freedoms are central to another element of what is lost in the act of sexual violence: choice. Automatic neurophysiological survival mechanisms mean that there is no choice in how the physical facet of the self responds whilst the act is taking place and thereafter. The psychological facet of the self also becomes stuck in the traumatic past, rather than being able to focus on or respond to the present.

Assisting a survivor to re-configure their self, relationships with other selves, and the world on their own terms in psychotherapy includes creating points of relatedness to widen such limits placed by sexual violence. Human-made systems can be disempowering simply because the survivor is coming into contact with processes and people that hold more power than them. Disempowerment can be felt by survivors in the mental health system just as much as any other system, which once more places an onus on the individual psychotherapist to offer opportunities to recover rather than re-traumatise wherever practically and ethically possible.

Overall, the psychotherapist is encouraged to consider the ways they enable survivors to feel more empowered across several domains. Being trauma-informed includes understanding that psychotherapy aims to create a new baseline within bodies and minds as a starting point for confidently and competently venturing further in other spaces. As this new baseline has been co-constructed with the client's consent (actioning their choices), this allows for construction of a new sense of their multi-faceted self in which the experience of sexual violence resides but does not overwhelm.

Freedom of movement: increasing accessibility and engagement

Psychotherapists ask clients to literally and figuratively make the necessary steps towards services to receive the kind of support offered there. However, extending accessibility to survivors in a trauma-informed manner requires sensitively moving towards such persons at times to meet them when fully stepping forward from their side is too difficult. In this sense it is worth extending the notion of accessibility to include practical, relational, and dialogical interventions that can promote empowerment of the survivor's self in psychotherapy.

After sexual violence the opportunities to disconnect as a safety mechanism can be triggered by contact with facets of the self, traumatic material, spaces in the wider world, and contact with other selves. Therefore, we can reasonably expect clients to feel triggered by aspects of the work, including the psychotherapeutic relationship. When a survivor comes up against a point of disconnection they are unable to move freely psychologically or physically.

The systems psychotherapists operate in and service provision are not helpful when they require clients to be compliant despite being traumatised. When this occurs, we misunderstand a survivor's needs. We also miss opportunities to facilitate recovery at each step found in formal procedures and psychotherapeutic relating.

Trauma-informed service delivery is actively understanding that psychotherapists need to adapt and increase the ways in which we step towards clients given the impact of sexual violence. Specifically: when a relationship contextualises what is on offer, we cannot expect all survivors to respond from a place where relatedness is possible.

Transparency and consistency can each assist in promoting a more accessible service via relational means. Services and psychotherapists become more known and safely familiar when this is achieved. The result can include less need for hypervigilance on the part of the survivor, as the psychotherapist's role in relation to them is clearer. Increased visibility of psychotherapeutic support and the people delivering such support is important in increasing accessibility within communities. The more visible we are outside of appointments in the mental health system, the less recovery remains an inaccessible concept to those who seek it.

Transparency about what a client can expect, why certain questions or interventions are being made, and needs that fall outside of a psychotherapist's role can be communicated verbally and in writing. The notion of safety and trust can be assisted via these concrete examples a client can view, hold, and keep. The latter can begin with written correspondence, the contract to formally agree to the terms of the work by all sides, and any written materials created together in appointments.

Within the dialogue, the psychotherapist explaining why they are considering a specific train of thought includes the survivor in the process, rather than potentially replicating a dynamic of being done-to as per the original traumatic experience. Explicitly offering places in the co-created dialogue for the survivor to feed back on the process of psychotherapy and ask questions about any element of the work is essential. Psychotherapists can then re-affirm our position as supportive in action, along with a safe embodied presence, in relationship with clients.

The value of consistency is established in modelling a baseline of safety based on predictability. Physical spaces offered must stay the same wherever possible and can be changed in negotiation with the client. Negotiation of change can take place in the psychotherapeutic relationship, for example movement of furniture to try and reduce the intensity of relatedness as the dialogue takes place.

When working online, to negotiate turning off the camera and audio periodically by all sides can achieve the same effect. When there is unavoidable change in a physical space it is helpful for many clients to hear why this change has taken place, preferably before it occurs. The window of tolerance (Siegel, 1999) is widened at a neurophysiological level thus giving more choice in moving freely within the self and in relationship with the psychotherapist's self, whilst both navigate the shared physical space.

Consistency in what is offered within the psychological spaces of a survivor's appointment includes the start of the dialogue beginning in the same way. Asking seemingly everyday questions such as 'How are you?' can offer a chance to fully attend and facilitate authentic responses to what is usually a casual question with an automatic answer. It also offers an insight into the details of clients' everyday lives, which increases understanding of how trauma has personally impacted them.

For clients who struggle to transition into or out of an appointment because of the severity of their post-trauma symptoms, it can also be helpful to offer the first and/or last sections of an appointment as time to do something other than traditional psychotherapeutic talking therapy. The aim is to either down-regulate from a hyper-aroused state (fight, flight), or up-regulate from a hypo-aroused state (freeze).

This can be a non-verbal activity such as focused breathing exercises, talking a short walk in a corridor, playing a card game, or making something using one's hands. Wherever possible and with the client's consent the activity could be another shared process in the spirit of co-createdness and relating together. If the client would prefer to talk, a topic of choice not related to their presenting concerns can be decided on, ideally one which they feel confident in leading.

The psychotherapist demonstrating a respectful curiosity about the chosen topic is a good way to facilitate a sense of empowerment from a base the client already has. Psychotherapists should not be concerned about not knowing much about the topic, as the relationship is a space to learn and to get to know a client's personal identity amongst presenting concerns.

For survivors whose personal identity is invested in something they are able to do, this is a way to practise relatedness to facets of their self they feel more empowered in. As examples this can be professional work, hobbies, or family life. For the psychotherapist these are ways of role modelling empowerment of the self, successfully relating to the multi-faceted self of their client amongst their trauma, and offering an opportunity to learn that there is the ability to move freely even in small ways. The choice and mutual agreement on how these sections of appointments are used is a way to practise a choice in how a survivor moves within their self, whilst in the presence of another self, without being disabled by shame, fear, or helplessness.

Any scheduled time away from attending to difficult facets of the self and self-experience enables practising control of which neurophysiological system is more active. Increased use of the front brain, rather than being stuck in the survival modes of the back brain, is a part of this practice in psychotherapy. There is more opportunity, therefore, to practise moving freely without feeling unsafe in several ways.

Often the process of accessing a psychotherapeutic service involves stepping towards and stepping back again. This can occur many times for the individual survivor, until they feel ready to do this kind of work. Despite the diversity of its population British society is predominantly structured to cater for white, western, cisgender, heterosexual, monogamous, and non-disabled ideas. Similarly, the mental health system caters far more for individuals that fall into these categories of identification rather than those outside of it. This includes variations of religion, faith, and spirituality that can sometimes be seen as having no place within such a system.

Familiarity is another way to assist survivors to step towards the mental health system and psychotherapists placed within it. It is then there for the client to use when they are ready and more empowered to do so as a free movement of choice. One instance where this is especially important is with communities that fall outside of the above categories.

Stepping forward towards clients outside of the rooms in which we see them can feel like the antithesis of traditional psychotherapy, but in fact it can be managed ethically to actively welcome different kinds of survivors into this process as it is offered in formal services. That is not to propose at all that psychotherapists poach or solicit survivors into the physical and psychological spaces they offer as to do so would sit too closely to the dynamic of forced participation in the process of another.

What is being proposed is an appropriate level of visibility of the individual psychotherapist, or the service offering psychotherapy, in the communities they can support so that potential clients feel more able to access the kind of support on offer. Visibility primarily fuels familiarity in making services accessible to communities that may not feel psychotherapy is a viable option for managing the impact of trauma.

As psychotherapists we are pressed to respond to the unique nature of working with the traumatic impact of sexual violence given its dynamic interplay within one's self, between selves, and in multiple spaces within the wider world. Offering a professional service within the mental health system, whether this be within an organisation or private practice, asks any client to follow internal procedures in a set sequence so that they can access psychotherapy.

This sequence is heavily boundaried because it can assist in supporting the gradual development of a safe relationship within which effective psychotherapy can occur. However, there are additional elements to consider when adapting service provision, wherever and however we work with survivors in our communities. This allows for the psychotherapeutic, relational, theoretical, and ethical benefits of psychotherapy to be extended to any kind of client we may meet:

> They're not 'hard to reach' victims, you don't try hard enough to reach them. I didn't go for therapy because I felt it was available to me, I just thought I'd try it because I needed it.
>
> *Rob*

Communities that are less enabled to step towards psychotherapy, mental health services, or support services in general demonstrate an unmet need. Inequality in accessibility further demonstrates that there is work to be undertaken by professionals to ensure needs are met. The ways in which we step towards survivors lessens the relational jump members of such communities need to make in order to begin the contactful process of receiving support.

Doing this for individuals and the communities they belong to can equate to a larger reduction in gaps found in overall service provision when actioned by enough psychotherapists. There is no safety, power, or choice when (for whatever reason) the option of accessing psychotherapy is out of a survivor's reach. An absence of these three factors reinforces the restrictive limits of personal worlds put in place by sexual violence and perpetuates the forced reconfiguration of the self without hope of reparative change.

Establishing a back-and-forth, negotiated, and evolving relational process by which to enable stepping towards selves on all sides is the foundation of achieving the above. An active respect for the needs and values of a community where survivors exist is a starting point for ethically extending psychotherapeutic support. This also integrates the truths of lived experience into such support in whichever spaces it is offered within communities.

Safety and trust need to be established for survivors to enter the physical and psychological spaces on offer by psychotherapists that we traditionally understand as engagement with services. Increasing the visibility of psychotherapy as a form of help and the psychotherapists available to offer it needs to be maximised in community spaces as a starting point. Stepping forward to be present in spaces occupied by the community should occur in repeated agreement with its members so that we are invited in, rather than intruding upon.

The role of psychotherapists in such spaces is to raise awareness of sexual violence as a societal issue, including expressing truths about it to push back against myths. Delivering psychoeducation on the impact of trauma and providing information about local services are ways to offer routes to further recovery in line with what a survivor may find practically, somatically, and emotionally possible at a given point.

Finally, a psychotherapist's role could also include encouraging facilitation of peer support that survivors wish to extend to each other within their own communities. This should only be done with the consent of survivors, as sexual violence being known within a community may put individuals' confidentiality and thus personal safety at risk.

Psychotherapists can be invited in to do this work within spaces such as drop-in advice services, social events, and workshops. For communities that have limited or no English skills this should include the use of an interpreter, or co-delivery with members of the community (including survivors) who can manage contact with distressing material and avoid reinforcing shame-based myths.

Collectively considering how clinical terminology needs to be translated into accessible language forms the co-created dialogue about sexual violence and its impact in line with the needs of specific communities. This can include exploring the ways it can limit understandings of gender, sexuality, ethnicity, and culture to avoid disrespecting how the core identity of a community intersects with this sensitive issue.

For example: talking about consent in any kind of relationship can be a precursor to exploring sexual violations in communities where sex is not normally freely discussed. Providing information on elements of post-trauma symptoms such as sleep hygiene or feeling safe, rather than trauma as a wider concept, can assist in making information more applicable to communities where mental health is an unfamiliar or shameful concept. Using gender-neutral language with the LGBTQ+ community can promote inclusion on a topic that can affect anyone.

Providing psychoeducation about trauma, its impact, and ways to manage these does not need to be withheld behind the barriers of mental health systems. It can and should be freely available, including being a part of everyday dialogues. Stepping towards survivors can include providing such information verbally, supplemented by digital or hard-copy materials, to promote accessibility of specialised support in these small but significant ways. A survivor can use these in line with their ability and inclination to do so, both of which can be restricted by post-trauma symptoms.

Ongoing parallel work 'behind the scenes' to practically increase ways that survivors can step towards psychotherapists is important to maximise engagement and accessibility. Psychotherapists who recognise unmet needs of survivors within specific communities may work towards creating new referral pathways and strengthening existing ones.

This may include collaborating with other support services so that all are linked, resulting in less lone navigation of them on the part of a survivor who requires multiple services. It can also involve work from a top-down approach by influencing policies or law that directly affect survivors and their rights so that any positive impact is felt on the ground.

When a survivor requests access to psychotherapy appointments, there are additional options we can extend to facilitate safe relatedness even before this kind of work begins. Members of the community and individual survivors within it can be shown the premises where psychotherapy takes place. Becoming familiar with a location, physical space, and travelling there can remove much of the stress many clients experience in attending their first appointment.

Offering to complete any referral paperwork in conjunction with the individual survivor, rather than assuming they feel empowered to do this on their own, is appropriate in promoting accessibility. Screening, and/or assessment appointments within community spaces may be a sensitive middle ground by which to introduce psychotherapeutic work and the psychotherapist, prior to the client attending further appointments in the relevant service.

Lastly, we can consider providing more than one assessment appointment at times in order for the psychotherapist and what they offer to become more safely familiar. Such an approach is beneficial for survivors who experience more disconnect than relatedness and require more assistance to consistently stay in the present moment. Importantly, clients are thus provided time and thinking space to make an informed decision as to whether to move ahead with psychotherapy.

Freedom of autonomy and speech: language

Being a psychotherapist means that there is a primary responsibility when working with a client, namely: to treat mental ill-health and alleviate psychological distress. However, these are not the only elements that enter the psychotherapeutic space when we meet with a survivor. The forced re-configuration of the multi-faceted self is visible in psychotherapy and compounded by the forced re-configuration of the client's wider life, both of which are a direct result of sexual violence. Given this, the remit of the psychotherapeutic dialogue can cover any topic such as: housing, parenting, sex, access to benefits, staying safe if perpetrators are still present, reporting to the police, asylum applications, and education.

Having any space to speak about the personal impact of sexual violence has a huge value in promoting freedom of speech and freedom of autonomy. The privacy of psychotherapy can be experienced by any survivor as a mixture of liberating and intimidating. For those with more pronounced post-trauma symptoms, doing any thinking or talking about personal experiences of sexual violence is simply not an option as it is too much of a risk to the multi-faceted self.

However it manifests, stress can be reduced by letting survivors know that there is no pressure to say anything more about their experiences than is comfortable. It can help to also advise that it is possible to work with post-trauma symptoms without having to communicate such details.

This does not mean a psychotherapist does not want to know, or wants to reinforce the incorrect belief that such experiences should not be spoken of. Instead, clients are given control of the process as a form of personal power.

Supporting a developing ability to use words, thoughts, and emotions as skill sets is another element that can be practised together throughout at the client's pace.

Not knowing what to say, or what to think, about sexual violence occurs across three intersecting levels for all members of society. First, it is an occurrence that is prolific amongst humans but that is not to say it should be considered a normal part of human life. The result is widespread misunderstanding about what it is, how it happens, and who is involved or affected. There is simultaneous collusion with the factors that line up to not only enable sexual violence to occur, but permit perpetrators to avoid being held responsible.

Language, as a vehicle by which to understand sexual violence, leads to the second factor: what is being communicated in implicit and explicit ways between selves. Messages about sexual violence are communicated by all. Professionals in human-made support systems (including the mental health system) also have their own language for this issue and ideas on how best to respond to it.

Communications about sexual violence are loaded with assumptions that homogenise those who are affected by it. Therefore, any communications, including specific words, should be assessed and expressed carefully in psychotherapy on a person-by-person basis in collaboration with the survivor.

Lastly, a lack of spaces to speak openly about one's experiences creates more ambiguity and uncertainty for the person at the centre of them whilst they attempt to make sense of the trauma. Such negative outcomes increase the less often a survivor is responded to in a way that understands, respects, and supports them. Language can thus be a way to either relate or disconnect in relationships with other selves and spaces in the wider world.

By virtue of offering talking therapy, psychotherapists need to offer a mutually understood language as part of the co-created baseline of the shared work, to mitigate these three factors. Autonomy, as the internalisation of language and communications, is similarly shifted in accordance with the truths of sexual violence. In offering a co-constructed language we maximise the potential for freedom of speech and freedom of autonomy, which clients can extend to their wider lives as a skill learned in psychotherapy.

One way a psychotherapist can do so is via the language used at all stages of the process. In order for clients to approach any service there will be a choice of words dictated by this service to refer to sexual violence, in order to indicate that this is a suitable place to access support. From the point of communicating with an individual survivor within such services, care should be taken to mirror their language used so that each client builds a linguistic base by which to increase their sense of empowerment in their experiences. This can include not having any words at all, or using words that have a different meaning from how they are understood in law.

Stepping towards a survivor by adopting their language minimises the gap across which they have to work to be understood and welcomed into a space.

Language is also helpful in appropriately pacing appointments as certain words or phrases can be re-triggering, which places more importance on echoing language wherever possible. Psychotherapists can ask clients which words they would rather be said, or not, at the outset of contact. In negotiating the psychological space occupied together in this way, the psychotherapist also honours the personal boundaries of their survivor.

Language has the potential to evolve over time. This notion is also relevant to each individual's process in psychotherapy as they utilise words concerning what was experienced then and now. Experimenting with words that don't quite resonate with the client's position right now, but may do so in the future, can be done when such words are introduced by the client. This assists the personal considerations of legal terms and terms used in society, both of which risk alienating a survivor in the wider world rather than supporting them to exist within it.

Adopting the same language respects the subjectivity of a client's experiences. In this way psychotherapists avoid the silencing nature of myths about sexual violence, given they are societally-created misconceptions that objectify the phenomenon as well as the individual. Further explorations on challenging myths in psychotherapy are found in Chapter four.

The psychotherapist makes the move from directive to inclusive information that is firmly centred on the client's experience and personal wishes about the work. It also promotes using language that is culturally sensitive and open to traversing a traditionally gendered issue from a gender-neutral stance. Thus, we offer psychological spaces where survivors are enabled to retain personal identity within systems that aim to accommodate them as multifaceted selves and not simply symptoms to treat.

The inherent power dynamics within the mental health system often challenge freedom of autonomy and freedom of speech for clients. This transpires within the psychotherapeutic relationship where a psychotherapist appears to be relatively personally unaffected by the trauma of sexual violence, even when hearing explicit details about it in discussion with clients. The historic silencing of survivor's stories by the criminal justice system, via the restrictions on what can be said in talking therapy, serve to further increase disempowerment in recovery.

What assists in minimising the power imbalance is to interchange 'you' and 'we.' As an example, the psychotherapist can state 'When we go through something traumatic, our bodies respond in the following ways to survive it …' Doing so can also normalise the survivor's experiences by bringing them into the perspective of a human-wide phenomenon, rather than something only the survivor has been through. The mediation of power dynamics between persons also handles the isolating impact of shame which, when managed successfully, implicitly invites the client to stay in the shared psychological and physical spaces offered by the psychotherapist.

The dual impact of sexual violence on the body and minds of individuals is a factor to consider when aiming to promote freedom of autonomy. A client's physical capacity to think is impaired when the brain and body are in a hyper- or hypo-aroused state. In these moments there is increased activation within the two older layers of the brain concerned with survival, coinciding with increased or decreased physical movement to achieve this.

As a repeated physical experience occurring outside of the survivor's control, there is an embodiment of a decrease in freedom of movement in physical spaces. Combined with a lack of freedom of movement in psychological spaces, the survivor is forced to face once again how small their personal world has become. In maintaining relatedness when this occurs, the psychotherapist once more needs to step towards their client in supporting them to regulate the physical facet of their self so that everything else is enabled to follow.

References

Siegel, D.J., 1999: *The Developing Mind: How Relationships and the Brain Interact to Shape Who We Are.* New York: Guilford Press.

World Health Organization, 2019: *International Classification of Diseases for Mortality and Morbidity Statistics (11th Revision).* Geneva: World Health Organization.

Chapter 7

Delivering pre-trial therapy in the United Kingdom

This chapter was written with the understanding that many psychotherapists would be finding out about pre-trial therapy here for the first time given that there is currently no standardised, mandatory training for trainee nor qualified practitioners on this topic within the field. Others will read it with the experience of professionally managing the emotional and practical conflicts that arise along the way for them as well as clients. Psychotherapists who are survivors themselves may have personal experience of accessing talking therapy pre-trial and what this entails.

For clarity, a client is considered as pre-trial when they have an active report with the police, are having their case investigated by the police or assessed by the Crown Prosecution Service (CPS), or are participating in a trial in court about the sexual violence they have disclosed to the legal system. The term 'pre-trial' is set by the CPS and is adopted by those offering talking therapy to formalise working within specific considerations with clients who come under this category.

Supporting survivors of sexual violence in psychotherapy necessitates an understanding of how such clients can come into contact with the criminal justice system, whether by choice or otherwise. This necessity is enforced by our ethical requirement to be aware of and work in line with any relevant guidance or law that applies to the clients we support. Within the United Kingdom there exists a set of guidelines set by the CPS, who investigate and manage criminal cases from the point at which a report is made. Once involvement with the criminal justice system ends, for whatever reason, the guidelines do not apply.

There is no universal statute of limitations which applies to the prosecution of sexual offences in the United Kingdom justice system. The implication is that a crime can be reported, investigated, and potentially prosecuted no matter how long ago the incidents occurred, provided the act constituted a criminal offence at the time it was committed. For survivors who need time to think about whether they want to report, or need time to feel ready, there may be the benefit of unlimited time available. For clients accessing talking therapy, the decision to report can therefore sit alongside or outside of this process.

DOI: 10.4324/9781003202943-7

It is worth being clear that these guidelines should be adhered to when working with any person reporting any kind of criminal offence. They are therefore not limited to those coming forward to disclose sexual offences to the police and therapeutic service providers. Another significant point to be made is that these guidelines do not apply to a perpetrator, as they are not the person making the report. Thus, there is freedom on their part to access talking therapy or any other form of support without consideration beyond their immediate emotional or psychological needs.

In what might be regarded as a nationwide example of systematic discrimination, the guidelines are often only discussed and applied in relation to survivors of sexual violence. As such the public push-back against the issues the guidelines have caused in delivering talking therapy pre-trial has been predominantly voiced by services, organisations, and individuals who support this client group along with survivors themselves.

It is the survivor's responsibility to advise the police and/or CPS that they are accessing talking therapy whilst legal proceedings are taking place. Therefore, therapists should be clear in contracting verbally and in writing that this is the case. Making this agreement contributes to the necessary psychotherapeutic frame required to proceed with work appropriate to the client's needs. Doing so also places vital supportive control in the hands of clients within systems where disempowerment is possible.

On the legal side it is usual for the police to signpost support services, especially at the early point of a report being made. In addition, it may be the case that the victim is asked whether they have in the past or are currently accessing any support services where a disclosure may have been made.

The original guidelines, issued in 2002, were called 'The Provision of Therapy for Vulnerable and Intimidated Witnesses' (Crown Prosecution Service, 2002) and applied to adults. Separate guidelines on the same matter for children were published in 2001 (Crown Prosecution Service, 2001).

Almost two decades later these were revised and combined by a panel comprised of professionals from the CPS, National Health Service, and several third sector organisations. This update included a public consultation of the revisions in late 2020, titled *Guidance on Pre-Trial Therapy* (Crown Prosecution Service, 2020a). At this point anyone could submit written feedback directly to the CPS for their consideration, to influence further revision.

Details on the core themes affecting therapeutic service provision present within both sets of guidelines will be discussed in this sub-chapter, for the purpose of educating psychotherapists on the historical challenges the guidelines posed which reflect systemic barriers to justice and talking therapy. It is likely that we will meet survivors who tell us they couldn't, or didn't want to, access talking therapy under the original guidelines because of the issues caused in practice.

As with any other material the client brings into the room, being introduced to the nuances of the criminal justice process adjusts the psychotherapist's attention accordingly. That is, our shared awareness includes the larger reality of working with sexual violence as a societal occurrence rather than simply an individual issue. It is something that happens in the world which aims to be addressed by multiple systems, as well as aiming to be addressed by the person we are sitting with in appointments.

The subjectivity of a client's narrative on sexual violence and its impact as communicated in psychotherapy comes into stark contrast with the objectivity of the criminal justice system, which is concerned with evidence based on facts that can be proven. The language used within this sub-chapter illustrates the collision of these two very different human-made systems with 'survivor' reflecting our empowerment-based approach, versus a person being a 'victim' of a criminal act.

Similarly, any mention of 'perpetrator' is not prefixed by 'alleged' in the spirit of a psychotherapist's belief in survivors' accounts and unconditional support of voicing their lived experiences as truths. Use of this prefix would however be applicable in any context where belief is primarily found in the weight of evidence, as per the criminal justice system.

Each of these words has a valid place in the psychotherapeutic dialogue and points to equally valid elements of being a person who has experienced any kind of sexual violence. For individual clients the choice of words is theirs, given the resonance or meaning attributed to it which encapsulates their subjectivity. In this sub-chapter these words are used in accordance with the respective mental health and criminal justice systems being discussed. Additionally, the word 'therapist' is used to reference any kind of provider of talking therapy such as psychotherapists, in line with the language used in the legal system.

The guidelines themselves reflect the central challenge discussed in this book, which is how psychotherapy with survivors of sexual violence is managed inside and outside of the room. The overlap with another human-made system and the professionals within it is counter to the assumed separateness of psychotherapy as a space in the world. This central challenge tends to cause uncertainty, anxiety, and ethical dilemmas for each psychotherapist working with this client group. For survivors who simply wish to speak privately and gain confidential support, becoming aware that accessing talking therapy may have implications on their involvement with the criminal justice process is often shocking and daunting.

Concrete examples are the request for therapy notes by the police or CPS as a potential form of evidence to back up a victim's report, which can feel intrusive to both psychotherapist and client. The use of the psychotherapeutic process as a means by which to provide evidence is a move away from the clinical focus of alleviating symptoms of stress and distress. For many psychotherapists this is the first mark of a compromise in practice.

When taking on an activist role outside of psychotherapy appointments, the conflict between acting ethically via adhering to relevant guidelines and pushing back against injustice is one to be considered thoroughly. Both are applicable to the role of the psychotherapist who wishes to work competently in support of survivors both inside and outside of the rooms in which we meet them. Although a seemingly impossible and emotive task at times, it is possible to do both.

An important note to be made at this point is that the reality of the criminal justice system in the United Kingdom rarely meets the expectations of survivors, practitioners, and the general public. Investigations can take months and it may be years until trials take place, if a report reaches these stages at all. Additionally, conviction rates for all types of sexual offences are low.

Such a reality is at the least a shock for clients who invest in reporting as a form of guaranteed justice, personal safety, or closure. At worst it is re-traumatising and disempowering, especially when this is not the outcome. It is helpful for psychotherapists to be aware of all of this as part of the emotional impact on clients of reporting, in particular the pause it can create in moving forward with one's recovery.

Overview of the criminal justice system for sexual offences

The terminology used within this section represents that which is used in the criminal justice system to enable therapists to become procedurally familiar with the basics of the process, as well as to better contextualise a client's experience. Reference to other support services for survivors who report are made here to further enhance a therapist's understanding of other professionals their clients may have contact with. These are also options for signposting and referral to meet a client's additional needs alongside talking therapy.

When a victim approaches the police to make a report, they are initiating a formal process by making a disclosure of sexual violence which is a criminal offence. There are many types of sexual offences including those listed under the Sexual Offences Act 2003 such as rape and sexual assault, each with their own statutory or legal definitions. As mentioned previously, in the United Kingdom criminal offences are not subject to a statute of limitations, so a survivor may be able to approach the police even decades after sexual violence takes place. Long periods of delay between an offence being committed and being reported are frequently encountered in cases of institutional abuse, for example.

In the British criminal justice system, the burden of proof always lies with the prosecution, meaning that there is an obligation on the prosecutor to present evidence to prove that any allegation is factual. By reporting, a survivor is trusting the state to use its resources to handle their case, and those resources include the police and the CPS. Conversely a perpetrator has no responsibility to produce evidence in the initial investigation stages and this includes not having to answer questions when interviewed by police. In part because of this, the pre-trial therapy guidelines are only applicable to the survivor.

Once a criminal offence has been reported to the police, they are under an obligation to investigate that offence and to pursue 'all reasonable lines of enquiry' in doing so. At the same time the police will be considering whether the evidence they have obtained is sufficient to result in a conviction, which is a 'guilty' verdict in court.

A victim of a sexual offence can be asked to recall the events at various stages, including cross-examination by the defendant's (perpetrator's) barrister in court. Their first report will typically be comprised of an interview with a specialist police officer and tends to be video recorded, although a written statement can be completed instead. This Video Recorded Interview (VRI) is re-played, or their written statement read out, in court should the prosecution reach this stage.

Once this report has been made, the victim should be given the opportunity to make a Victim Personal Statement (VPS) either straightaway or at any time before the perpetrator is sentenced. The VPS is the victim's opportunity to formally state how the crime has affected them and is completely optional. It can later be shown to the CPS and court along with the victim's report. If a VPS is prepared, it will be considered by the judge before sentencing.

The role of the police is to investigate the crime and gather evidence that may later be used in court. From this a two-stage 'Full Code Test' must be satisfied in order to proceed from a police investigation to CPS assessment and then satisfied again to proceed from a CPS assessment to prosecution. The Full Code Test can be summarised as follows:

1   The police/CPS must be satisfied that, based upon the evidence, there is a realistic prospect of success; and
2   The police/CPS must be satisfied that a prosecution would be in the public interest.

Should a case not pass both points of this test, a decision will be made to take 'No Further Action' (NFA) and the victim's engagement with the criminal justice system will end. Therefore, a NFA can come at the earlier stage of a police investigation or further on following an assessment by the CPS.

If the Full Code Test is passed following police investigation, any evidence gathered in total is then handed to the CPS, who hold responsibility for charging decisions with the application of the Full Code Test for the second time. This means that they decide whether to charge a perpetrator and, if so, with what sexual offence specifically. If a perpetrator is charged, they will be prosecuted (taken to court).

Once the case reaches court, the prosecution is represented by a barrister tasked with prosecuting whilst the perpetrator is represented by a barrister whose role is to defend them. Again, it is important to remember that the

Delivering pre-trial therapy in the UK 131

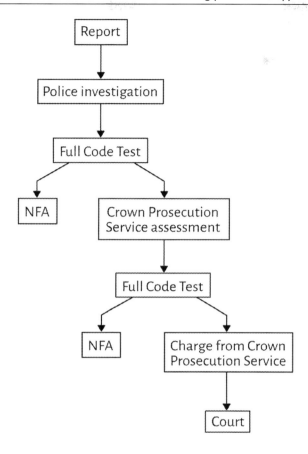

Figure 7.1

burden of proof lies with the state/prosecution which reflects the resources they have on their side. There is no burden on a defendant to prove their innocence, nor any obligation on the defendant to give evidence in court, although they may choose to do so.

Criminal offences of a sexual nature can be tried in the Magistrates' or Crown court depending on the nature of the offence and length of sentence. The Crown court is where the most serious sexual offences such as rape are heard, whereas for example some sexual assaults can be tried in a Magistrates' court. In every criminal case that proceeds to court, its first hearing will be in the Magistrates' court, which is attended by either three Magistrates or a district judge. At this hearing, a defendant can plead guilty, in which case the defendant will be sentenced in the appropriate venue.

If a not guilty plea is entered, the Magistrates' court will decide where the case should be tried. All criminal offences are categorised as one of three types of offence, which helps the court determine where the case should be tried based on the severity of the offence as quantified in law. For clarity these are: summary only (heard in Magistrates' court), indictable only (Crown court), or either-way offences (Magistrates' or Crown court).

If a perpetrator is charged with an either-way offence, they have the right as a defendant to choose to be tried in the Crown court without having to justify this choice. This is because a defendant charged with an either-way offence always has the right to a jury trial, which would only take place in the Crown court.

A defendant can always choose to have the trial escalated up to the Crown court, but cannot choose to remain within the Magistrates' court if the nature of the either-way offence they are charged with is too serious to be tried there. Summary only offences are always tried in the Magistrates' court (subject to very limited exceptions) and indictable only offences are always tried in the Crown court.

When a trial takes place either in the Magistrates' or Crown court, the evidence is presented there. Within the Magistrates' court this would be heard by three magistrates or a district judge once more. They are tasked with deciding whether a guilty or not guilty verdict is applicable, based on the evidence presented.

Within the Crown court the evidence is heard by a judge and a jury. Here, the role of a judge is to ensure all parties are complying with procedure and the law. A jury, which is made up of randomly selected members of the general public, holds the responsibility to examine all of the evidence presented to them in court. This includes forensic evidence (if any), the victim's VRI, as well as statements made by the victim or perpetrator whilst being cross-examined by barristers.

The standard of proof which a jury is required to apply when considering whether to return a guilty verdict is 'beyond a reasonable doubt.' That is: the jury must be sure, based on the evidence put forward by the prosecution, that guilt on the part of the perpetrator has been established. They are asked to return a unanimous verdict wherever possible, but in the absence of this a majority verdict is sometimes sufficient.

Within the Magistrates' and Crown courts a guilty verdict means a perpetrator has been convicted of the crime. The magistrates and/or judge will then proceed with sentencing, which can include imprisonment. A not guilty verdict results in the case being closed.

At the point the police or CPS decide that a case is NFA'd, the complainant can ask for a 'Victim Right to Review.' A police officer and/or CPS lawyer, different to that which made the decision to NFA a case, would undertake review of the decision to not continue with a case. This is a review of the evidence and the application of the law and would not include another trial. Once the review is completed, the victim is advised accordingly.

On the perpetrator's side, as a defendant they or the CPS can decide to appeal against a conviction or sentence. Appeals are a specialised area of law

Delivering pre-trial therapy in the UK 133

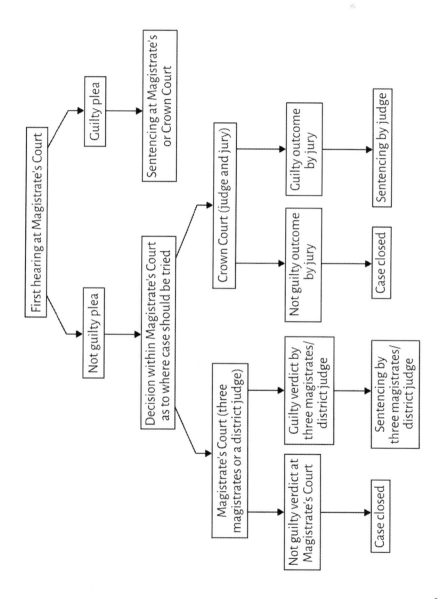

Figure 7.2

and need to be managed by appropriately qualified legal professionals. Making an appeal is distinct and different to a Victim Right to Review as it occurs after the outcome of a trial. The victim cannot request an appeal of the court's decision.

No matter the outcome of a report, a victim is able to apply to the Criminal Injuries Compensation Authority (CICA), which can provide compensation for psychological and/or physical injuries sustained as a result of the reported crime. A victim can apply themselves, or gain assistance from an Independent Sexual Violence Advocate (ISVA) or specialist organisation to do so. Upon receipt CICA will look into the case, including speaking to the police officer who undertook investigations, in order to confirm the details given on the application.

It is worth highlighting the fact that a survivor may choose to pursue a civil claim as a means of obtaining compensation for any damage or loss which they have suffered. This would involve an individual privately suing another for damages within the civil law system, which is separate from the criminal justice system.

Where a civil claim is pursued the process is completely different from a criminal prosecution. Importantly, if a survivor is successful in a civil action, it will not result in imprisonment or even punishment of the perpetrator. The civil court would be concerned solely with awarding monetary damages for loss suffered by the survivor, which would be met by the unsuccessful defendant or, potentially, a relevant insurer.

Psychotherapists are not legal professionals, meaning our remit is very much focused on a client's mental health above all else. However, knowing the above enables us to better support survivors as we begin to understand the prolonged stress caused by this process. Such stress can exacerbate pre-existing post-trauma symptoms, so care must be taken to address this as a pre-emptive measure, in the early stages of psychotherapy. In this way a client is assured of at least being in control of their physical self and psychological self amongst the potential disempowerment the criminal justice system often brings.

A helpful addition for survivors who report is the assistance provided by an Independent Sexual Violence Advocate (ISVA). This is a highly specialised role where a trained professional offers emotional listening support (not counselling or psychotherapy) and practical support to victims who are thinking about or have reported to the police. They are bound to the CPS guidelines on pre-trial therapy despite not being therapists themselves as, according to the 2002 guidelines, any discussions of the details of the case with professionals (or even friends and family) may result in this evidence being challenged. Further specialisms are available such as FISVAs (family ISVAs) and CHISVAs (ISVAs for children).

ISVAs offer a service free of charge and are typically found within rape crisis centres, women's centres, and national organisations supporting victims of crimes. The practical support they provide can be information on what to expect when reporting, accompanying a survivor to a police station, liaising with the police or CPS on their behalf, and accompanying them to court should a trial take place.

An ISVA can also support a survivor to make an application to request special measures to be put in place during the trial when a survivor feels unable to advocate for this themselves. Examples include use of screens to shield the survivor from the perpetrator's view, or using a live video link outside of the court room, to give evidence. Such measures make the process of appearing in court feel less traumatic if such stress responses are likely. They also maximise a victim's sense of safety when they are in court along with the perpetrator and members of the latter's personal network who may also pose a threat. These measures are ultimately at the discretion of the judge who decides the outcome of the application.

In terms of a suitable network for survivors accessing talking therapy as well as reporting, the partnership of a psychotherapist along with an ISVA not only gives a client what they need but also alleviates any pressure on the former to know every detail of the criminal justice process. They can be accessed via a self-referral and the police typically signpost or refer to them too.

There are several routes to address the physical impact of sexual violence, each of which can be accessed alongside or independently of a report to the police. A Sexual Assault Referral Centre (SARC) offers specialist medical and forensic services. Their services are free and run twenty-four hours a day. Medical assessments and care is offered in any case when someone visits. This can be accompanied by specially trained in-house support staff, in acknowledgement of the psychological impact of trauma.

Forensic evidence can be gathered at a SARC if a survivor visits within a set time frame (usually several days) and is kept for a period of time regardless of whether a report is made to the police. The length of time for which forensic evidence is kept is dependent on the individual SARC and can be several years. Such evidence can be used in legal proceedings. Similarly, a Forensic Medical Examiner (FME) collects evidence from sexual crimes that can be presented to a court. The option of seeing a FME is dependent on making a report to the police and may be utilised in lieu of a SARC centre being available.

One's GP or local accident and emergency service can be approached as a third option in treating the physical impact of sexual violence. Confidentiality as usual is applied here, so there is no requirement for a medical practitioner in these settings to report a crime.

Exceptions to this are the victim lacking the ability to decide to report through an impaired mental capacity; the victim cannot report because they are unconscious; and when reporting is in the interest of protecting the public from further harm from the perpetrator. Should a report be made in this way, the victim is not required to answer any questions or make a statement.

Contextualising the Crown Prosecution Service guidelines

As an overview, the original version of the guidelines for adults was published in 2002 as a response to an interdepartmental report called 'Speaking Up for Justice' (Home Office, 1998). A point in this report noted that there should be guidance on how vital emotional support is delivered to adult and child victims. Throughout the first conception and subsequent adjustment of the guidelines this theme is explicitly repeated many times.

This touches on another key element of the guidelines, which aims to ensure that the victim remains at the centre of the process throughout. The importance of gaining consent to proceed with therapy, knowing that ultimately it is the victim's choice whether to do so, is stated as one essential part of this centring of the person amongst the process.

So far there is an alignment between the criminal justice system and psychotherapy in its aims for those who are undertaking both systems simultaneously. However, the original guidelines posed a significant challenge to survivors and those offering therapeutic services in meeting these aims consistently. This stemmed from the inclusion of a clause whereby a victim was not allowed to have discussions about the offence pre-trial, either formally or informally.

In practice this meant that a survivor who had chosen to report was not able to talk about the details of what happened to them with family, friends, or professionals including psychotherapists. The reasoning for this was that a victim's oral account needed to be protected given that it is their evidence in their case. A concern for the legal process was that a victim's account might be subject to influence as a result of any such discussions, specifically that 'pre-trial discussions may lead to allegations of coaching and, ultimately, the failure of the criminal case.'

Within psychotherapy this meant that freedom of speech was severely restricted and the primary reason why someone might ask for support would be removed from them. Often when a client is ready to ask for professional help this means they want to and are ready to talk to some degree about the root cause of their presenting issues. Under the previous guidelines the focus for talking therapy would be limited to only the emotional and psychological impact of sexual violence experienced as well as the impact of undertaking the criminal justice process.

The result within organisations and individuals providing talking therapy pre-trial to survivors meant there were variations in what was available from service to service, including whether anything could be delivered at all for this client group. Understandably, many psychotherapists held concerns about potentially jeopardising a case in offering appointments where the sexual violence might be discussed, or didn't consider that effective or appropriate talking therapy could be offered at all with this significant restriction.

In such cases survivors were denied this form of support and advised that they could access it once their involvement with the criminal justice system had come to an end. As a middle ground, many services offered brief, structured work to address specific concerns related to trauma such as disturbed sleep, or general mental health self-care. Both guidelines advise against the use of group therapy, particularly if it is unstructured work, given the extent to which a pre-trial client's experiences may be discussed amongst multiple persons as well as what they may hear from others with similar histories.

All of the above, combined with the fact that a psychotherapist might not even be aware of the guidelines' existence, meant that the kind of service survivors of sexual violence received was hugely inconsistent. It was also true that a client might refuse appointments when offered given the impossibility of their being able to voice their experiences in order to psychologically manage them, or even withdraw their report to bypass this issue.

The barriers to accessing psychotherapy in an equitable manner for those pre-trial are obvious here, but worth citing so that psychotherapists are at least aware of the historical context of these guidelines. What is more important is an active acknowledgement of the impact of this restriction on clients, as it effectively reprimanded them for making the choice to seek justice whilst receiving talking therapy.

Clients would of course be shocked to learn that they could not speak freely in the private, confidential space of psychotherapy. Their wish to speak up would be forced to shut down against their will. At the same time many psychotherapists would struggle with this conflict in trying to meet their client's needs and working in contradiction to the ethos of the profession. Although a client may not wish, nor feel able due to post-trauma symptoms, to discuss the details of their lived experience, the effects of the removal of this option were significant.

Recalling experiences of sexual violence

From a trauma-informed perspective one can gain the understanding that sexual violence as a violating and life-threatening experience affects how memories of such events are processed. The body automatically responds to threats with an influx of hormones which sets off neurophysiological responses to ensure survival of the person. This includes an over-stimulation of parts of the brain involved in memory processing. For further details refer to Chapter two.

Recollection is therefore subsequently affected, manifesting along a spectrum from traumatic recall, where one relives the past as if it is happening now, to having impaired recall. Having gaps in one's memory, or even a complete lack of memories, is normal as well as common. This can be due to many factors including the neuropsychological survival mechanism of dissociation, or to surrounding elements of the incident such as excessive substance use or unconsciousness incurred via physical violence from the perpetrator.

A major source of misalignment between the talking therapy profession and the criminal justice system is how each regards recollection of what happened at the time sexual violence took place. For psychotherapists what a client states about anything is an insight into the presenting material and their corresponding subjective perspective on it. The shared work is to address the impact of such material and understand its cause wherever possible, beginning from any views the client has. Additionally, in relational psychotherapy a client's subjectivity enables psychotherapists to understand, empathise, and work through any psychological or embodied distress via an honouring alignment with the client's multi-faceted self.

Recall can take many forms in psychotherapy, including talking about the specifics of past experiences of sexual violence. Responding to this recall can concurrently take as many forms on the part of the psychotherapist whose role is to alleviate the distress and disruption to their client's sense of self, relationships, and wider life. Some trauma-based techniques for example require the client to recall in detail any memories, flashbacks, or nightmares about past traumatic experiences. This can be silently to themselves in thought, or out loud with their psychotherapist, for the purposes of alleviating post-trauma symptoms.

For individual survivors, recall reflects the degree of one's ability and need or wish to do so in service of re-configuring their selves in psychotherapy. There is a lot of variation amongst clients in this respect, from those who have an urgency to share in order to feel unburdened, to people who cannot go anywhere near memories nor the wider topic because it is too overwhelming. There may be instances where a psychotherapist is unaware of what happened beyond how long ago it was and that a type of sexual violence occurred.

With traumatic experiences, including those that took place a long time ago, missing information or uncertainty from this part of a client's history can be expected. In any case, a client's inability or unwillingness to recall to any degree their experiences of sexual violence in psychotherapy are not taken as a sign that they are mistaken or it did not occur. Simply put, psychotherapists start from the point of believing a survivor, whereas in the criminal justice process belief only occurs if there is enough evidence available to support a victim's account.

As a personal experience, this in itself is often the core of re-traumatisation whilst undertaking the criminal justice process, as disclosure is not always responded to in ways a survivor may want or expect:

> In the past I felt 'I can't verbalise this' and some things were literally unspeakable for me. I have never been able to verbalise it until I was in therapy. That was in a safe place. I couldn't imagine doing it in a police station or in court.
>
> M

Both versions of the CPS guidelines so far are cautious about the purpose of recalling incidents of sexual violence in talking therapy, with an explicit worry about how doing so might result in changes to a victim's account. A need to keep a victim's report consistent is understandable from a legal viewpoint, as any changes may weaken it, especially should it come up against opposing evidence from the perpetrator's side.

There are considerations in both guidelines on the normalcy of the impact of traumatic stress on memory formation, recall, and how a traumatised person may present. However, this is significantly undermined by the inclusion of information on false or recovered memories within the same guidelines as a seemingly routine intention or consequence of undertaking talking therapy. These phenomena have a long history of being highly disputed, to the point of being redundant in modern psychological treatment.

The issue here is that its inclusion is an attack on the truth of any survivor's account, as well as the integrity of talking therapy as a support mechanism. Such attacks replicate the victim-blaming perspective found in many spaces within the wider world once again, including within a process that is seemingly concerned with securing convictions wherever appropriately possible.

A distinction must be clearly made between the nature of anyone's memories of any event to be subject to influence at large by many factors, and the incorrect inference that therapy is a place specifically where survivors' memories are deliberately or habitually influenced. Being caught in this crossfire means that talking therapy is mistakenly seen to be at high risk of malpractice, which undermines it as a form of appropriate psychological intervention as well as undermining a victim's report.

This is of course extremely unhelpful in creating a mutual, supportive intersection of two very different systems that seek to support survivors albeit in different ways. Any mention of false or recovered memories within the guidelines increases the risk of this misunderstanding occurring for a survivor, legal professional, talking therapy provider, and any layperson.

This element of both guidelines presents a difficulty for psychotherapists wishing to respond to the truth of any survivor they meet, whether it is their account of sexual violence that is voiced or a focus on how it has affected them. The wording presented in the guidelines, in particular the original version, is quick to provide caveats in a victim's account where it could be dismissed as untrue.

For example, within the original version a therapist is advised against taking the responsibility to separate fantasy from reality on behalf of or with a victim. At the same time, recalling the incidences with this in mind is equated to a possible distortion of the truth expressed on the part of a victim. A therapist is encouraged to bear in mind that it is just as likely that a victim's material can fall into the category of fantasy or distortion, as it does to being reality or truth.

It is correct to say that the role of a therapist does not include assessing facts in the same way the criminal justice system does by way of managing evidence. The piecing together of information in talking therapy is not to establish a chronology to prove what happened, but to assist in processing its impact. For some clients wanting to do so is part of consolidating the integration of traumatic experiences into their history and personal narrative or sense of self. On the whole therapists do not ask the same questions as the police or CPS do in their investigations, nor barristers or judges within trials.

Truth is therefore defined differently by each system, which poses a particular difficulty when they intersect pre-trial. For therapists a survivor's truth is in their account of it whether expressed verbally, emotionally, or somatically. This includes clients who have incomplete recall, or none at all, but know that sexual violence took place.

The sympathetic stance of the mental health system when help is offered, compared with the adversarial nature of the criminal justice system, is a source of distress for many survivors who need others to recognise what happened in order to move on:

> I did feel vindicated on the unanimous decision of the jury. I can't imagine how I would have felt if they had said 'not guilty'... A not guilty verdict would have fed into the myth that I deserved what happened to me.
>
> *Crystal*

The nature of Crystal's experience of sexual violence meant that she was not conscious whilst it occurred although there were witnesses present before and after the event. Coming to terms with what happened included a reliance on others to piece together its chronology so that adequate evidence was gathered for her trial. In turn this supported her personal consolidation of its impact on her mind, body, and sense of self.

The message from the CPS guidelines in general is that recall should be doubted. This is understandable given the criminal justice system requires all statements to be considered and investigated until sufficient evidence can objectively prove them as true. Only then can the next step occur, which is sentencing. However, this is far from the stance of a relational psychotherapist wanting to respect a client's experiences so as to facilitate better management of their impact.

Whilst it is possible to address the impact of sexual violence in psychotherapy without voicing the details of what happened, the weight of such events bears down upon the multi-faceted self. The weight becomes heavier in a wider world that demands survivors move on with life and forget what happened, regardless of any struggle in doing so. For many survivors simply being able to talk to someone openly about what it's like to live such a life is part of feeling less alone in spaces within the world, and the weight becomes shared with their psychotherapist rather than something for them to hold in isolation.

A sense of being forced to re-live what happened, rather than move forward, is a reoccurring theme in the mental and somatic health of each survivor we meet in our work. A huge part of recovery is recollection without distress and recollection that occurs in the control of the client rather than simply relentless re-living. Being asked to recall what happened as a part of the criminal justice process, including very specific details, can unfortunately trigger post-trauma symptoms. Therefore, therapists can regard management of these as an essential focus of pre-trial work and empowerment of a client when this becomes within their control.

Record-keeping and requests for therapy notes

Part of a therapist's general responsibility is the management of records, including appropriate note-taking, for each client they support. Another relevant theme in delivering therapy pre-trial is directly linked to this as therapy notes may be requested as part of investigations or a trial. They can be requested by the police or CPS, or court-ordered by a judge, as part of the overall evidence considered in a case. The same applies to visual or audio recordings of appointments, or any artwork/images produced as part of the work undertaken.

For the purposes of clarity, only therapy notes will be referred to here but in practice the same rules apply for this range of materials. In the instance that therapy notes are requested by the police or CPS, this request can be declined by the victim and/or the therapist. If a court order is issued by a judge, then it is mandatory to disclose therapy notes even if a client and/or therapist does not consent to this.

The decision on whether to use notes, or have them remain as 'unused material,' is dependent on whether they are assessed by the CPS to contain anything that can assist the victim's defence case, or undermine the prosecution of the accused. This means that any information within them that corresponds with, or contradicts, the victim's or perpetrator's accounts is taken into consideration. Should notes be used, any information irrelevant to the case will be redacted so that it is not visible to those viewing them.

As has been noted above, whilst therapy notes could be relevant to an investigation into any criminal offence, they are disproportionately requested in the context of sexual offences. This is perhaps due to the fact that such cases will often turn on one person's word against another's, with little to corroborate either account. Juries may simultaneously be reluctant to return a guilty verdict in such circumstances, knowing that to do so would have serious repercussions for the defendant.

In navigating the criminal justice process, many survivors feel that their privacy is excessively intruded upon because of this high standard of evidence. The standard of evidence required to secure a 'guilty' verdict in sexual offence cases is no higher than any other criminal offence cases. However, in practice therapy notes became routinely requested by the police and CPS at the point when a victim stated they were undertaking talking therapy. Similarly, the volume of requests for victims' electronic devices, including all of their mobile phone use history, to search for evidence caused public alarm. From this the phrase 'digital strip searches' was coined in the late 2010s (Big Brother Watch, 2019).

The frequency and practical steps by which to retrieve both of these types of evidence constitute incorrect procedures being followed within the criminal justice system on a large scale. In this way they are speculative enquiries rather than requests proportionate and reflective of the need to only gather evidence related to the crime being reported. Doing so correctly would mean a request is being made from a suitable legal basis, which is a 'reasonable line of enquiry.' A related conflict for therapists is the requirement to record notes that are court-ready when (and just in case) a client is pre-trial, when clinical notes are taken to support the nature of the work offered which is focused on symptom alleviation and emotional support.

Given the above, therapists working with survivors can face the potential or actual disclosure of therapy notes with varying levels of anxiety or uncertainty. It is a significant responsibility to be involved in any element of a client's life, including legal proceedings. This can be exacerbated when requests or disclosures of therapy notes are felt as intrusive to the therapeutic process by the client and/or therapist. One example is requests and disclosures being felt as an attack on the privacy or safety of therapy for the client, which are essential elements of its efficacy.

From an empowerment-based perspective the therapist is concerned with extending choices and freedom wherever possible. The intersection of the mental health and criminal justice systems in a pre-trial scenario both agree that the needs of the survivor are paramount. This includes their wish to access both systems and their ability to give consent throughout their engagement with each.

Therapists are able to facilitate empowerment via providing information on what a client can expect from accessing therapy pre-trial, so that informed consent can be given should the client wish to proceed. Such information should be given verbally and in writing as many times as is required, including contracting accordingly. As an example, designated time should be given in appointments to discuss a request for therapy notes to explore any thoughts on the client's part. Being clear about which person is responsible for a task at any given point is also prudent given the different professional, personal, and procedural requirements throughout.

For example, the police should ask whether a victim has ever disclosed their experiences of sexual violence to anyone including a therapist. It is simultaneously the police's responsibility to inform a victim that they are required to notify the police or CPS should they access talking therapy whilst managing the legal process. The therapist should echo this. Advising clients on what to expect should notes be requested, or court ordered, well in advance of this occurring ensures that the client is aware of how the nature of the work might change. They can thus give informed consent to proceed at points along the way, should they wish to each time.

In terms of the aforementioned personal requirements that can arise from the client, this can be understood in the traditional question: what does the client need to support management of their health via therapy appointments? Addressing this question thoroughly sets the focus for the work as well as maintaining an appropriate contractual boundary between therapist and client. Here consistency and certainty are qualities the client can be in receipt of.

When the criminal justice process cannot mirror these qualities at times and the client's presenting concerns are overwhelming, there is at least one space that can provide them within the context of a relationship. The unfamiliarity of the criminal justice system to most people and the outcome of a report not being within a victim's control are ways that inconsistency and uncertainty can affect clients' wellbeing in seeing the process through.

Should the client decide to consent to release of their notes it is appropriate and ethical to schedule time to go through these together before this takes place. Therapists should be mindful that a client can have any kind of emotional reaction to seeing the notes that have been made about them, and of what impact this might have at conscious or unconscious levels to the working relationship.

The therapist themselves may have difficult feelings about this element of the work becoming visible to their client, as it is not usual. Signing a release form in consenting to therapy notes being passed on to the legal professional making such a request is appropriate here too. A copy of the notes, and a corresponding release form, should be provided to the client if safe to do so as a respectful way of giving them ownership of this material.

With regards to the timing of this dialogue, including information-giving or contracting, this can be done in the early stages of a client's engagement with a service regardless of disclosures of being a victim of a crime, to avoid any unexpected changes in the service being provided. Doing so also establishes a channel by which reporting may be spoken about at a later date, in the spirit of collaborative support.

The therapist can explicitly state their generally neutral position on reporting so as to avoid the problematic myth of 'You should report to the police,' which may induce blame, shame, and guilt for clients. At the same time, clients can be informed that exceptions to this neutrality may be made if safeguarding becomes relevant under legal or ethical circumstances.

The same conversation can be had with a survivor who is explicitly thinking about reporting, so that they are aware of the additional factors that may come into play under the CPS guidelines should they take this step whilst working together. Further information on instances where a client may have contact with the criminal justice system and whether or not this means they are pre-trial, are detailed in the above section on 'Overview of the criminal justice system for sexual offences.'

A usual concern for therapists is how best to record notes, especially when they may be viewed or used outside of a talking therapy context. Notes are a record of when an appointment or communication took place, the topic of what was discussed, any specific techniques applied by the therapist, how the client presented, and whether anyone else attended the appointment. In the case of a disclosure of risk, details on what the presenting risk is and how this was managed are appropriate.

As a personal experience, sexual violence is made sense of at an individual level, with corresponding language assigned to it by the survivor. What they have been through may or may not have the same definition as that used in the criminal justice system, which has clearly defined terms for different types of sexual violence such as rape and assault. Furthermore, language can change as a survivor processes the impact of their trauma on their own or with any form of personal and professional support. Again, this is not reflective of a survivor's account being unsound, but a natural by-product of coming to terms with one's own narrative, including trauma's place within it.

Concurrently a therapist will approach working with the impact of traumatic experiences in a similar way no matter what type of sexual violence took place. For the purposes of note-taking it is therefore more suitable to use umbrella terms such as 'sexual violence' or 'sexual abuse' across one's entire caseload. Details that only serve to locate the incident within a client's history are appropriate to make, such as how old a client was when this took place, or the perpetrator's relationship to them. As such, there is a record of sexual violence being disclosed in therapy without elaboration, which is clinically sufficient. Should the CPS guidelines state that further details need to be recorded in any instance, such as including verbatim quotes when first disclosures are made, therapists are ethically required to comply.

In the meantime, the therapist is not drawn into subjectively evaluating or interpreting on their part what took place. As a potential form of evidence that could be used in criminal proceedings, ambiguity or inconsistency is avoided wherever possible as a record of discussions whilst therapy itself maximises its ability to be a place to speak freely. This protects the privacy of the individual survivor and their conversations in therapy, whilst also being suitable evidence should notes be used in assessing their case.

The purpose of notes is to be a brief, factual record of client contact. Therefore, they should not include a therapist's theoretical interpretations, emotions or feelings occurring on the part of the therapist, nor specific details or identifying information that elaborate on the main themes of an appointment. The focus therefore remains on the therapist's task, which is to provide psychological treatment of mental health difficulties, with an appropriate level of comment in their notes to support the ethical delivery of such work.

The therapist is required to take in and process information on many levels in an appointment with any client, including those with lived experience of sexual violence. As such, each of us will make decisions on what needs responding to in any given moment and attending to these in the dialogue as required to alleviate presenting concerns. This can be via verbal communications, facial expressions or body posture, and the use of specific advice or techniques.

A similar approach can be taken in recording notes for clinical purposes. There is no need for a therapist to give an excess of details outside of demonstrating the work being completed in written form, although disclosures around significant matters such as incidences of sexual violence or other risk may require details to be noted for the purposes of appropriate safeguarding. The bulk of the work is undertaken live between a therapist and client whereas notes are an overview of work completed appointment by appointment.

A request/court order and release of therapy notes can be emotive for the therapist along with their client. The sensitivity required to manage this effectively can be explored within the context of relational psychotherapy, as an intersubjective experience that also requires interaction with others outside of the room. Visibility of therapeutic material and the client–therapist relationship, outside of the physical spaces we work, has a symbolic function as well as being the fulfilment of a practical action.

A helpful question to ask here is: what would it mean for the client, particularly within their relational style, to be part of the therapist–client dyad outside of the room? This question can be explored by the therapist on their side as well as between them and the client as part of the work being traversed pre-trial.

Consideration of this question sheds light on any personal value that the survivor places on their therapist, as a professional taking up a specific role within their process of recovery. It also sheds light on any transference material which demonstrates developmental needs, power dynamics, and relational patterns of the past that can come to life in the present work. Such transference material can heavily contextualise the experience of the working relationship on both sides, as well as the many levels of a survivor's conscious and unconscious needs when accessing talking therapy.

Along with the above practical steps, therapists can encourage conversations as often as required to check in on the impact of the criminal justice process on the survivor's multi-faceted self. An active interest in their client's search for justice is in the least a demonstration of their not being alone in the stress and uncertainty that this can cause. A request, court order, or release of therapy notes can be solidifying of amplifying a survivor's voicing of lived experiences as much as it can be experienced as an intrusion on the physical and psychological spaces provided by psychotherapy.

A survivor's placing of trust in the therapist and therapy as a supportive process must be honoured throughout. Transparency and the sharing of information becomes part of being collaboratively prepared to navigate the criminal justice process however far an individual client goes with this. Both of these factors feed into the offering and facilitation of consent as a form of respecting the client's wishes to counter the non-consensual violation of what has brought them into the room.

Providing clients with a copy of their notes and release forms provides the opportunity for a concrete understanding that these are taking up space beyond the therapeutic work. Paperwork forms representations of what is known about clients in multiple spaces in the wider world, particularly as someone who has experienced sexual violence. It is prudent to facilitate conversations about paperwork within appointments pre-trial, as it may give space to expressions of what it is like to be a person with lived experience and what being a 'victim' or 'survivor' means on an individual basis.

The interweaving of the procedural and experiential aspects of working pre-trial is another way of ensuring that the survivor remains central to the therapeutic process. It also ensures that the boundaries and function of therapy are retained, rather than being fully hijacked by an external force. Dynamically, this would sit too closely to the original incidents of sexual violence, which increases the potential of traumatising disempowerment.

It would be easy for a therapist to be pulled into a position of professional disempowerment too, given the above, and become worried about the level of responsibility in adhering to the CPS guidelines within their role. However, the criminal justice system and mental health system are not completely incompatible. Equally, there are occasions when therapy notes assist in securing a conviction, meaning that they can have an influential place in a disempowering system.

Survivors' experiences of reporting

A person's decision to let anyone know they have experienced sexual violence is an extremely personal one. There are many survivors who do not make disclosures until years, or even decades, after it has occurred due to internal or external barriers. This is the case even if there is a strong desire to let someone know and knowing the reasons motivating this feeling. When reporting to the police is a decision made by the survivor as a form of disclosure, it is accompanied by an intense mix of emotions, thoughts, hopes, and concerns.

There are of course times when a report is made on behalf of a survivor, perhaps without their consent. This may be via a neighbour who becomes aware of domestic violence and is concerned for the person's safety. Therapists may be in a position where they are required to report whenever an adult makes a disclosure, as deemed mandatory by their place of work to appropriately safeguard clients, even if there is no concurrent legal obligation to do so. Both CPS guidelines chime with this given that there is an emphasis on therapists encouraging victims to report should a disclosure be made whilst offering talking therapy.

At one level this is consistent with the notion that justice is achieved via legal interventions by the state, including imprisonment of perpetrators who harm the general public. As a protective measure for all and a recognition of the harm done to a survivor who makes a report, when justice is secured in this manner it can be hugely reparative. For many survivors what this means is a kind of closure and a personal narrative that is re-aligned with one's experiences following its disruption. In short, it makes sense that there are consequences for a perpetrator's actions.

Justice through criminal proceedings can also mean the beginning of some kind of normalcy following the forced re-configuration of one's multi-faceted self, life, and relationships within the wider world that comes with the impact of sexual violence. The possibility or actuality of making a disclosure to the police is, however, often a very difficult means to this hoped-for end. In this sense our attention is brought to the vital element of control, which sits closely to the equally vital element of trust. These are both important to consider in the reality of navigating the criminal justice process for our clients when supporting them.

Therapists may resonate strongly with their client's distressed feelings at times due to uncertainty of what the criminal justice process entails and therefore what it can mean for their clients. A therapist may also have gone through this process personally or professionally with varying results. Collectively as a profession we become acutely aware of the value of control and trust as it plays out within the working relationship when clients are pre-trial or they make a disclosure to us in the privacy of an appointment.

There is the potential for the therapist to feel disempowered along with their client around responding to disclosures, whether they are tentatively made in appointments or formally with the police. The tension between wanting to respect a person's individual choice in reporting alongside adhering to statutory requirements, legal obligations, and organisational procedures required to do so can bring disempowerment into the working relationship and psychological space offered by therapists.

The ongoing interplay between the power of myths and the burden of proof being the victim's responsibility points to common themes expressed by survivors in therapy whilst they consider reporting, or have current or past contact with the criminal justice system. An exploration of the power of myths in all the spaces it can emerge in the wider world is more fully completed in Chapter four. It is, however, certainly worth mentioning here as the criminal justice system is a space that is negatively influenced by myths about sexual violence.

A triple disempowerment is in place for survivors who have reported to the police. The concurrent responsibility for recovery, achieving justice, and managing everyday life is placed primarily onto the survivor for having been the victim of a crime within a victim-blaming society. A low conviction rate for sexual offences within the United Kingdom means that there is a societally-sanctioned lack of responsibility on the part of those who create the issue, and therefore perpetrator's lives remain largely unaffected.

As a personal experience, the criminal justice process can exacerbate the lonely position of disempowerment because one has to prove that what one is saying is the truth so that it can be responded to:

> Once I reported straight away as I was attacked by a stranger. Then two men found me and they took me to a police station. I found talking to the police okay then. They were really kind and supportive. But there's also lots of things I didn't report from my childhood because I felt ashamed and I didn't think they would believe me. I had no evidence so it felt pointless.
>
> *M*

If there isn't a guilty verdict or a case is NFA'd, there is no recognition of sexual violence having taken place by the criminal justice system and there are no consequences for perpetrators set by the state. As an individual experience, the incidents remain with the survivor for them to hold whilst the rest of the world remains unmoved:

> The public don't appreciate what happens behind closed doors. If there's no bruise or cast, it's like the damage is invisible.
>
> *Anna*

The repeated denial of a client's traumatic experiences in multiple spaces within the wider world means there is little proportionate recognition of what happened. Thus, there is little chance of humane consolidation of its impact externally within human-made systems nor internally within the multi-faceted self. Being listened to at the very least means trusting one's own experiences in being witnessed by another self. Trust is forged within one's self, as well as between selves, rather than internalising disbelief or minimising what took place.

Regardless of whether or not a criminal case does result in a conviction, the process of putting the pieces together can be helpful to a survivor in recognising the specifics of sexual violence as a way of processing its impact:

> I was able to accept that it happened and knowing more about the stranger who assaulted me was helpful in making sense of it.
>
> *Sam*

So far, we have considered survivors' experiences of the criminal justice system in relation to its outcome. It is useful to also become more aware of what it is like to undergo the process of reporting itself and the subsequent steps. The procedures in place to respond to reports of sexual crimes may not be what a client expects. This can add to the difficulty in emotionally and practically seeing the process through even if the survivor is determined to do so:

> The process wasn't what I expected at all. I wasn't properly informed of what was happening nor why ... The disadvantages of reporting are that it takes a lot of time and a lot of energy when there's a lot more going on in your life besides the assault. I also had to ask for time off from work, which included making excuses as to why I had to be off work. Once I had to make something up for a family member about why I was appearing in court.
>
> *Sam*

Contact with the police through related incidences, such as physical assault, may lead to a loss of faith in the criminal justice system as a protective mechanism overall. Tayba's experience of this occurred within a marriage where different types of violence were routine. One such incident occurred whilst her child was in the home:

> It was the first time he grabbed a knife and in that moment I had a clear sense of 'This is the end' – either for our marriage, or my own life. I'm still left with the feeling of wanting my child to be safe, away from him, even if I wasn't around.

After the police were called her husband was removed from the home and she was asked if she wanted to have him arrested. On reflection of this event in her life, and after having professionally supported other women who have had similar experiences, Tayba deeply contends the idea that responsibility for deciding whether or not an abusive man is arrested lies with the woman:

> Surely if someone has overpowered a woman with a knife in front of a child then the police should just arrest them?
>
> *Tayba*

The personal decision to report often comes with having to face the fact that one's status as a victim or survivor will be known to others. Therapists should be mindful of what this personally means to a client, as well as any practical consequences that may further disrupt their lives, including an increase in risk to personal safety. This is of note given that most survivors know the perpetrator in some way prior to sexual violence happening, including it occurring within the family:

> I was put off reporting because I was worried about what other people would say about me.
>
> *Amanda*

I didn't want to upset our children. It didn't seem relevant or important to unearth everything so long after the abuse.

Anna

Why would I do it? I don't want my family to know, or disrupt family relationships.

M

The notion of 'justice' is helpful to explore in order to widen our shared understanding of what constitutes a proportionate reaction to sexual violence from others we have relationships with and wider society. Such reactions are at best affirmative and reparative too. Within therapy this can be part of addressing the injustice of sexual violence as framed by the individual client and as a wider societal phenomenon.

Many clients describe the urgent need for sexual violence and its impact to stop in some way. Ending the cycle of inter-generational abuse within a family via therapy can be part of becoming empowered as a survivor of it, similarly to how action in other spaces in the wider world can achieve this sense of control being within one's reach. Reporting can be one type of such action, as can activism or taking up a professional support role for other survivors.

A recognition and response to what happened is often at the heart of justice for survivors of sexual violence. There are survivors for example who decide to confront perpetrators or those who knew sexual violence took place but did nothing. Here there is usually the citing of a need to hear others confirm what they have done as going some way towards mitigating the disempowerment the survivor felt whilst it occurred and then repeatedly afterwards in its invisibility or denial.

The seeking of a resolution to injustice does not have to be limited to reporting to the police. There are many spaces in the wider world where this can be an option and therefore it can have many different definitions aligned with what is meaningful to each survivor.

The core of humane justice is being able to speak when one was previously silenced, being in control when one was previously disempowered, and being able to take action when previously one had no options. For clients, the provision of therapy and their relationship with their therapist is where hope for this can be maintained even when the criminal justice process is disappointing, re-traumatising, and disempowering.

Collaboration between two systems

There is an increased probability of contact with the criminal justice system when working with survivors of sexual violence. Therapists therefore have a specialised role to undertake in meeting the needs of this client group, including the additional responsibilities of appropriately delivering therapy services pre-trial.

Although contact with the criminal justice system and its guidelines on pre-trial therapy precipitates stress at times, therapists are required to respond to stress with clear thinking and appropriate action rather than replicating the reactive survival strategies of trauma. This is part of appropriately modelling and offering a reparative relational experience to survivors whilst the reality of the wider world enters the room with them at each appointment.

Individual practitioners in private practice and teams within organisations working pre-trial should create processes and paperwork in advance of delivering therapy in this way. Consistency afforded by standardisation is reflective of an ethical service supported by its practical boundaries. Such boundaries can be helpful in minimising the manifestation of any stresses such as anxieties on the therapist's part.

A lack of preparation here can be disruptive or injurious to the client–therapist relationship, and the process of undertaking therapy together, at a highly sensitive time. The uncertainty and disempowerment of contact with the criminal justice process need not be replicated within therapy if it is boundaried and transparent between all parties involved from the outset.

Part of addressing the issue of sexual violence with survivors means being well-informed about the routes available to do so, as it enables a sense of control whilst pursuing such routes. The least that therapists can do for survivors is to raise their professional awareness of the criminal justice system as a formal process, as well as it being a personal experience via what clients tell us about how it feels to report or go to court. We can therefore remain solid as a form of support rather than falling into a state of disempowerment within our selves, along with our client's selves that are under pressure.

As a profession, therapists are severely under-trained in working with any clients pre-trial, including survivors of sexual violence. This puts us at risk of working unethically seeing as we are required to be aware of and work within the CPS guidelines in these circumstances. The creation of standardised and mandatory training for practitioners is key in the role of therapists collectively stepping up to managing this often-complex work. Legal professionals and the general public may similarly be assured of the standard of such work on offer via the creation of a register of appropriately trained therapists.

Knowing survivors' truths about the criminal justice system can reinforce any pre-existing mistrust and lack of faith in reporting from the therapist's perspective. Naturally the meeting of two very different human-made systems can result in an 'us versus them' dynamic from both sides. One way this dynamic is apparent in the CPS guidelines is not only its doubt of the victim's account until proven true via evidence, but its simultaneously casting doubt on the reliability of the role of therapists pre-trial.

From the CPS's perspective we simultaneously have the power to provide evidence via notes to reinforce the validity of a victim's report and also have the power to jeopardise its consistency by simply giving victims space to talk about what happened. This creates an impossible position which many therapists have encountered in applying the guidelines since they were published in 2002.

If the position of the CPS is that therapists have an explicit role in the support and evidential process then the element of trust via continued three-way collaboration would be of benefit to legal professionals, therapists, and survivors. This can be achieved in individual therapists' interventions with clients pre-trial at specific stages to emotionally support their client's participation in the criminal justice system and ultimately their case.

Therapists' involvement at all the stages of the reporting, investigation, and trial process would be helpful in educating a very different system on the reality of the work undertaken. For example, a brief report on the type of therapy provided, and how it addresses post-trauma symptoms, contextualises therapy notes rather than simply being a place where the details of the sexual violence are discussed to the concern of the criminal justice system.

Replication of good practice in criminal proceedings could enhance understanding of the content of therapy notes provided to barristers, judges, magistrates, and juries alongside other evidence presented to them in court. One example could be the use of ground rules hearings, which are typically used to ascertain how a vulnerable witness (such as a victim reporting a sexual offence) can be enabled to give their best evidence.

A ground rules hearing at the beginning of a trial can be a place where the therapist verbally explains the nature of the work undertaken, how much or little the details of sexual violence was discussed, for what purpose the sexual violence was discussed, post-trauma symptoms treated, and how the victim's presenting concerns in therapy align with what is recognised as a normal response to sexual violence. This would assist in minimising misconceptions about the integrity of the therapy, dispel myths about the impact of sexual violence, and allow the therapist to be an advocating voice along with the survivor's own account in court.

The idea of appearing in court as a witness is another anxiety-inducing position for therapists, although its occurrence is an exception rather than the rule. On the legal side, having set questions, rather than an unstructured conversation, about any relevant areas ensures standardisation of how each victim's case is treated and that the criminal justice system is adhering to its own procedures of enquiry. It also enables therapists to adequately inform clients in advance, within the safety of an appointment, about what questions will come up plus consider together how they will be responded to wherever possible or appropriate.

The therapist maintains their position as a supporter of the survivor, rather than yet another person who doubts their account or wishes to challenge them. Maintaining a three-way process with the survivor at the centre in this hypothetical instance means transparency, preparing in collaboration within the client–therapist relationship, and gaining consent to participate in the process in line with the survivor's wishes. The therapist can continue to be an ally rather than an oppositional figure, especially if the therapist is the only person in their client's support network (as can be the case).

Trust can be facilitated from a top-down approach in influencing the criminal justice process as a collective profession, alongside the input of individual therapists from the ground up on a case-by-case basis. Both versions of the guidelines were created via input from the CPS, therapy providers, and organisations supporting survivors. However, the absence of survivors' voices in the creation of the guidelines in both versions so far is notable despite input from organisations serving this client group.

It is not clear whether individual survivors, or groups of survivors, have ever been approached by the CPS to contribute to the guidelines, although it is implied that they were able to do so via the public consultation of late 2020. In order for their needs to be met and for trust in justice or support systems to be facilitated, survivors must have as much power as professionals on the topic of pre-trial therapy.

Thus far considerations have been made here on how to improve collaborations in service of survivors between the criminal justice system and those providing talking therapy. An equally valid argument to be made is that the disclosure of therapy notes should only be a rare exception rather than the rule. A move towards the police and CPS refraining from requesting therapy notes speculatively is helpful as a starting point.

However, in practice any mention of accessing therapy is viewed as an opportunity to suspect discussions of the offence. Suspicions have long been sufficient grounds to make a request for therapy notes, as they form part of the justification for making a reasonable line of enquiry under the disclosure test. This is cemented by the police and CPS's instructions to victims that if talking therapy commences they should be notified immediately.

Pre-emptive assumptions are therefore made on the appropriateness of applying internal procedures to request therapy notes, as well as the appropriateness of frequently approaching therapists as a type of professional a survivor might speak to. An emphasis on trauma therapy in both versions of the CPS guidelines legitimises the targeting of survivors of sexual violence as a specific group of victims accessing therapy pre-trial.

Although the CPS guidelines are changing, the legacy left by the original version will be seen in therapy rooms and the public consciousness for many years to come. More importantly, the barriers they have created to recovery from the traumatic impact of sexual violence will be felt by survivors throughout their lifetime. Not having access to talking therapy as it is usually delivered for almost two decades, purely because of the restrictions created by the original guidelines, is an injustice in itself that needs to be righted on all sides.

There is a gap in understanding between professionals who create formal systems to address sexual violence and survivors who are subject to the rules of such systems. This is a gap that many survivors fall through, including to the point where reporting isn't seen as a viable option so an attempt to do so is never even considered. The criminal justice process that encourages victims to always report can be seen to lesser but significant degrees in individual therapists, therapeutic organisations, and the general public. Ultimately, this is a reflection of reporting being the only assumed route to resolution of the issue of sexual violence by the state.

This assumption is cemented in the societal myth that one should always report and report straightaway. Failure to do so can then be seen as a valid enough reason to disbelieve a survivor. For these internalised misunderstandings to change, ongoing work is required within both the mental health and criminal justice systems as well as between them. Listening to survivors' experiences is important in itself as a humane response to injustice, so that the truth is heard. In this fundamental way therapists meet the people behind the statistics of low conviction rates and respond accordingly in the person-to-person encounter of therapy.

References

Big Brother Watch, 2019: *Digital Strip Searches: The Police's Data Investigations of Victims*. London: Big Brother Watch.

Crown Prosecution Service, 2001: *Therapy: The Provision of Therapy for Child Witnesses Prior to a Criminal Trial*. Available at: https://www.cps.gov.uk/legal-guidance/therapy-provision-therapy-child-witnesses-prior-criminal-trial (accessed November 2020).

Crown Prosecution Service, 2002: *The Provision of Therapy for Vulnerable and Intimidated Witnesses*. Available at: https://www.cps.gov.uk/legal-guidance/therapy-provision-therapy-vulnerable-or-intimidated-adult-witnesses (accessed November 2020).

Crown Prosecution Service, 2020a: *Guidance on Pre-Trial Therapy*. Available at: https://www.cps.gov.uk/publication/guidance-pre-trial-therapy.(accessed November 2020).

Crown Prosecution Service, 2020b: *Special Measures*. Available at: https://www.cps.gov.uk/legal-guidance/special-measures (accessed November 2020).

Home Office, 1998: *Speaking Up for Justice: Report of the Interdepartmental Working Group on the treatment of Vulnerable or Intimidated Witness in the Criminal Justice System*. London: Home Office.

Sexual Offences Act 2003. Available at: https://www.legislation.gov.uk/ukpga/2003/42/contents (accessed November 2020).

World Health Organization, 2019: *International Classification of Diseases for Mortality and Morbidity Statistics (11th Revision)*. Geneva: World Health Organization.

Chapter 8

Vicarious trauma

Impact and management

All psychotherapists are required to be aware of and manage the impact of their work no matter what clients or presenting concerns they encounter. Professionally this is part of being an ethical practitioner, as one is always seeking to work within one's own margins of competency. This concept points to one's ability to successfully complete the demands of one's workload, whatever this looks like. It is an active task that evolves along with these demands and can therefore change over the course of a psychotherapist's career.

There are three levels by which to assess competency for supporting individual clients on a case-by-case basis and wider client groups characterised by similarities in presenting issues. The first is whether one's training, qualifications, and experience appropriately prepare them to meet the needs of each of their clients at any one time. Competency in this manner indicates a psychotherapist's professional remit and, as such, should be used to decide whether or not to undertake work with a client.

The nature of relational psychotherapy requires practitioners to utilise their multi-faceted selves in the process of addressing a client's mental health difficulties. How we are with each other with regards to relational dynamics, and the information gleaned from the intersubjective experience of working with a client, both feed into the ongoing assessment of a client's presenting material. Such assessments translate into interventions made by the psychotherapist in the effort to facilitate change in accordance with a client's needs and wishes.

Therefore, the second level of competency takes into account the psychotherapist's ability to respond to the client's relational needs as they emerge consciously or unconsciously. The aim is to do so in ways that are reparative rather than colluding with the presenting issue, and are respectful of the person as a multi-faceted self. This includes giving due attention to what is occurring intersubjectively in order to avoid causing harm person-to-person in any way.

Being immersed in a relational process during the treatment of post-trauma symptoms is a significant task, as the nature of the mistreatment caused to the survivor originally happened between persons. A blueprint for how people

DOI: 10.4324/9781003202943-8

are with each other is traumatically altered and can be felt even if the client knows they are in a safe physical or psychological space. Working relationally is where the personal and professional collide so care must be taken at all times to fulfil competency at this level.

Finally, the third level is an ongoing consideration of the overall health of the psychotherapist as a multi-faceted self. A sufficient baseline of physical and psychological health needs to be maintained as part of being able to provide a consistency of service provision. If there are personal difficulties in these areas, the psychotherapist's clinical remit and the ways they practically carry out their responsibilities must be taken into account so that they operate within their margins of competency.

A general principle related to health is that psychotherapists need to be well enough to physically and psychologically manage their work. Equally, the work may be part of what makes them unwell through various forms of stress. In this sense it is prudent to consider the impact of working with sexual violence in psychotherapy, specifically the risk of vicarious trauma.

Understanding vicarious trauma

In qualifying what vicarious trauma means in order to enhance our working understanding of it, the language used in this chapter is reflective of language used elsewhere in this book. The aim is to explicitly demonstrate similarities in the ability of sexual violence to impact all of us as multi-faceted selves, no matter where or how we are confronted with its truths. Such truths can be felt within the many facets of our selves, including the physical and psychological facets.

Psychotherapists undertaking work on the issue of sexual violence inside and outside of the rooms in which appointments are offered are subject to developing symptoms of vicarious trauma. The interpersonal contact required in the psychological spaces we extend to survivors equates to contact with the truths of sexual violence, whether this be details of the incidents or details of their impact.

These can be felt within and between each self on either side of the client–psychotherapist relationship. This context not only informs the interventions a psychotherapist makes to provide effective treatment, but is a stark reminder of the context of the shared wider world where sexual violence takes place. Reminders of this nature can be a significant factor in transforming a workload from manageable to unbearable.

Vicarious trauma is a form of stress response arising from acute or prolonged exposure via contact with others who have experienced traumatic events. Stress indicative of vicarious trauma can reflect post-trauma symptoms such as: distressing thoughts or memories, disturbed sleep, hypervigilance, dissociation, physical pain, flashbacks, irritability, disrupted concentration, and difficulties in managing emotions.

When experienced by the psychotherapist, vicarious trauma can represent a direct triggering of one's own existing stress responses, including post-traumatic stress, and/or an internalisation of the client's traumatic material. Working relationally in the person-facing arena of psychotherapy can increase the possibility of experiencing elements of what our clients experience which, when it is mediated carefully, can lead to reparative interventions delivered empathically. In instances where contact with traumatic material is literally too close for comfort, a psychotherapist may begin to feel overwhelmed.

Earlier in this book we acknowledged the ability of sexual violence to forcibly re-configure a survivor's multi-faceted self and personal world. Within this there are significant changes to one's sense of self, relationships with others, and ability to freely occupy spaces within the wider world. In the case of psychotherapists affected by vicarious trauma, all of this can be replicated at their end of the working relationship. Akin to the survivors we work with, it is felt during and beyond the boundaries of appointment times.

Further to the aforementioned post-trauma symptoms, vicarious trauma is also characterised by changes in one's behaviour in relation to one's work. Another mirroring of the impact of sexual violence takes place here, in that a psychotherapist may become hyper- or hypo-aroused at a neurophysiological level when they become stressed. Falling outside of one's window of tolerance (Siegel, 1999) in response to traumatic material is an attempt to psychologically and physically survive it.

Attempts to survive are made using a combination of unconscious, automatic responses or conscious, intentional reactions to manage its impact. Such attempts can be a way of getting back in control through an active push back against traumatic material, which is similar to a fight or flight response. Examples are irritability in taking up a support role including whilst hearing clients' accounts of sexual violence and working increased hours to keep busy.

Alternatively, having this distressing kind of material come into contact with you whilst passively trying to suffer as little harm as possible reflects a freeze response. This can be experienced as feeling numb or shutting down emotionally, a loss of hope for individual clients, and a loss of hope on the wider scale of sexual violence as a societal phenomenon that can be tackled.

In any case the demands of the work undertaken begin to fall outside of a psychotherapist's competency at levels two and three. If we are responding in survival mode, we are more likely to replicate unhelpful or unhealthy patterns of relating with clients or end up not meeting their needs at all. Both of these are missed opportunities to offer reparative support in a relational context.

The ability of the psychotherapist to be fully present and stay solid as a multi-faceted self to hold the boundaries of the work is impaired. Concurrently the health of the psychotherapist needs to be good enough to sustain this self, as well as their clients' selves. Being caught up in automatic or intentional efforts to deliver psychotherapy whilst needing to protect one's self makes the psychotherapist less available to clients in all the ways that are required in their role.

A lack of control over the ways we can successfully sustain the impact of working with the truth of sexual violence as professionals can expand into a lack of control in other ways within personal lives. More than anything else this reflects the power of the issue to move any of us that come to know it, whether from personal and/or professional experience.

In this way vicarious trauma is not a sign of personal or professional failure. It is an indicator of the limit of one's capacity to tolerate contact with distressing material and the subsequent attempt to survive it. Where a psychotherapist's capacity lies can change over time and is influenced by a number of factors. For example: current life circumstances including any stressors, physical health, mental health, and how much a client's material resonates with a psychotherapist's own personal experiences.

A notion of failure on the part of the psychotherapist is in any determination to continue to proceed in an adaptive way under the pressure of vicarious trauma, rather than addressing it to regain a more controlled, sustainable way of working and living. Failures of this nature are not only detrimental to the psychotherapist's inherent commitment to their personal wellbeing as a private individual, but also has an impact on their commitment to practising competently as a professional. Both of these are important and have a direct influence on each other as facets of our selves.

Thus far we have considered vicarious trauma only in relation to appointments with clients. Many psychotherapists will engage in confronting the problem of sexual violence outside of these spaces, perhaps even in the public domain as activists. In addition to this, the truths surrounding sexual violence are visible within many spaces along our dynamic loops, such as the media and discussions within our communities.

It is not necessarily the case that we are vicariously traumatised because we hear multiple accounts, however detailed or vague, about sexual violence from survivors in multiple spaces. Psychotherapists are also absorbed in its impact as part of the relational experience. Explorations of this impact can be completed to varying degrees of depth with clients in order to collaboratively address them.

The insidious nature of sexual violence holds the power to permanently change not only the survivor, but those around them. Psychotherapists who have worked with family members or partners of survivors, or have survivors in their personal network, will know this well. Another notable effect of vicarious trauma therefore is its ability to change one's perspective, accompanied by revised ways of living.

At worst this means existing in small personal worlds and only feeling able to move within narrow margins (literally and figuratively) because of the reconfigurations to one's self forced by sexual violence. We may find ourselves on a train wondering how many perpetrators or survivors are around us, or may take a different route home because it somehow feels safer than our usual one. We may also re-evaluate our past relationships that included sexual contact, or shy away from what might have previously been welcome forms of physical intimacy with partners, because we now feel unsure.

The impact of vicarious trauma can be surprising, even for experienced psychotherapists. It can arise from contact with one particular client, or manifest in a successive accumulation of contacts with the matter over a period of time. Additionally, the onset of vicarious trauma can be delayed rather than being an immediate response to the work being undertaken with survivors.

Should vicarious trauma be experienced severely enough and for a prolonged period of time, a diagnosis of post-traumatic stress disorder can be relevant as a form of traumatising exposure (American Psychiatric Association, 2013). As such we may at one time feel comfortable with a full caseload and then at another better manage with a reduced number of clients. Of course, watching survivors struggle is emotive when we are invited in to their processes as witnesses and are asked to respond with help.

Above all, being moved by suffering is a normal response to injustice and knowing that the people we meet have suffered significant violations of their human rights. The challenge for psychotherapists includes mediating this adequately on a consistent basis in order to keep clients at the centre of the work, maintain levels of good relatedness within our selves as an indicator of good health, and continue to work effectively with the complexity of sexual violence wherever we have a responsibility to do so.

Relational responses within and between selves

Relational psychotherapy requires an emphasis on the nature of the relating taking place between the multi-faceted selves contributing to the process, whatever their role. Each self influences this via their own relational patterns or attachment style as a template by which to understand and respond to others. The accumulation of person-to-person interactions throughout one's lifetime shapes this significantly, particularly in early life. Each self will have a similar template by which to relate to the different facets of their self as an internal experience.

Both types of internal and external relating provide valuable information as a context for psychotherapeutic work. It is known consciously and unconsciously between all parties. For the psychotherapist such information influences their responses so that their clients' needs are adequately attended to. This is provided alongside specific interventions that come from the psychotherapist's training and experience.

What this relational context entails is contact as a psychological act between multi-faceted selves, wherever it is possible. The psychotherapist and client also individually have contact within their self between different facets which are experienced primarily in their body or mind. Encouragement to develop consciousness or create change around internal relationships between facets of the client's self may be part of the work taking place.

When a person is subjected to sexual violence the relationships between facets of their self, and between multi-faceted selves, are violently disrupted. The relational or attachment template between selves is forcibly transformed and the multi-faceted self becomes a difficult place to inhabit comfortably. Contact with the subjectivity of one's experience and the intersubjectivity of contact with multiple selves may only be possible intermittently rather than consistently when trauma has an impact. This is true for both clients and psychotherapists.

What is often overwhelming about trauma, and indeed vicarious trauma, is losing control over one's circumstances as well as one's responses to it. For a psychotherapist affected by vicarious trauma from their workload, contact with clients plus their presenting material feels relentless and distressing.

What happens as a response is disconnection between facets of one's self and between other selves to create a distance from contact that is felt as threatening. As a survival mechanism, disconnection is an automatic attempt to forge a sense of safety or control through distancing. The same distancing can be caused by sexual violence as a societal phenomenon outside of psychotherapy appointments.

Another automatic response is increased psychological contact with clients, their material, and the wider issue of sexual violence. This may not be what a psychotherapist intentionally seeks in the case of persistent thoughts or images that cannot be pushed to the back of one's mind. As a more visible pattern of responding to the personal distress stemming from increased contact, a psychotherapist may work harder in the face of survivors' distress. Disconnection and increased psychological contact are therefore both indicative of the ability of trauma to remove control from our personal power.

One's definition of relational work includes an acknowledgement of any communities the psychotherapist is involved in as a space where such work is delivered. This is particularly applicable to psychotherapists who are activists, or engage in other forms of work in support of survivors outside of appointments or traditional services. In this sense there are many spaces within the wider world where the aforementioned protective mechanisms of disconnection or over-relatedness can manifest.

A loss of control is of course closely linked to disempowerment as negatively impactful experiences. The reality of working with sexual violence as a psychotherapist includes literally sitting with its truths as voiced and embodied communications from survivors. Such survivors have had their lives on hold due to the actions of perpetrators and barriers to accessing support or justice in multiple spaces.

Contact with this sense of being on hold can add to our own experiences of a loss of power in treating the impact of sexual violence and in taking care of our multi-faceted selves as we do so. Interruptions to progress of the work, even if completely understandable, can feel like a further loss of power in resolving the issue of sexual violence in collaboration with survivors. This is the case whether we address the issue in clinical or other societal spaces.

Psychotherapist example: George

George's psychotherapeutic work with survivors of sexual violence was based in a third sector service for clients identifying along the LGBTQ+ spectrum. As a trainee practitioner George was pleased to be able to support people of their own community in a service such as this given that they were non-binary, used they/them pronouns, and polyamorous themselves. They felt their lived experience of these parts of their self enabled them to better understand the material presented by clients from a diverse range of sexualities, genders, and relationships.

Although George enjoyed the setting and meeting with clients, towards the end of the academic year they found themselves becoming physically tired along with eating less and sleeping more. This continued for several weeks to the point where George felt a back pain for much of the day, which in turn caused muscle tension in their shoulders.

George also thought a lot about their workload during the week, including specific clients. They put this down to wanting to do well on the course and considered it relatively normal, as other trainee colleagues said they felt tired at times too. However, as a result their concentration worsened which added to the pressure of getting things done.

On the whole George felt that the course tutors were openly understanding about the challenges of training and placements when trainees voiced them. This included explicitly offering support on an ongoing basis. At this point George wasn't sure what they would be asking for help for and that in general the stresses they were experiencing would pass.

One of George's clients was a cisgender male, gay survivor called Leo who they had been working with for seven months. Leo was once again in the process of leaving a household where domestic violence (including sexual violence) was being inflicted by multiple family members. There were two previous occasions during the work when Leo left his home but he would always end up back there, whereupon the violence would begin again.

George often struggled to gain a sense of moving forward in their shared work because of the frequent crises brought about in practically managing Leo's safety and the repeated steps taken to help him live independently of the perpetrators. Leo trusted George, and said he was glad he could talk about things openly because this wasn't possible elsewhere. George would sometimes extend the length of appointments, which Leo also said he appreciated given the safety of being in a queer-friendly space.

Although their working relationship was good, George began to feel frustrated with Leo at times. They also began to forget details of his material, which made it harder for George to keep up with the pace of the dialogue or the chronology of events being disclosed. When at home on the weekend George would research other support services for Leo to access alongside psychotherapy and would once again become frustrated if unsuccessful.

During supervision George chose not to talk about Leo given that they usually ended up discussing how best Leo could manage the practical tasks around leaving again, which George considered was them responding to their client's needs whilst being in crisis. As the local LGBTQ+ community was very small, George was also worried about Leo being identifiable if they spoke about him in further detail which would compromise his confidentiality.

Within the service amongst colleagues George was irritable, preferring to stay in the room where they saw clients instead of going into the office as part of the team. George felt that they couldn't bear to hear more stories of abuse in addition to the details of Leo's experiences, which were often at the forefront of their mind. The clinical lead at the service noticed that George was somewhat absent and approached them to open up a conversation.

During this she was transparent about the levels of stress that can come from knowing that so many of their clients were vulnerable or traumatised in some way. George felt a little relieved as this meant it wasn't just the trainees that struggled. She asked how they were doing on their course, to which George said there was a lot to do but they were managing. They thanked her for her time and knew the offer to speak more was there if needed.

In their part-time job George arranged to work remotely from home more often as this would help them conserve time and energy. George's partners began to comment on seeing them less and that when they did see each other George would start arguments. George's response was to say their priority was meeting deadlines and seeing clients so that they didn't fall behind on their course. Privately George felt annoyed that their partners were being so demanding and they were angry that none of them were more supportive.

Thus far we can see several ways in which George's response to vicarious trauma manifested in multiple spaces in their personal and professional lives. The sense of being alone with their client's material was exacerbated by the fact that they were the only person in Leo's support network and George's simultaneous declining of professional support with colleagues.

Feeling out of place within their personal networks, such as partners and the LGBTQ+ community, was indicative of the traumatic pushing out of spaces for George. Losing a sense of one's self, including tangible relatedness with the ways one identifies, can occur from living in survival mode for sustained periods of time. Humans lose the ability to manage and enjoy socially engaging, which can be hugely compromising when the communities we live in reflect fundamental elements of our identity.

As a result, the isolation in holding all of this brought George to capacity within their psychological self via decreased concentration, forgetting, rumination on traumatic material, irritability, and anger. Its impact also began to seep into the physical facet of their self in decreased energy, sleeping more, eating less, and pain in their body.

George's response as a professional was to try harder to manage their workload in an adapted way. Requesting to work from home was a conscious effort to manage emerging stress, as was distancing from others around them to maximise the chance of completing deadlines for their course. Looking up additional services for clients to access is usual practice for psychotherapists, but doing so excessively may point to an active protective response to the intrusion of vicarious trauma rather than a due diligence to clients.

Overall, narrow margins were automatically created in response to traumatic material. In this way George ended up having to sustain their disconnected multi-faceted self on limited internal and external resources, alongside a client that was living in the same way. Two bodies and minds operating in this way will unfortunately continue the cycle of living from a depleted baseline because of the power of sexual violence to disrupt normal life.

The implications of vicarious trauma for individual psychotherapists and the survivors in their care are considerable. Within relational work there are also implications for how its impact may manifest between all parties. This is the case even if the psychotherapist does their best to retain and manage any negative impact within their own self or professional support networks. In holding the material clients bring in order to lessen the impact on them (momentarily in sessions and overall as a goal of trauma work), we hold it in the facets of our selves.

In relational psychotherapy any changes to the experience of our own multi-faceted self and relationships between selves with clients can be indicators of vicarious trauma. The use of one's multi-faceted self as a tool by which to maximise the efficacy of relational psychotherapy therefore requires a huge amount of care, in the same way we extend care to survivors.

Assessing our own dynamic loops

Given that we live in a shared world with clients where sexual violence occurs, a psychotherapist's proximity to sexual violence can occur in multiple spaces along dynamic loops. Examples are sexual violence as: lived experience, societal issue, psychotherapeutic material, exposure to media including the internet, and contact with survivors in our personal networks. It is not only a clinical issue but a prolific global phenomenon that can be encountered inside and outside of the rooms in which psychotherapy appointments are offered.

Sexual violence being a human rights violation means that working with the issue as a psychotherapist includes coming into contact with human rights injustices. For some this is part of the pull to work with survivors by offering psychotherapy appointments. For other practitioners this pull can also include work outside of mental health services, again in support of survivors.

Explicit acknowledgment of your own motivations for working with sexual violence is important, as this can illuminate the level of proximity to it as an issue. Such proximity can be maintained even when vicarious trauma takes effect, because of our personal responses to it. When working moment-to-moment in appointments, empathy is a relational channel by which psychotherapists can be pulled into a client's process, including being traumatised.

Tied into explorations of what pulls us into working with survivors are more practical factors such as needing to earn a living, or meeting the allocated number of clients one is required to see in one's role. There may be no negotiation possible on these factors at times due to the reality of service delivery, particularly when organisations determine the size of one's caseload.

Notes on pushing back against the limits of the mental health system to better suit the needs of survivors are made in Chapter one. Similar considerations can be made to widen the limits of service provision with regards to overloaded practitioners who need flexibility to work competently. This points to an issue with the mental health system at large and thus is likely to require a collective effort to make changes for all affected by the ways it perpetuates stress including vicarious trauma.

Although our human reactions to sexual violence can be constructive when offering reparative empathic responses to survivors, it also indicates how much the personal can be used to inform the professional when engaging in relational psychotherapy. It may feel counterintuitive to do less as a human in response to injustice or suffering so we move closer to specific clients, their material, and the wider problem.

However, increased contact with sexual violence as an issue can overwhelm to the point of personal disempowerment, which is of concern when operating as a professional. In psychotherapy we are tasked with responding to distress empathically. The challenge here is being psychologically contactful without losing our own position in relation to the client, nor becoming overwhelmed by the force of trauma between the facets of our selves.

Managing the impact of sexual violence as a psychotherapist starts with adequate preparation in advance of beginning any kind of work with survivors, and continued assessment of this throughout one's career. Preparation minimises having to adapt in a reactive way once vicariously impacted by trauma, as doing so exacerbates the feeling of being out of control over what is happening.

Adapting, reacting moment-to-moment, and becoming out of control are some of the dynamics of traumatic experiences which we aim to mitigate with clients. We are required to do the same for ourselves as people and professionals. Given the nature of psychotherapeutic work it is likely that we will be affected by sexual violence in a secondary manner when supporting survivors. Psychotherapists therefore have an ethical responsibility to manage this well for all selves involved.

A helpful starting point is to reflect on the specifics of one's dynamic loop which begins and ends in contact with a client. The time frame of travel around one's dynamic loop is one week, if you see clients on a weekly basis. As you travel around your dynamic loop over your time frame in between meeting with a particular client, make a note of all the spaces within it:

Figure 8.1

Attention should be paid to spaces where contact with the issue of sexual violence is made from internal and external sources. Next to each of these spaces reflect on how you were impacted by this contact in the physical and psychological facets of your self:

Figure 8.2

Lastly, notice any patterns in how you were impacted in terms of the level of disconnection or increased connection between any facets of your self, between other selves, and the wider issue of sexual violence. Going on to consider the following questions will provide an indication of how you physically and psychologically respond to stress throughout the week:

How much are these responses within your control, if at all?
Are these responses effective in resolving the impact on a long-term basis, or only effective short-term?
Which responses are usual, or atypical, for you?
Are any responses similar to or the same as post-trauma symptoms experienced by survivors you support?

The last question can be helpful in separating our own personal responses to a client's traumatic material from the client's responses, to their lived experiences. Within relational psychotherapy there is an interplay between selves as they dialogue. It is here where transference, countertransference, and projection can play a role. Further information on how each of these dynamics can manifest in psychotherapy with survivors is provided in Chapter five.

Any similarities in lived experiences the psychotherapist can resonate with requires additional care in staying appropriately alongside, although separate from, their client's process. Identifying with, understanding through lived experience, and empathising with a client can be useful in sensitively meeting their needs as a mental health professional. However, these can at times precipitate one too many steps towards a client's traumatic material.

The result is a de-centring of survivors from the process and also mis-aligns the psychotherapist in their responsibilities towards them. Typical responses are feeling as though we know best for a client rather than maintaining a collaborative stance, not responding to elements of their material including disclosures of risk, or offering additional help outside of psychotherapeutic support where it may not be appropriate.

A helpful question to ask here is: 'Is there anything going on between us that could helpfully be discussed within our shared dialogue?' Additionally: 'What is best for me to continue holding and resolving with my networks outside of the client–therapist relationship?' is a vital notion to consider given that clients should primarily be in receipt of the support we are offering.

Management strategies

The practice of incorporating management strategies for stress, including vicarious trauma, is a task for the individual psychotherapist as well as the wider networks within which they operate. Professional networks found in spaces along dynamic loops are usually formalised as training courses, personal psychotherapy, clinical supervision, and discussions with colleagues within the same field.

For practitioners working outside of psychotherapy rooms, a professional network may also include colleagues or allies of a different kind. This may be a grassroots survivor-led group, fellow activists, or professionals aiming to support survivors within other human-made systems such as the criminal justice system.

In addition to this, formal or informal support within one's professional network can include some overlap into a personal network. It is common for personal connections to be created when collectively aligning to support survivors. This has an impact on one's dynamic loop as most, or all, of the spaces within it may be orientated around the issue of sexual violence in some way at a given point.

Once again, appropriately mediating contact with traumatic material which comes from knowing the truth of sexual violence is the challenge of working with the issue, whilst avoiding or minimising the impact of vicarious trauma. A first step is referring back to your dynamic loop and noting who you can approach to negotiate the possibility of support with. Creating an ongoing process of negotiation between selves is in part a recognition of the ability of traumatic material to force us to think, experience, and act differently upon contact. Therefore, there may be times when we are available for supporting others or need to have some space to recuperate.

Being proactive in this manner adds a layer of participation in a network that inherently includes checking in and managing any emerging stress for our selves or others around us. It also invites those in our networks to actively ask how we are managing, which is helpful for psychotherapists who struggle to reach out for help or stay hidden underneath their workload as a safety mechanism.

There is value too in adding or subtracting spaces along dynamic loops as required. The impact of vicarious trauma can forcibly re-configure our personal worlds so that they become smaller and perhaps this means feeling pushed out of spaces because they cannot be inhabited nor enjoyed to the usual degree.

Reviewing which spaces you occupy along your dynamic loop on a regular basis can assist in identifying spaces that are just for your personal needs, amongst professional commitments. This can include spaces for respite on your own, or to be looked after by others. Care is then required to place boundaries around these spaces in order to protect them and your self as much as possible from the impact of vicarious trauma.

Practically, scheduling in breaks during the week in the same way as you would schedule work is a concrete way to create this boundaried space. This commitment is a practice of alternating potentially stressful work with rest, which counters the survival mode that vicarious trauma places our bodies and minds in. As a practice in itself this is a form of staying in control wherever possible via self-regulation, and produces a sense of empowerment in our personal worlds.

Boundaries also promote empowerment for clients, as our selves resist becoming traumatically intertwined with their material or their selves. Incorporating a trauma-informed approach to psychotherapy includes explicit attention to the physical facet of the self, with the benefit of knowing that humans have the ability to co-regulate at this level. One body's presence can significantly influence the physiology of another body whether this is felt consciously, or unconsciously, for example.

A state of hypervigilance represents what happens when the physical facet of the self needs to be on alert for danger. For clients with sexual violence in their history, this is re-experienced long after the incidents in order to promote safety even when there is no threat present in their environment. The automatic stress responses activated in clients can be regulated with the assistance of their psychotherapist, who needs to begin with their own regulated state of homeostasis to achieve this.

The ability for the truth of sexual violence to traumatically re-configure our selves, relationships, and personal worlds should not be underestimated. Pushing back against this re-configuration should involve spaces where a psychotherapist does something normal, even mundane, to provide a different experience to the ones coloured by the impact of sexual violence.

This can include physical movement to promote a freedom of movement in one's body. For psychotherapists that become hyper-aroused (anxious, agitated, physically mobilised) when stressed, employing the same grounding techniques we encourage clients to do is helpful on two counts. First, it upholds the integrity of one's work as we literally practice what we preach.

Second, there is an increased sense of getting back in control of at least one facet of the self. For the hypo-aroused psychotherapist, physical movement will be harder to achieve from a state of shutting down. Therefore, an uptake of oxygen is required to increase muscle mobility as a starting point, followed by small movements in a part of the body that one feels neutral or positive towards.

The benefit of a body-based approach is that it enables our nervous system to operate from a place of homeostasis, which includes optimal functioning of the brain involved in cognition rather than simply surviving a stressful moment. Even if a client becomes disconnected from the psychological facet of their self because their body is overcome via re-living sexual violence, the psychotherapist can make use of all the facets of their self to respond appropriately.

Outside of engaging the body according to one's stress responses, the mundane can include everyday tasks done in a safe environment. Making a meal and sitting with a trusted person to enjoy it, is far different from the truth of sexual violence where threat is ever-present. These are regular reminders that there can be a range of elements comprising personal worlds amongst the injustices we know of through our work and lived experience.

Staying in contact with both of these as concurrent realities is part of creating the necessary balance to respond proportionately to sexual violence without becoming overwhelmed by it. The more this balance is achieved, the more our multi-faceted selves can inhabit spaces along dynamic loops in an empowered way, which ultimately assists in supporting survivors wherever we undertake such work.

References

American Psychiatric Association, 2013: *Diagnostic and Statistical Manual of Mental Disorders 5*. Washington, DC: American Psychiatric Publishing.

Siegel, D.J., 1999: *The Developing Mind: How Relationships and the Brain Interact to Shape Who We Are*. New York: Guilford Press.

Index

Figures indexed in italic page numbers

abuse 37, 45, 66–8, 80, 98–9, 150, 162; human-to-human 74; institutional 129; inter-generational 150; organised large-scale 19; of persons 34; ritualised 39, 65; sexual 39, 86, 99, 103, 144
abusive relationships 66
accessing 6, 8, 15, 21, 24, 87, 93, 95, 105–6, 119, 126–8; psychotherapy 8, 11–12, 16–17, 19, 44, 49, 119–20, 137; support services 47, 57, 77; therapy 126, 142, 153
ACTH *see* adrenocorticotropic hormone
activism 1, 42–62, 115, 150
activist work 52, 56
acts and regulations, *Sexual Offences Act 2003* 129
addictions 98
adrenocorticotropic hormone 30
agreements 6, 41, 52, 96, 127; contractual 62; mutual 118; psychotherapist's 45; repeated 120
Ainsworth 61, 94
amygdala 24, 29–30, 41
anxiety 15, 39, 70, 109, 128, 142, 151; pre-existing 70; primitive 70
appointments 4–5, 16, 23–4, 27, 39–40, 43, 45–7, 53–4, 56–62, 89–90, 96, 101–4, 111–13, 117–18, 122, 141–2, 144–7, 151–2, 160–1; assessment 23, 39, 96, 122; client 42; completed 145; offering 136; psychotherapy 13, 16, 23, 51, 54, 57, 59, 121, 128, 160, 163; scheduled 64; structuring 41; survivor's 118; traditional 1, 11
asylum 8, 103; applications 8, 13, 122; process 105; refugees 35

attachment styles 6, 37, 91, 94–5, 159; client's 94; individual 94; observable 94
authority 17, 21, 45, 81
autonomy 9, 13, 34–5, 44, 46, 51, 56, 71, 78–9, 83–4, 111, 114–15, 122–3; exercise of 41; and freedom of movement 51, 65, 82, 84, 103, 122–5
awareness 28, 32–3, 50–2, 68, 73, 76, 82, 91, 95–6, 100, 120; client's 73, 82; internal 95; professional 151; psychotherapist's 91; raising 33, 50–1; shared 68, 128

barriers 6–9, 11, 14–17, 21, 23, 41, 48, 50, 86, 105, 111, 153, 160; dialogic 16, 21; evaluating 48; external 36, 49, 146; multiple 14, 46; practical 11; significant 21; societal 16; strong 72; systemic 8, 127
baseline 35, 75, 92, 102, 116–17, 156; co-created 40, 102, 105, 123; collaborative 96; consistent 102; depleted 163; personal 71; relational 16
behaviour 48, 59, 66, 68, 76, 85, 98, 101, 113, 115, 157; bad 70; client's 113; feminine 87; observable 113; partner's 99; pre-determined 87; sexualised 27, 40, 73, 95, 98
beliefs 71, 116, 128; incorrect 122; psychotherapist's 128; religious 18, 66; survivor's 82
binary theoretical framework 11
biological processes 28
birth 17, 19, 86
bisexuality 8
black 67, 78

Index

blame 9, 22, 27, 31, 32, 46, 57, 67, 69, 71–77, 83, 85, 96, 108, 143
blood flow 29
bodies 2, 17, 22–3, 26–7, 29–31, 34, 38–41, 72–5, 77, 79, 98, 100–1, 103–4, 124–5, 167–8; human 28, 30; and minds 15, 21, 32, 73, 90, 116, 163, 167; physical 32, 34, 56, 79; survivor's 40
body language 112
boundaries 40, 44, 56–7, 62–3, 80, 90, 94, 146, 151, 157, 167; clear 9; contractual 143; multiple 65; personal 94, 114, 124; practical 151; relational 113
brain 26–32, 39, 104, 119, 125, 137, 168; front 119; human 28; neo-mammalian 28, 31, 39; paleo-mammalian 28; regions 30; reptilian 28; triune 28
brain structure 81
British criminal justice system 18, 129

capacity 22, 89, 91, 158, 162; client's 24; impaired mental 135; low 68; neo-mammalian 32; physical 125; psychotherapist's 158
careers 59, 89, 155, 164
central nervous system 28–9
change 1–2, 4, 27, 29, 43–4, 46, 48–51, 55–7, 59, 111–13, 118, 143–4, 154–5, 158, 160; effective 42, 54; influencing 42; internal 90; positive 51–2; reparative 120; social 1, 42, 47; societal 48–9, 62, 89; supportive 52; unavoidable 118
child victims 136
childhood 20, 37, 39, 73, 94, 100, 103, 148
children 40, 65, 82, 98, 104, 108, 116, 127, 134, 149–50; grooming 67, 73; protecting 20
choice 10, 12, 15, 18, 75, 79, 85, 87, 96, 114, 116, 118–20, 132; client's 91; deliberate 76; individual 79, 147; lack of 13, 15–16; personal 15; psychotherapist's 92; victim's 136
Christianity 11
chronology 34, 81, 140, 162; linear 69; physical 27
CICA *see* Criminal Injuries Compensation Authority
cisgender 45, 95, 119, 161; categories of 7; male or female 4; women 86
civil claims 134

civil disobedience 32
client contact 144
client groups 27, 32, 36–7, 58, 127–8, 136, 150, 153, 155
clients 56, 69, 74, 90, 94, 100, 108, 140; ability to be in contact with their self 71; advising 142; experiences of 4, 122, 124, 129, 157; female 100; fictional 2; individual 3, 6–7, 33, 39, 47, 54, 59, 62, 145, 150, 157; life of 2, 6, 11–12, 56, 76, 105, 142; processes 4, 62, 88, 91, 164, 166; psychotherapy 20, 58, 72; relationships 42; safeguarding 146; supporting 11–12, 14–15, 18–19, 21, 31–2, 48, 51, 69–71, 83, 86–7, 117, 119–22, 155, 158, 160–2; teaching 75; traumatised 76, 157, 156; welcoming 63
clinical responsibility 27
clinical work 58–9
CNS *see* central nervous system
collaboration 33, 56, 150, 152–3, 161;
collaborative 17, 21, 43–4, 63, 68, 75, 77, 80, 84, 89–90, 96, 143, 145; efforts 44; opportunities 68; process 17, 21, 111; support 45, 143; work 43
communities 11–12, 15, 18–19, 21, 48, 51, 67, 70–1, 117, 119–21, 158, 160, 162; global 17; local 34; non-white 67; supportive 84
competency 155–6; margins of 155–6; professional 12; psychotherapist's 157
Complex Post-Traumatic Stress Disorder 37, 94, 111
concealment (level of) 65–6
confidentiality 6, 53, 56–8, 106, 121, 135, 162; compromising 11, 57; principles of 45; of the process placed by other human-made systems 13; and upholding the professionalism of psychotherapy as a field 53
consciousness 76, 96, 160; enhanced 33; public 153; shared 6
consensual acts 19, 36, 61
consent 5, 18, 32, 39–41, 103, 107, 121, 136, 141–3, 146, 152; client's 116, 118; informed 18, 43, 103, 142–3; personal 75
consenting relationships 21
contact 2–6, 8, 15–16, 33, 35–8, 40–1, 49–50, 53–5, 59, 69–71, 90–1, 93–4, 98–9, 113–14, 116–17, 149–51,

156–60, 163, 165, 167–8; client 144; clinical 89; consensual 17; direct 13; human 13, 16, 24, 93; impaired 115; interpersonal 156; mediating 167; person-to-person 102; physical 6, 19, 27, 39, 98; psychological 3, 41, 60, 70, 97–8, 100, 160; relational 7, 39, 91; safe 65; sensitive 73; sexual 2, 5, 17–18, 32, 36, 66, 73–5, 159; sustaining 49
contract 57, 61, 114, 117; contracted 43, 94, 102; contractually 61; contractual 62; contracting 123, 142
contradictions 69, 77, 137
control 5, 7, 9–10, 22–3, 30–1, 40, 71–3, 79, 84–5, 112, 141, 147, 160, 164, 166–8; client's 8; coercive 104; lack of 9, 158; loss of 30, 76, 111, 160; personal 30, 84; practising 119; regaining 85; survivor's 103, 115, 125
conversations 6, 18, 29, 45, 56, 79, 90, 99, 112–13, 143–6, 162; co-created psychotherapeutic 3; global 1, 86; open 62; shared 18; unstructured 152
conviction rates 129, 147, 154
convictions 130, 132, 139, 146, 148
countertransference 96–7, 166; embodied 40; responses 98–9
court orders 141, 145
court rooms 135
courts 20, 126, 130–2, 135, 138, 142, 149, 151–2; civil 134; Crown courts 131–2; decisions of 134; Magistrate courts 131–2
CPS *see* Crown Prosecution Service
crime 35, 70, 126, 130, 132, 134–5, 142–3, 147; hate 78; sexual 135, 148
Criminal Injuries Compensation Authority 134
criminal justice process 20, 106, 127–8, 135–6, 138, 141, 143, 145, 147–8, 150–1, 153–4
criminal justice system 13, 15, 19, 106, 124, 126, 128–30, 134, 136–7, 139–40, 142–4, 146–54
criminal offences 126–7, 129–31, 141
Crown courts *see also* courts 131–2
Crown Prosecution Service 35, 106, 126–30, 132, 135–6, 140–2, 151–3; assessment 130; guidelines 138, 140, 143–4, 146, 151, 153; instructions 153; lawyers 132
cultural customs 105
cultural practices 17

damages 76, 134, 148
defence mechanisms 101
defendants 130–2, 141
delivering pre-trial therapy in the UK *131, 133*
depression 15, 21, 109
diagnosis 21, 109, 111, 159
diagnostic criteria 2, 24, 33, 37, 94, 109
dialogue 1–2, 20, 41, 75–6, 86, 92–3, 99, 117–18, 143, 145, 162, 166; co-created 117, 121; global 16; internal 57; professional 2; shared 1, 64, 166; societal 44; therapeutic 33; wider 59; worldwide 20
differences 15, 60, 74; cultural 21; significant 12; vital 17
difficulties 8, 11, 24, 32, 34, 37, 91, 94–5, 111, 156; client's 2; mental health 21, 106, 144, 155; personal 156; presenting 106
digital media 20
disclosures 2, 5–8, 15, 21–2, 24, 31, 59–60, 70, 72, 100–1, 138, 142–7, 153; of the psychotherapist's self 60; of therapy notes 142, 153
disconnection 9–10, 22, 33–4, 37–41, 67–8, 71, 73, 75, 83–5, 91–3, 97–8, 100, 106–7, 114–15, 160; forcing 77; and **increased psychological contact 160**; levels of 98, 165; precipitating 18; premature 91; psychological 65; and states of relatedness 97, 115
disempowering 1, 7, 22, 79, 95, 116, 129, 150; dynamics people 7; injustices 8; survivors 15, 69
disempowerment 5, 7, 9, 13, 15, 17, 34–5, 45, 48, 50, 64–5, 71, 77–8, 147–8, 150–1; experiences 14; mass 17; personal 164; potential 108, 134; professional 146; societal 8; stemming from sexual violence 115; traumatising 146
disengagement 8–9, 14, 109; increasing 16; partway through the work 90; survivor's 77
distress 22, 28, 33–4, 41, 48, 67–71, 83, 138, 140–1, 160, 164; embodied 138; feelings of 74, 147; mediating 16; mental 68; psychological 15, 19, 37, 70, 122; significant 83
domains 2, 31, 33, 55–6, 97, 107, 116; multiple 11, 68; physical 31; psychological 34; public 59, 158

drug addictions 98
dynamic loops 52–4, 56, 59–60, 64, 66, 73–8, 81–5, 88, 158, 163, 165–8; information 77; and selves 69; silencing 76
dynamics 101, 106, 164, 166; complex 7, 9; internal 97; intersubjective 61; oppressive 5; relational 7, 155
dysregulation 68–70, 77

e-mails 94, 112
electronic devices 142
embodiment 58, 66, 125; of the client's link to the wider issue of sexual violence 62; psychotherapist's 51
emotions 22, 26, 72, 74–6, 83, 85, 104, 112, 123, 144, 146; heightened 112; managing 156; spectrum of 58; and thoughts associated with physical symptoms 27
empowerment 40, 47, 49, 51, 56, 84, 87, 90, 114–15, 117, 141–2; increasing 85; internal 116; in psychotherapy 51, 108–24; role modelling 118; sense of 118, 123, 167
engagement 16, 36, 48, 95, 108, 113, 116, 120–1, 142; client's 143; social 82; survivor's 93; victim's 130
environments 40, 96, 104, 168
ethical benefits 120
ethical dilemmas 15, 36, 128
ethical framework 57
ethical requirements 126
evidence 52, 128–32, 134–6, 138–42, 144, 148, 151–2; CPS as a potential form of 128; forensic 132, 135; managing 139; oral 19; potential forms of 128, 144; victim's 35
experiences 2, 4–5, 7, 9, 19–20, 26, 28–9, 31, 40–1, 47–8, 75–6, 79, 97, 159–60, 167–8; common 49; diminished 115; disempowerment 14; embodied 27, 115; forced 92; human 15, 26, 93; individual 87, 93, 148; internal 22–4, 26, 113, 159; intersubjective 145, 155; life-threatening 137; personal 92, 126, 138, 144, 148, 151; professional 45, 114, 158; psychological 115; psychotherapist's 54, 82; relational 24–5, 38, 151, 158; reparative 65; working 12, 61

face-to-face 23, 45, 57; client work 60; interactions 84
facets 2–3, 22–3, 26–7, 31–4, 38–9, 59–62, 65, 67–8, 71, 73–4, 76–80, 83–6, 91–4, 96–7, 100, 104–5, 107, 117–19, 158–60, 163–5; disconnected 82; individual 68; intolerable 34; multiple 35, 54, 91, 115; pathologising 88; primary 26
facial expressions 29, 145
facilitators 42, 45, 59
failure 87, 104, 136, 154, 158; institutional 20; professional 158
faith 8, 11–12, 19, 93, 98, 105, 113, 119, 149, 151
faith groups 36
family 22, 70, 73, 95, 98, 100, 104, 134, 136, 149–50; homes 22, 98; and Independent Sexual Violence Advocates 134; life 81, 118; members 96, 100, 104, 149, 158, 161; relationships 150
flashbacks 22, 30, 72, 102, 138, 156
FME *see* Forensic Medical Examiner
forced re-organisation 2, 31, 36–7, 90, 92
forced reconfiguration of the self 84, 120
Forensic Medical Examiner 135
formal psychotherapeutic spaces 58
freedom 74, 79, 87, 116, 127, 142; of autonomy and speech 122; decreased 35; exercise in 44, 79; impacting 71; impaired 71; of movement 13, 51, 103, 114–16, 125, 168; personal 15, 49; restricted 35; survivor's 115
Freud, Sigmund 96–7, 101
Full Code Test 130
functions 29, 81, 146; reductionist 72; symbolic 145
funding 12, 14, 19, 113; consistent 14; cycles 46; personal 12–14; public 13; ring-fencing of 47; of therapy services 14

gender 4, 7, 9–10, 12, 17, 19, 66–7, 78, 93, 95, 102, 106, 113; expressions 36, 113; issues 124; misunderstandings 19
genitals 19
goals 84, 116, 163; individual psychotherapeutic 116; personally meaningful 116; of recovery 81; of societal change 62
grooming children 67, 73

group psychotherapy including the loops of all participants 55
groups 17, 42, 45, 52, 69–70, 73, 78, 83, 85, 153; client 27, 32, 36–7, 58, 127–8, 136, 150, 153, 155; communal 83; societal 43, 70, 74, 94; survivor-led 166
guidelines 19, 52, 126–8, 134, 136–7, 139, 151–3; original 127, 136, 153; pre-trial therapy 106, 130, 134; set by the criminal justice system 19, 126
guilt 9, 22, 27, 31–2, 46, 57, 67, 69, 71–7, 83, 85
guilty pleas 131–2
guilty verdicts 130, 132, 140–1, 148

health 35, 143, 156–7
health care 11, 13, 50
heterosexual 7–8, 45, 119
hippocampus 30
homeostasis 30, 34, 168
hormones 29–31, 137
HPA see hypothalamicpituitary-adrenal
human contact 13, 16, 24, 93
human interactions 7, 39
human life 78–9, 123
human-made systems 6–8, 11, 13, 35–6, 45, 50, 64, 92, 128, 148, 151
human responsibility 28
human rights 58, 159; infringements 17; violations 79, 89, 163
human trafficking 5, 39, 103
humane justice 150
humans 4, 7, 26, 28–30, 35, 37, 50, 103–4, 123, 162, 167
hyper-arousal *38*
hypo-arousal *38*
hypothalamicpituitary-adrenal 29
hypothalamus 29

IICSA see Independent Inquiry into Child Sexual Abuse
incidents 5, 7, 15, 27, 30, 44, 70, 126, 137–8, 148–9, 156; original 35, 69, 106, 146; random 5; single 37
Independent Inquiry into Child Sexual Abuse 20
Independent Sexual Violence Advocate 134–5
inequalities 14, 50–1, 56, 120
information 27, 29, 37, 39–40, 43–4, 47–8, 52–4, 75–6, 81–2, 92, 94, 111, 120–1, 139, 141–3; first-hand 1; identifying 144; inclusive 124; missing 138; sharing 42; truthful 43
injustice 7–8, 10, 28, 62, 129, 150, 153–4, 159, 164, 168; human rights 163; societal 9
internalised shame 57
interventions 6, 13, 16, 75–6, 88, 92, 101, 103, 105, 152, 155–6, 159; body-based 38; dialogical 117; healthcare 9; inclusive 104; legal 147; psychological 139; psychotherapeutic 43, 56, 88; reparative 40, 157; supportive 10, 12
intrusive memories 22, 30
Islam 66
ISVAs see Independent Sexual Violence Advocate

judges 130, 132, 135, 140–1, 152
juries 132, 140–1, 152
justice 44, 50, 127, 136–7, 145, 147, 150, 153, 160

Klein, Melanie 70, 101

language 2–3, 11, 18, 21, 28, 31, 39, 122–4, 128, 144, 156; clinical 21; co-constructed 123; colloquial 18; formalised 18; forms 121; gender-neutral 121; primary 7; professional 1
legal process 3, 106, 136, 142
legal professionals 134, 151–2
LGBTQ+ community 121, 161–2
local governments 47
loops 54–8, 64; of client and psychotherapist 54; creating a dynamic live feedback system 55; reinforcing an explicit understanding about psychotherapists and clients 56

Magistrate courts 131–2
magistrates 131–2, 152
management 10, 29, 59, 140–1, 155
management strategies 166
marginalisation of survivors 47, 50
masturbation 40
media 20, 90, 158, 163
medical assessments 135
memories 20, 22, 30, 34, 81, 99, 137–9, 156; intrusive 22, 30; recovered 139; sensory 30; somatic 96; traumatic 30
mental health 12, 18–19, 21, 24, 42, 44, 47, 49, 58–9, 105, 108, 154, 158;

difficulties 21, 106, 144, 155; issues 109; practitioners 35; problems 43; professionals 44; self-care 137; services 10, 120, 163; spaces 4; support 8, 13; systems 6, 8–10, 43, 45–7, 90–2, 94–6, 99, 109, 111, 113–14, 116–17, 119, 121, 123–4, 164
MeToo movement 20
misconceptions 44, 88, 105; descriptive 77; minimising 152; societal 13; societally-created 124; and society's myths 105
misdiagnosis 46, 109
Mohammed, Prophet 66
monetary damages 134; *see also* damages
multi-faceted selves 22, 32–3, 35–9, 59–61, 68–9, 84–8, 91–2, 106, 108–9, 113–14, 122, 147–8, 155–7, 159–61, 163
muscle mobility 168
muscle tension 27, 72, 161
muscles 29
Muslim woman 10
Muslims *see also* Islam 11
myths 15, 17–19, 36, 44, 49, 52, 54, 64–87, 93, 95, 97, 124, 140, 143; collective 65; common 101; effects of 66–7; interacting with other presenting material 64; internalised 50, 74, 77, 85, 88; interrupting the recovery of those impacted by sexual violence 65; power of 69, 78, 147; re-configuring 74, 88; rejecting 83; societal 9, 19, 27, 32, 154; societally-constructed 74

national governments 47
nausea 99
negative outcomes 68, 123
negative reactions 49
neo-mammalian brain *28*
nervous system 28–9, 31–2, 168; parasympathetic 29; sympathetic 29
networks 135, 166–7; client's support 153; personal 35, 45, 49, 115, 135, 158, 162–3, 167; wider 166
neurobiological level 81, 157
neurobiological processes 31
neurobiological safety mechanisms 22, 24
neurobiology 34, 75
neurophysiological mechanisms 4, 118
NFA *see No Further Action*
nightmares 22–3, 30, 72, 99, 102, 138

No Further Action 130, 132; NFA'd 132, 148
non-binary 17, 161
non-disabled 7, 45, 119
non-consensual sexual contact 2, 18, 73–4, 146
non-heterosexual orientation 78
non-monogamy 8

offences 14, 129–32, 136, 153; criminal 126–7, 129–31, 141; sexual 20, 126–7, 129–31, 141, 143, 147, 152
online 51–3, 59
oppress 45, 52; oppressed 9; oppression 45, 50, 64; oppressive 5, 7, 16, 21; oral accounts 35, 136
organisations 23–4, 43, 52, 94, 111, 119, 127, 136, 151, 153, 164; charitable 10; national 134; specialist 134; therapeutic 154; women's 23
orientation 8, 34, 36, 78, 93; non-heterosexual 78; sexual 8, 36, 93; theoretical 34

pain 21, 71–2, 87, 102, 156, 161; body 163; chest 21; physical 21, 27, 72, 102, 156
Paleo-mammalian brain *28*
paperwork 146, 151
parasympathetic nerve 29
parents 98, 108, 116
partners 17, 66, 70, 74, 95, 98, 104, 158–9, 162; caring 67; female 18, 98
patriarchal structures 45, 66
peers 18, 43; learning 88; support 121
peripheral nervous systems 28–9
perpetrators 5, 19–21, 31, 36–7, 43, 45, 65, 67–70, 99–101, 103–4, 127–30, 132, 134–5, 147–50, 160–1; accounts 141; avoiding responsibility 123; individual 72; intruding on the self of the client 106; judgements 104; male 70; multiple 37; potential 99
person-to-person 7, 15, 24, 59, 89, 93, 102, 154–5, 159; interactions 59, 159; process 15; relationships 93
personal identity 6, 8, 62, 65, 68–9, 73, 78, 83–8, 115, 118, 124
personal meaning 27, 57, 81
personal power 16, 56, 85, 113, 122, 160
personal processes 33, 68, 114
personal relationships 34–5

personal worlds 43, 46, 50, 53–4, 56, 77, 79–80, 84–5, 87–8, 90–1, 98–9, 104–5, 167–8
perspective 2, 43, 68, 74, 82, 124, 158; empowerment-based 86, 142; empowerment-facilitating 111; neurophysiological survival 70; personal 82; physical 28; psychological 27; relational 10, 21, 91, 106, 111; subjective 138; therapist's 151; trauma-informed 94, 137; victim-blaming 139
physical contact 6, 19, 27, 39, 98
physical facets 35, 38, 40, 69, 71–3, 75–7, 80, 83, 97–8, 100–2, 107, 163, 167–8
physical self 27, 32, 34, 96, 99, 134
physical sensations 22, 74, 76, 90, 101, 112
physiology 34, 75, 168
pituitary gland 30
PNS *see* peripheral nervous systems
police 15, 98, 106, 122, 126–30, 132, 134–5, 140–2, 146–50, 153; and the Crown Prosecution Service 130; investigations 130
police officers 132, 134
police station 135, 138, 148
polyamorous 161
polyvagal 29
population 3, 64, 87, 119
post-trauma symptoms 18, 21–2, 24, 27, 83, 85, 93–4, 109, 118, 121–2, 137–8, 141, 152, 155–7; common 70; pre-existing 134; pronounced 122; psychological 28; re-framing 111, 113; somatic 28
post-traumatic stress disorder 159
power 10, 42, 44–6, 50, 56–8, 77–8, 81, 113–14, 116, 151, 153, 158, 160–1, 163; dynamics 50, 114, 124, 145; hierarchy of 10; imbalance of 40, 56, 90, 124
practitioners 12, 15, 45–6, 49, 87, 92, 96, 102, 113, 151, 155, 163, 166; ethical 155; individual 24, 151; lone 46; medical 135; in non-specialist services 46; overloaded 164; qualified 126; unpaid 14
pre-trial therapy 35–6, 106, 126–130, *131, 133,* 154–153
professional 11–13, 15–16, 18–19, 35–37, 42–51, 78–9; commitments 167; credentials 13; ethics 53; networks 35, 114, 166–7; outcomes 79; registration 15; responsibility 47; standards 58; support 1, 144, 150, 162; training 61
projection 96, 100–1, 166; psychological 70; re-framing 101
projective identification 101
promoting empowerment in psychotherapy *110*
Prophet Mohammed 66
protective safety mechanisms 71, 73, 149, 160
psychological 26, 68–9, 73, 75, 102–3, 105, 116, 156, 165, 168; concepts 72; contacts 3, 41, 60, 70, 97–8, 100, 160; experiences 115; expressions 103; processes 33–4, 76, 96, 99; self 32, 34, 134, 162; self-facets 95; spaces 49, 54, 59, 94, 96–7, 99–104, 106, 113–15, 118–20, 124–5, 145, 147, 156; support 10; tasks 71; treatments 139, 144; work 75
psychotherapeutic 2, 97, 117, 120; benefits 49; change 40, 102; contact 55, 64; dialogue 3, 17, 43–4, 51, 58, 76, 104–5, 122, 128; information 48; interventions 43, 56, 88; process 3, 27, 128; relationships 37, 43, 51–2, 59, 61, 66, 90–1, 96, 103, 105, 109, 117–18, **124;** services 48, 119; spaces 3, 16, 33, 58, 83, 89–91, 97–8, 106, 122; support 86, 88, 113, 117, 120, 166; work 1, 4, 21, 27, 33, 36–7, 62–3, 65, 85, 92, 159, 161, 164
psychotherapists 1–8, 10–14, 16, 18–24, 27, 31–6, 38–54, 56–64, 68–71, 73–100, 102–9, 111, 113–29, 134–40, 155–61, 163–4, 166–8; beliefs 128; careers 155; decisions 60; educating 127; experienced 46, 159; female 95; hypo-aroused 168; individual 37, 106, 109, 116, 119, 163, 166; poaching or soliciting survivors 119; qualifications 12; relational 3; relational work 3; relationships 31, 109, 156; responsibilities 38, 50, 56, 59, 62; role 106, 117, 121; training 159; understanding of the individual's re-configured self 38; undertaking work 156; unpaid 14; welfare 61; work in spaces outside of appointments 59
psychotherapists self 59, 62, 80, 97, 114, 118; access to facets of the 60;

disclosures of the 60; supportive 72; various facets of the 59
psychotherapy 2–3, 15–16, 36–7, 59, 61, 81, 84, 119, 138, 155, 159, 163–4, 166; accessing 8, 11–12, 16–17, 19, 44, 49, 119–20, 137; appointments 13, 16, 23, 51, 54, 57, 59, 121, 128, 160, 163; clients 20, 58, 72; empowerment 51, 108–24; ethical 48; freedoms of 9, 23; inclusive 86; long-term 15; modern 91; open-ended 12; personal 102, 166; private 35; services 1, 9–10, 15–16, 23–4, 44, 52, 65, 85, 94–5, 111; traditional 119
punishment 104, 134

qualifications 12, 155
Quran 66

race 36, 67
racism 7, 67, 78
rape 18, 51, 65, 129, 131, 144
rape crisis centres 65, 134
re-configuring 74, 79, 82, 138; the facets of the self following sexual violence 62; internal sense 33; myths 74, 88; one's self in relation to other selves 74, 84, 120; the self through their personal perspective 82
re-traumatising 8, 15, 33, 116, 129, 138, 150, 164
recollections 30, 33, 81–2, 137, 141
relatedness 2, 4, 7–9, 15–16, 31, 33, 57–8, 61–2, 65, 76–7, 84–5, 87, 91–2, 97, 113–18; comfortable 33, 38, 93; forced 22; good 159; increasing 31; maintaining 125; safe 13, 43, 77, 114, 121
relational injuries 2, 8–9
relational styles 61, 93, 145
relationships 2–5, 9–10, 16–19, 21–4, 31–8, 40–5, 59–62, 74, 80–3, 90–100, 102–5, 107–9, 113–19, 123–4, 143, 145, 147, 150–2, 156–7, 159–61; clients 42; consensual 36; consenting 21; family 150; healthy 95; human 16; managing 37; observable 94; personal 34–5; positive 18; safe 9, 119; same-sex 65; sexual 35
release (adrenal) 30
religion 8, 78, 113, 119
religious practices 95, 105
remits 48–9, 58, 105, 115, 122, 134; clinical 156; narrow 86; professional 155; psychotherapist's 89; wider 42, 47

reparative 7, 9, 16, 20, 61, 65, 105, 111, 147, 150–1, 155; efficacy 16; elements 16; empathic responses 164; interventions 40, 157; relationships 45; support 35, 157; work 44, 93
reports 76, 126–7, 129–30, 134–7, 143, 146–9, 151–2, 154; concerning a reduced ability to manage in body and mental distress 68; involved in the criminal justice process 106; to the police 15; victim's 128, 130, 139, 151
reptilian brain *28*
resources 27, 44, 47, 61, 114, 129, 131; external 115, 163; financial 35; internal 46, 56, 115; limited 113; practical 11
responses 29–30, 44–5, 49–50, 57, 59–60, 84, 87, 89, 96, 99–101, 157, 159–60, 163–4, 166; authentic 118; automatic 30, 39, 157, 160; client's 166; embodied 34; emotional 40; explicit 76; fight-flight-freeze 23, 29–30, 34, 157; human 78, 98; humane 154; individual 4; injurious 15; mother's 22; negative 109; neurophysiological 137; normal 26, 70, 152, 159; personal 164, 166; police's 98; primal 28; psychological 27, 31; psychotherapist's 39, 96–7; repeated 77; socially-influenced 101; somatic 103; stress 38–9, 113, 135, 156–7, 168; trauma-informed 111
responsibility 47–8, 50, 52, 69–71, 73, 75, 101, 104, 129–30, 132, 139, 141, 146, 148–50, 156; concurrent 147; ethical 164; police's 142; primary 122; significant 142; survivor's 127
restrictions 13–14, 74, 78, 124, 137, 153; forced 36; literal 103; significant 136
risk 3, 8, 15, 66, 69–70, 76, 78–9, 106, 114, 121–2, 144–5, 149, 151; alienating 124; high 139; management 42, 79, 94; presenting 144

safe spaces 14, 23, 90
safety 10, 22–4, 34–5, 40–1, 70–1, 75, 78, 81, 94, 96, 103, 106, 116–17, 120, 160–1; lack of 94, 98, 106; mechanisms 24, 41, 71, 117, 167; personal 23, 78–9, 121, 129, 146, 149; relative 44; signals 12
same-sex relationships 65
SARC *see* Sexual Assault Referral Centre

self-disclosure 53, 60
self-experience 26, 48, 68, 71, 85, 93, 96, 119
service deliveries 16, 108–9, 111, 117, 164
service provision 14, 24, 117, 120, 156, 164; constrained 90; therapeutic 127
services 8–16, 24, 43, 46–8, 56–7, 60, 89–90, 92–6, 102, 105–6, 109, 112–13, 116–17, 119–23, 134–8, 143, 161–3; accessible 117; emergency 135; ethical 16, 151; feminist 87; forensic 135; formal 48, 86, 119; generic 13, 15; multiple 11, 52, 121; private 12–13; professional 47, 51, 119; psychotherapeutic 48, 119; psychotherapy 1, 9–10, 15–16, 23–4, 44, 52, 65, 85, 94–5, 111; public 12–14; specialist 20, 46, 52, 90; support 3, 8, 24, 35–6, 41, 94, 98, 113–14, 120–1, 127, 129; therapy 14, 150; traditional 4, 160
sex 17–18, 27, 73, 121–2
sexual abuse 39, 86, 99, 103, 144
Sexual Assault Referral Centre 135
sexual contact 2, 5, 17–18, 32, 36, 66, 73–5, 159
sexual offences 20, 126–7, 129–31, 141, 143, 147, 152
Sexual Offences Act 2003 129
sexual orientation 8, 36, 93
sexual relationships 35
sexual violence 1–40, 42–54, 56–8, 61–79, 81–95, 97–8, 101, 103–4, 107–9, 113–17, 119–26, 128–9, 135–8, 140, 144, 146–50, 152–3, 156–8, 160–1, 163–4; ability of 156–7; accounts of 139, 157; act of 9, 14, 116; activists 51; complexity of 7, 159; disclosure of 1, 129; domino effect of 12–13; existence of 19, 68; experience of 8, 17, 30, 40, 82–3, 100, 106, 108–9, 116, 146; experienced 8, 17, 82–3, 100, 106, 108–9, 146; forces reconfiguration of the self 83; historical 30; hypervigilance 23; incidences of 6, 76, 145; issue of 4, 9, 36, 47, 53, 151, 154, 156, 161, 165, 167; nature of 39, 45, 98, 158; repeated 39, 94; results of 41, 56, 68, 71, 113; seeking support following 11, 35, 48, 54, 62, 90; truth of 4, 11, 44, 65–6, 77–9, 84, 88–9, 93, 156, 158, 167–8
shame 8–9, 18–19, 22–3, 27, 31–2, 65, 67, 69, 71–7, 83, 85, 95–6, 112

silence 45, 52, 56–7, 66, 76, 93; oppressive 16; preferred 57; professional 48, 57; psychotherapist's 56; unwavering 57
skills 27, 43, 45, 89, 91, 116, 123
sleep 11, 21, 34, 40, 99, 102, 121, 137, 156, 161, 163; disturbed 21, 102, 137, 156; hygiene 121
social media 20, 51–2
social responsibility 49–50, 53, 56–8, 64, 71, 78–9, 115; extending the role of psychotherapists into a wider remit 42; outward-facing 47; proactive 57
societal damages 76; *see also* damages
societal dysregulation 68–9
societal issue 59, 61, 71, 77, 120, 163
societal issues 59, 61, 120, 163; complex 77; wider 71
societal marginalisation 16, 50, 67
societal myths 9, 19, 27, 32, 154
societal phenomenon 50–1, 150, 157, 160
society 2–3, 14, 16, 18–19, 31–2, 34, 36, 44, 46, 49–52, 57, 66–71, 73–4, 81, 123–4; global 9, 47, 68; victim-blaming 13, 36, 69–70, 78, 147; western 108; wider 34, 50, 65, 68, 108, 150
spaces 1, 3–11, 20–1, 32–3, 35, 38–41, 43–6, 48–62, 64–6, 71–9, 81–6, 88–90, 93–7, 102–3, 115–18, 120–3, 146–7, 157–8, 160–2, 165–8; alternating 101; boundaried 44, 167; community 1, 120, 122; confidential 44, 137; formalised 17; hidden 11; identifying 167; multiple 35, 44, 54, 61–2, 81, 91, 146, 148, 158, 160, 162–3; navigating 66; online 88; personal 98; physical 21, 23, 40, 42, 44–5, 52, 54, 60, 62, 103–6, 109, 114–15, 117–18, 122, 124–5; private 13; professional 79; psychological 49, 54, 59, 94, 96–7, 99–104, 106, 113–15, 118–20, 124–5, 145, 147, 156; public 1, 44, 49, 51–3, 58, 61–2; public-facing 59, 81; regulated 79; relational 103; societal 161; supportive 62; therapeutic 97; victims 151
states 29–30, 32, 34, 73, 75, 102–3, 114, 116, 129–30, 147–8, 151, 154, 168; hyper-aroused 118; hypo-aroused 29, 118, 125; physiological 32; regulated 168
stereotypical characteristics 19

stress 22, 29–30, 39, 122, 128, 134, 145, 151, 156, 161–2, 164–6; emerging 163, 167; extreme 29, 34, 81; post-traumatic 157; pre-trial therapy precipitating 151; prolonged 134; psychological 22
stress responses 38–9, 113, 135, 156–7, 168; automatic 168; post-traumatic 38
Stolorow and Atwood 100
suicidal feelings 114
support networks 84, 163
support services 3, 8, 24, 35–6, 41, 94, 98, 113–14, 120–1, 127, 129; accessible 90; local text 23; practical 36; signpost 127
support systems 20, 36, 54, 153; human-made 34, 123; multiple 47; professional 96
supporting survivors 1, 57, 89, 139, 153, 164, 166–8
'Surah Al-Nisaa' 66
survival 26, 28–9, 31–3, 38, 40, 68, 115, 125, 137; aid 72; automatic 31; client's 27; mechanisms 86, 89, 137, 160; mode 69, 119, 157, 162, 167; physical 82; strategies 34, 85, 151; of traumatic experiences 26
survivors 1–24, 26–7, 30–41, 43–54, 56–64, 66–79, 81–98, 102–6, 108–9, 111, 113–30, 134–6, 138–61, 163–4, 166; ability to exist comfortably 34; accessing services 43, 135; accounts of 57, 66, 72, 139, 144; cases of 136; disempowering silence of 66; female 86; gay 65, 161; hyper-vigilant 41; individual 1–2, 5, 44, 49–50, 58, 64–5, 72, 119, 122–3, 138, 144; instances of 84; material 30, 92, 114; self 31, 60, 73, 77, 82, 95, 98, 104, 111, 115, 117; soliciting 119; supporting 1, 57, 89, 139, 153, 164, 166–8; truths 5, 39, 47, 51, 72, 111, 140; younger 20
symptoms 22, 34, 93, 99, 109, 124, 128; cognitive 109; developing 156; embodied 66, 75; linking the body back to the traumatic past 72; physical 27, 99; somatic 27, 29, 37, 75
systemic barriers 8, 127
systems 7–8, 10, 35–7, 46, 49–52, 72, 75, 94–5, 105–6, 124, 126–7, 139–40, 142, 150, 152–3; alarm 29; civil law 134; diagnostic 21; disempowering 18, 146;

endocrine 29; formal 153; human-constructed 94; inaccessible 10; individual belief 74; legal 2, 19, 35, 126, 128; neuroendocrine 29; neurophysiological 119; peripheral nervous 28; pressured mental health 47; psychotherapists 117; societal 92; tracking 41; wider mental health 37

talking therapy 6, 10, 12–13, 15, 18–20, 35, 106, 124, 126–9, 135–9, 141–2, 144–5, 153; clients accessing 126; courses 15; offering 123, 126, 146; profession 137; providers 128, 139; regulatory organisations for 10; services 20, 109
technology 52, 89
telephones 113
television programmes 20
theoretical framework 21
therapeutic process 98, 142, 146
therapeutic relationships 92, 97
therapeutic work 3, 146
therapist relationships 145, 151–2, 166
therapists 24, 95, 127–9, 134, 139–47, 149–54; female 95; individual 152–4; involvement at all the stages of the reporting, investigation, and trial process 152; male 95; private 11; role of 151; trained 151
therapy 120, 136, 138–9, 141–2, 144–7, 150–2, 154; accessing 142, 153; pre-trial 35–6, 106, 126–53; provision of 127, 150; rooms 153; services 14, 150
therapy notes 15, 128, 141–3, 146, 152–3; client's 144; contextualising 152; disclosures of 142, 153; release of 145
threats 16, 22, 26, 28–31, 36–8, 69, 79–80, 102–4, 135, 137, 168; actual 31; constant 79; perceived 5, 29, 31–2; potential 31; verbal 52
tolerance 32, 38–40, 82, 118, 157
trafficking 5, 37, 39, 103
transference 60, 96–7, 100, 166
transgender 17, 86
transparency 61, 63, 117, 152; and consistency 117; public 108; and the sharing of information 145
trauma 6, 12–13, 26–9, 34, 62, 67–8, 79, 83–7, 95–9, 105, 108–9, 118, 120–1, 123–4, 160, 164; based techniques 138; informed approach 167; informed

therapy service 108, 114; original 41, 93, 109; psychological 99; survived 57; therapy 153; vicarious 40, 47, 70, 91, 100, 155–68
traumatic 2, 4–5, 28, 81, 103, 124, 135; circumstances 46; experience 27, 32, 106, 117; human-to-human contact 102; incidences 21, 30; memories 30; recall 3, 18, 22, 30, 38–9, 41, 72, 102, 137; stress 29, 139
traumatic events 21, 37, 65, 70; enduring 3; experiencing 156
traumatic material 38, 69, 117, 162–3, 167; client's 157, 166; contact with 40, 157; and the pressured mental health systems 47
trials 19, 126, 129, 132, 134–5, 140–1, 152
trust 2, 9, 24, 40, 45, 48–9, 57, 61, 74–6, 80, 90, 92, 94, 98, 112; building 19, 25; lack of 41, 49, 75, 94; lost 62; priority in re-establishing 57
truths 1–4, 10, 42–4, 46–7, 51–2, 54, 57, 64–70, 72–86, 88, 90, 139–40, 154, 156, 158; expressing 120; personal 51, 82, 84, 87; of significant value in psychotherapy 65; spoken 45; of survivors 5, 39, 47, 51, 72, 111, 140
Turner, Brock 70

unconscious levels 3, 35, 73, 107, 143
unconscious processes 26, 32–3, 97, 99–100
United Kingdom 8, 19–20, 35, 106, 126, 129, 147

vagus nerve 29
value 1, 7, 14–15, 43–4, 56, 60, 71, 113, 116, 120, 122; human 57; misplaced 7; personal 145; significant 65; western 10
vicarious trauma 40, 47, 70, 91, 100, 155–68
victim personal statement 130
victims 3, 19, 127, 130, 132, 134–6, 139, 141–3, 146–7, 149, 152–4; accessing therapy 153; accounts subject to influence 136, 138–9, 151; child 136; of criminal acts 35, 128; defence case 141; of a sexual offence 130; spaces 151; supporting 134

video recorded interview 130, 132
visibility 3, 32, 48, 50, 58, 60–2, 119–20; increased 59, 117; professional 58; psychotherapist's 60; of therapeutic material 145
voices 1, 15–16, 20, 51, 56–8, 81, 88–9, 104, 111, 137, 152–3
volunteers 14
VPS *see* victim personal statement
VRI *see* video recorded interview

wars 37, 65
weight 13–14, 31, 43, 50, 71, 77, 85–6, 101, 109, 128, 140; fluctuating 93; isolating 75
white 7, 8, 45, 119; non-white 21, 67
WHO *see* World Health Organization
window of tolerance 32, 38, 39, 40, 82, 118, 157
witness 27, 29, 51, 140, 152, 159; second-hand 39; vulnerable 152
witnessing 27, 47, 56, 89, 98
women 8, 19–20, 66–7, 95, 101, 149; black 78; cisgender 86; Islam 66; lesbian 18
words 2–4, 8, 17–18, 21, 26, 31, 41, 47, 104, 123–4, 128; choice of 123, 128; client's 82–3; person's 141; use of 123
work 6–8, 10–12, 14–16, 18–19, 39–42, 45–6, 48–9, 51–2, 56, 58–62, 89–93, 95–100, 105–6, 117, 119–24, 141–6, 151–2, 154–7, 159–64, 168; activist 52, 56; client 51; trauma 8, 163; unstructured 137
working online 118
working relationships 2–3, 40, 44, 80, 83, 86, 91, 143, 145, 147, 157, 161; developing 113; psychotherapeutic 97; security of the 19
workloads 155–6, 160–1, 163, 167
world 6–8, 10, 20–1, 31, 33–5, 37, 44–6, 58, 62, 76, 82–4, 90, 98–100, 104–6, 128; dangerous 10; disempowering 50; figurative 34; internal 33, 97; re-traumatising 63; shared 46, 56, 63, 82–3, 106, 163; unsupportive 70
World Health Organization 17, 37, 70, 94, 100, 111

Printed in the United States
by Baker & Taylor Publisher Services